The Application of Social Sciences

About the Author

Ralph Tanner has a B.Sc. and Diploma in Social Anthropology from Oxford University and a D.Phil. in Law from Stockholm University. He has done fieldwork in Thailand, the Philippines, Guyana, Zambia, Zimbabwe, Tanzania, Uganda and Kenya as well as in Britain and EIRE. He was Chairman of the East African Institute of Social Research and Lecturer in Comparative Religion in the University of London. He has published books on murder in Uganda, witchcraft killings and religions and successful change and a cross cultural study of the Roman Catholic Mass. He has co-authored books on the social ecology of religion and the environment. He has written numerous articles on the social aspects of religious change, translation and language use in religion, as well as on behavioural theories in the *Journal of Modern African Studies*, *Africa Journal of the Social Sciences*, *Nordic Journal of African Studies*, *Antropos, Studia Missionalia* and others. He is currently working on a study of recent mass murdering of suspected witches in Tanzania, as well as religious behaviour as a working misunderstanding and the common place nature of religious experiences.

The Application of Social Sciences

A GUIDE TO ITS PROBLEMS

R.E.S. Tanner

CONCEPT PUBLISHING COMPANY PVT. LTD.
NEW DELHI-110059

ISBN-13: 978-93-5125-164-4

First Published 2015

Published and Printed by

Concept Since 1974

Concept Publishing Company Pvt. Ltd.
A/15-16, Commercial Block, Mohan Garden
New Delhi-110059 (India)
T: 25351460, 25351794, *F*: 091-11-25357109
E: publishing@conceptpub.com, W: www.conceptpub.com
Editorial Office: H-13, Bali Nagar, New Delhi-110 015, India.

Cataloging in Publication Data--Courtesy: D.K. Agencies (P) Ltd. <docinfo@dkagencies.com>

Tanner, R. E. S., 1921- author.
The application of social sciences : a guide to its problems / R.E.S. Tanner.
pages cm
Includes bibliographical references (pages) and index.
ISBN 9789351251644

1. Social sciences--Research. I. Title.

DDC 300.72 23

SHARON CURE

The Librarian

Trinity College Oxford

for prolonged back-up help

Contents

1
Introduction

Most of us are conscious that much knowledge can have immediate benefits to us in the here and now. In medicine, design, agriculture and indeed in every field of social behaviour there have been repeated changes which have been created by men and women which have benefited others outside their own environments.

The social sciences, as in all professions, have a division between hypotheses which are possibly no more than ideas produced by more or less socially isolated thinkers which may or may not have some future relevancy; they come and go through the pages of professional journals for the stimulus of their professional colleagues and who in the end modify or demolish them.

Their main field is the acquisition of pragmatic information about social behaviour and to use this knowledge in the present day for the benefit of some people, communities and societies.

The application of social science understandings and methods to explain, adjust and predict human behaviour is widespread in the professions of sociology and psychology. It is predominantly used in secular settings in which there are three parts; those who want this knowledge, the individuals and societies from whom information is sort, and the results.

Each of these three sectors provide different difficulties in motivation and how information is obtained and indeed how it is used. This is a pragmatic concentration of issues with which the social sciences have endeavoured to provide answers to social difficulties ever since Comte had formulated sociology as a science that would provide laws for human behaviour found by regulated and pragmatic enquiry.

We take applied social science to be any research work that is not done for purely personal reasons such as the work done for a higher degree. There is also the acquisition of knowledge for its own sake which might be highly abstract but which indeed might be moved from some library years later for an applied application to some contemporary problem. The conclusions that Malinowski made about the concentric circles of ritualised exchange in the Trobriand Islands (Malinowski, 1961) cannot have had any or indeed do not have any applied relevance as they are now no more than part of Pacific history. However his field work methods have been used subsequently in many applied analyses.

This book is a study of how the professional understandings of social scientists, principally in the Asian context, are being used to apply their knowledge and expertise to the solution of difficulties and to the improvement of the living conditions of some people. Some examples will show the success of what has been done while others make recommendations of how improvements might be achieved. Others make suggestions that are far too broad to accomplish in any communal setting without wholesale changes in national social behaviour.

Whenever there is a gap between what people want for their own benefit and what they experience, the social sciences have a role to apply their expertise to these gaps and to make suggestions as to how the situation might be changed for the benefit of those involved.

Many social scientists are qualified by temperament as well as by education to investigate human behaviour but they choose to take a more literary and detached approach to human behaviour. They may like Durkheim carry out comprehensive analyses of foreign cultures without any field work there, as in his authoritative study of Australian Aborigine religion (Durkheim, 1961). Many such studies have little influence beyond Western professional readers and even less in the professional and political circles in China, India, Indonesia and Japan. Much of this work on human behaviour in Africa and Asia has been done by Western researchers who may have unconsciously or consciously imported their own cultural biases into their work as in their use of such words as 'civilisation' and 'primitive'.

Even if a proportion of such work by foreigners is applied to the problems of their host societies, they come and go usually for their own professional needs without the emotional and pragmatic commitment of national social scientists. They propose what they want to research and the hosts can only accept or reject.

In Western societies enormous sums are spent in grants for research in social behaviour through national institutions, government departments and foundations which have no immediate applied relevance and is more or less part of national intellectual progress and an investment in what they hope will turn out to be investments in their own clever people.

Their publications usually contain thanks to the providers of the financial support enabling their work. A poorer nation cannot afford such diversions of scarce national financial resources unless it can be part of national purposes and what their power holders consider to be national needs.

Yet we can presuppose that in all societies there is a need for applied social science to discover the realities behind the social behaviour which decision makers and researchers consider to be important.

We can estimate that nationals outside the Western world will continue to use their positions to assess and publicize dimensions of the work in which they are professional interested and which have value to their own societies.

It is also likely that this valuable work will not be in matters of political and social sensitivity over which publication would endanger their own careers and families. Such dangerous research will continue to be made mainly by foreign researchers and nationals who publish their conclusions in the safety of other countries to which they have returned after their short residence in the country of their research; it is doubtful if their results have much influence over those in power.

The Scientific Weaknesses of the Social Sciences

The unknown as it relates to human behaviour is unlimited in scope and more importantly in the factors that may be involved. A basic problem for the social sciences must be this professional title—social science—as it leads outsiders to think that it may provide exact information about what it studies; this is not so. The definition of science refers to trained skill, a branch of knowledge and a branch of study concerned with a connected body of demonstrated truths or with observed facts systematically classified or more or less colligated by being brought under general laws and which includes trustworthy methods for the discovery of a new truth within its own domain (Oxford English Dictionary; 1956). It is certainly taken to cover a certain hardness of facts and conclusions that can be verified by others, but there can be no experimental repeatability for social behaviour which changes all the time almost as we watch it.

In reducing this unknown there has always been an uneven approach with some areas of behaviour receiving continuous or intermittent attention from researchers and some aspects none at all. Much research attention has been paid to the genetic results of inbreeding in many societies but little attention has been paid to domestic sanitary behaviour. Most of the research in the social sciences has been highly specialised and restricted to small samples while tending to become the foundations of more general conclusions within the hopefulness of Comte to provide rules that might govern all social behaviour.

So it is always a question of who does, what, when, where and how so that while the whole research process is theoretically open, it is in fact always severely restricted by personal, professional and place restrictions and variations. It may well be the fact that academic considerations have to be subordinated to factors that have nothing to do with what is chosen and indeed what can be researched such as fears for their own safety, tiredness and boredom.

Very little of human behaviour can be classified as exact enough to parallel inorganic chemistry or DNA analysis which would have effects independent of human variation. But even if we accept the accuracy of a DNA analysis, a medical diagnosis or a marriage certificate, the 'social' aspect of the social science label comes into the equation. The fact may exist but how it is treated or come into social existence is immensely varied in how it is observed, understood, and acted upon by those involved; a pool of potential knowledge with inexact boundaries and innumerable invasive factors all based upon research for which there can be no hard base line definitions.

The social sciences are faced with the problems of human variability at any stated time and that this variability is ongoing and continuous. Any research in its conclusions is tied to circumstances which have passed into history. Professor Evans-Pritchard has suggested that anthropologists are in fact historians as whatever they have studied was in the process of change, but those who are observing are also changing and are as varied as their research subjects. In practice what the social scientists observe has already past and they are reconstructing past events from written records and the inevitably inaccurate memories of those who may not have been directly involved in what they are describing. Even if they were involved they might well have reasons enough to change their memories to make it fit into their present social situation.

So it would seem that social science strains after a scientific exactness which is denied to them by the circumstances in which people are studied. Certainly there are facts, influential or not, round which there are not exact behavioural events but brief periods of coincidence which may have correlations which are created by the social scientists involved. However the key variability in all research are the researchers themselves in relation to the environments in which they work.

The citizen as a researcher involves two categories of people. The citizen category in law is a general one in which the individual is no different demographically to several million others. The value for researchers to have this legal status will involve positive assets which will enable them to do certain things, while at the same time will restrict them in other just as significant ways.

However the citizen as a researcher is entirely individual within the dimensions of their socialisation. Any group affiliation of researchers will be circumstantial. Their personal contributions to any research situation will be a combination of what they bring into it as individuals, as Bengalis or Brahmins, and the particular circumstances in which they are involved.

The importance of citizenship is only in theory a static value and much will depend will depend on the researchers awareness of what is involved nationally in not only their ability to do research but in their ability to manipulate the national social and political environment; the factors which officials and politicians want to employ at that time and which can be employed by those who want to do business with them. A Chinese and Indian citizen would have the necessary knowledge to get through bureaucratic restrictions. Citizenship is a card in the pack which has legally defined values but its value at any particular time and place depends on the value of the other cards which are being played in that situation. Foreigners would always have an inadequate knowledge of how to play these cards in particular situations. It took the American social scientist to realise after much coffee drinking goodwill expressed in Arabic that each authority in saying that he would agree if some other authority agreed was in fact refusing his application to study Islamic sermons in an Egyptian city because they could not guarantee his safety. While a Bengali woman was able to study a pre-Partition non-violent Muslim group in Pakistan because she knew someone's important brother but it took two years to engineer the necessary permission. An Austrian sociologist was able to live in an African township under Apartheid because his host with whom he lodged had a relative who wanted to further his studies of such poor communities.

The researcher on the other hand will be evaluated in entirely individual terms and in different ways in all the social and political levels of the society in which he or she wants to work. The permissions of a ministry will only be a start and there would have to be subsequent negotiations at district, town and neighbourhood level and indeed in how and where they are going to work and sleep. Srinivas has described how that in one case he ended up living in the cowshed because of complicated excluding possibilities of where he could live because of caste restrictions. Their personalities and approach to their research work are disparate by any social, psychological and physiological categories which people involved choose to bring into play and employ. In addition the research situations are by definition different and changing all the time while the research continues. Researchers studying farming methods in Uganda were brought back to the sponsoring university by the police as they did not want the responsibility when civil unrest made their position uncertain and thus a bureaucratic liability.

It is our contention that those who undertake research can be divided between those who are nationals of the country in which research is undertaken and those who are non-nationals with a third category of nationals who have left their country of origin and undertake research in or about that country from a position of citizenship in a third country whom we classify as 'half and half' researchers. We feel that this division is more important in influencing the nature of research than the more conventional divisions based on ethnicity, sex and age. This study is largely confined to Indian social scientists.

It is also our contention that since the social sciences originated in European thought, it is Westerners who have continued to dominate research not only from a theoretical perspective but through their greater access to research funding and peer reviewed publishing. So it would seem that in their Asian and African intellectual and political assessments there would be an element of unconscious exploitation.

Our study looks particularly at the advantages and disadvantages of citizenship for research in Asia and Africa comparing the methods and enablement of the three categories which we have defined. We will assume that citizens with their superior insider knowledge of the societies in which they work would have significant advantages over the non-national, while imposing balancing disadvantages which outsiders may be able to avoid. As far as is possible we look at social science research from the perspective of African and Asian academic and political realities and at the published work of nationals as much as non-nationals to illustrate these issues.

In every situation of applied social science there is the basic difficulty that the social scientists involved are social and linguistic aliens to the people they are investigating. There is no reason why they should give any information to these 'invaders' unless it is to their advantage to do so by gains of status, influence or money. The researchers have to use considerable ingenuity to get over these barriers of language and social distance apart from the general inclination to provide misinformation on any subject about which they have their own views.

Language and Obtaining Information

The linguistic code of the highly educated social scientist in both its vocabulary and its semantics almost inevitably bring difficulties into their relationships with their informants except when they are involved in in-house applied work. It is language that the social distance between researcher and the researched is most striking. Some cultures such as that of the Papuan Urapim believe that all speech is inaccurate and no one can speak the truth as there is a long social distance between heart and mouth (Robbins, 2001).

This issue of social distance is always there even if they are both using the same words. Social scientists often come to realise that there are different uses of many common words which are abstract rather than materially based. Getting school children to write sentences using the word 'God' shows that their views have a wide variation in their understandings of that word; even a single individual when asked to produce ten sentences using a single word shows that there may not be any consistency even within individual thinking.

In any society there will be linguistic codes related to age, gender, religion, status and education. There is always the fact that many people even in simpler societies who are multilingual. A study of language use in a Kampala housing estate (Parkin, 1971) showed that there were four languages in common use depending who was talking to whom.

The data used for a study of homicide in Uganda (Tanner, 1970) collated by the central police office was written in English by policemen who may have had an English vocabulary of not more than 500 English words so that the information in their reports was both brief and interpretations of the situations which they saw or had been given information about. In the classification of these data only information that might be seen as reasonably accurate was date and location and the name of the deceased. Everything else in those collated reports must be seen as doubtful and yet those involved were doing their best to provide accurate information for their superiors over these important and common offences since the conclusion was that the Uganda murder rate was substantially higher than that of New York as many murders were not reported and the absence of refrigeration led to the disappearance and deterioration of many bodies before the police were informed.

The Insider-Outsider Division between Social Science Researchers

This may be an unwise dichotomy however attractive it may seem to those who see researchers as fitting into such a classification dividing nationals from non-nationals. It is obvious enough that an Asian Indian anthropologist researching American Indians is an outsider and that in his comparative work with Indians in India he was an insider (Pandey, 1979), just as a Saudi Arabian woman with high American educational qualifications researching Saudi Arabian family life is an insider (Altorki, 1982) and as an insider subject to all the restrictions of a woman in that society within which she had to manipulate her research interests as she was just another Saudi woman in which her education could not override the restrictions on movement and dress to which she was subjected such as not being allowed to drive herself about or associated with men to whom she was not related.

But these are extremes and between them there are many gradations between the legal distinction of being a national or a non-national which have to be discussed. The vast majority of social science researchers in India are legal insiders while being internal expatriates in varying degrees at the same time according to the aspects of the topic on which they are working. An Afro-American studying Nigerian social life is both a quasi-insider and outsider at the same time just as a European studying European social life in East Africa (Tanner, 1964, 1966), made himself into a specialised outsider among other outsiders in terms of their nationality and the surrounding African majority.

It has always to be remembered that those taking on a research project in the social sciences are by self-definition making themselves into outsiders to those that they are studying. It is only by deliberate and difficult deception that someone can research without disclosing in some way that they are being inquisitive which in most societies is not viewed as an accepted activity. How far this 'outsiderness' goes is very much a matter for their personalised methodologies, a combination of personality, topic and fortuitous circumstances, but outsiders they remain from the moment that they start their research and inevitably when they put pen to paper. Cross that boundary line of professional detachment to liking or disliking the people with whom they are working and they have to consider whether they are any longer social scientists. It is indeed difficult to live closely with individuals in a community and to avoid the obligations which come from this closeness.

It seems likely, therefore, that there are analytical classifications of limited usefulness except in Merton's comment (Merton, 1972; 36) that 'the problem is not to ask whether it is the Insider or the Outsider who has monopolistic or privileged access to social truth but to consider their distinctive or interactive roles in the process of truth seeking'. A heterosexual researching a prison community has to immunise his socialised feelings in relationship to the permutations of institutionalised homosexual relationships.

The researchers are insiders when there is mutual interests which at least to some extent overlays their obvious differences as researchers and the researched; ethnic similarities; belonging to the same family, lineage or clan, shared birthplace, shared experience of understandable misfortune, shared interest in football or religion, and a shared dislike of certain categories of outsiders. The distinguished Indian sociologist

Srinivas had difficulties over his Brahmin caste status. In a study of cattle theft in Musoma, Tanzudyania, it was in the interests of informants to give as accurate information accurately as possible so that government might introduce a policy which helped to reduce the enormous amount of cattle stolen by insiders rather than by raiders from outside tribes.

In their field work do the researchers let the information come to them as at least partial insiders but never completely so or do they seek for information which makes them more distinctively outsiders; what are the dimensions of social acceptability in the roles of being accepted as curious outsiders to being outsiders who are curious. Religion is not a topic which most people feel able to talk about. Also in applied social science projects do they have the time to allow the reduction of this outsiderness.

Researchers are outsiders when they are known to be investigating matters which are not seen by those being researched as commonly accessible to outsiders; their dividing line between public and private curiosity. The question 'why' does not sit easily into any inter-relationship in any culture as it is intrusive. Once researchers take an active part in obtaining information they are automatically outsiders and becomes almost always a potentially hostile act since it has no part in their social lives and is related to the bureaucratic entanglements of modernising societies. The actively seeking researchers whether they are nationals or non-nationals are following on these people's experiences in schools, government offices and the presence of inspectors from a wide range of departments. The cards are marked against researchers when they are to go beyond the passive role of letting themselves to be slowly absorbed as far as they possibly can into the research environment and it is this which they will be involved in.

The Aims of Research

We must assume that the aim of social science research is the betterment of the lives of the particular parts of society which are being investigated by particular researchers and that they have some particular insights in this and that almost inevitably they have some personal concern; they are biased by their personal and professional commitment to their field of enquiry.

Further, that the aims of social science researchers should not in the first instance be professional success and career fulfilment. Of course this exists but surely this should be mainly secondary and should be kept severely subordinated to the essential aim of the betterment of the lives of those researched.

If we accept that the aims of social science research is this betterment of the lives of those researched, then we are immediately concerned with how this is to be brought about since we are not administrators nor political and social power holders. At whom are we directing the results of our research and who are we trying to make aware of how the people we have researched live.

The aim of this study is to examine the problems of applied field work by the well-meaning and socially aware national researchers who devote much time, money and effort, their social capital, to finding out about the social life of people whom they research. The inarticulate people who are researched know their own ways of behaving well enough but about whom the local power holders and initiators of change may know very little and should whenever possible use the suggestions and recommendations of detached social scientists.

Thus social science research has a threefold aim beyond the moral aim of enabling betterment. To find out what they want to know without disrupting the lives of those researched. To enable better understandings about these parts of society by those seeking to change it. Finally to persuade outsiders about these understandings which have been acquired by through social science research.

Of course in all this there is the need for foundations based on appropriate and acceptable methodologies and through this the ability of researchers to portray and persuade by combinations of their personal influence and recorded findings. The basis should be the possibilities enabled by methodology, not the methodology enabling the possibilities. The study of human behaviour can never be an exact science and forcing numerical exactness on to data by using the methodological approaches appropriate to working on inorganic material, is self-defeating. The data cannot cover the ranges of variation and is out of date almost as soon as it has been recorded. The aim of methodology should be to produce data that has some logical coherence between the views of the observed and the observer and not just one created by the intellectual imagination of the researchers.

The Dimensions of the Unknown

Let me start by referring to my own experiences of trying to find out about the people with whom I was involved for the applied project of reintroducing some semblance of administration destroyed by the three years of Japanese occupation in north Burma almost all records had been destroyed by accidents or deliberately during the Japanese invasion and the subsequent reinvasion by the British and Indian armies and United States Army Air Force bombers. Offices in the Northern Shan States were bare except for the recent productions of the British Military Civil Affairs directorate. Even if I had known that there had been studies of the Kachins (Naung, 1942), Palaungs (Milne, 1924) and Shans (Milne and Cochrane, 1910), it would have been useless since but there were no locally owned copies.

When I came to work later in the Kilwa coastal district of Tanganyika Trust Territory there was nothing in the office except recent records related to cases that had been heard in court and tax registers. The so-called District Book contained no more than a few unsystematic idiosyncratic reminiscences of previous administrators. There was some data on the Arab rule over the island of Kilwa Kisiwani and some published descriptions of the 1905 Maji rebellion against the German colonial occupation which had centred on Liwale and Kibata over a hundred miles inland (Bell, 1950) of which there were still some survivors of the subsequent famine alive.

Thus it seemed to me, as it must have occurred to almost any social science researchers, that whatever field work project I started the knowledge that I acquired would be a very small item in an enormous field of the unknown and however thorough I might be, it would be no more than a pebble thrown into a pool of ignorance.

This situation should not be seen only as an example of British colonialism but as paralleling the boundaries of knowledge faced by any social scientist applying their professional expertise to any contemporary problem, but the situation of any executive official or business manager wanting to institute some administrative policies of which political overseers had decided should be put into operation.

In both the two areas mentioned above there were small populations in an enormous area so that when this situation is seen in societies numbering many millions such as in China and India. this amount of the unknown must be multiplied. The situation must be much the same as that faced by any social scientist working on applied projects. Only in some small communities in which individuals have specialised such as the Manus islanders and some American Indian communities in the United States for which there is an accumulation of knowledge not much related to the issues for which decisions have to be made in the here and now about food, education and medical help.

The theories behind much contemporary applied social science fieldwork will have been based on the sporadic earlier coverage of a limited range of communities, may seem important in retrospect, particularly for those who do not have any personal knowledge of cultures or parts of cultures other than their own, but not nearly so important as new data which for most of the world still continues to be more or less blank slates. The examples of applied social science used to illustrate this study shows how little is known about social behaviour.

Developing Societies and Research

There is a basic difference between the research environment in poor or at least not wealthy societies and economically more successful ones in which those in institutions of higher education are able to develop their own ideas of how research should be conducted because they have the resources to be independent. In most of the world social science research is a hand to mouth improvisation by nationals of fleeting self-financing opportunities dictated by obvious needs and in-house applied research dictated by the needs of their employers. Opportunities to carry out research which are more or less dropped into the lap of potential researchers such as my Uganda homicide study (Tanner, 1970) and my reactions to the Buganda *coup d'état* (Tanner, 1978) heard through my office window.

A developing nation with its own limited revenues is often dependent on the major western nations for its own plans for social and economic development. They would agree to non-nationals researching inside their boundaries on subjects and producing results for which they have no immediate or indeed foreseeable use they would see research which has no obvious or potential use as a waste of money. They know that these researchers are furthering their own careers but it is not worth the political difficulties from trying to direct such work to areas which they consider important. Of course this happens to some degree in national committees vetting research topics before visas are granted, but they cannot be too bureaucratic about this because they need the good-will of outsider universities for exchange students and support for their own universities. Even then the popular feeling in Uganda about those researching foreigners is that they are sucking the blood of the host societies in which they work for their own advancement in getting higher degrees and further employment.

Most developing societies have immediate needs as do their universities and they want to maintain control of their own institutions so that they provide value for money in the opinion of political power holders rather than being the source of more than suppressed hostility. Of course there is the theory that education is a 'good thing' for all but in practice the cost of education beyond the primary level is so high that it is in fact always elitist and limited, even though they understand that education is the means to achieving higher standards of living for all or at least in keeping economic development in time with population growth. They would see little need to educate engineers and agriculturalists when national opportunities are limited and they would be financing a 'brain drain' in which these nations lose their best brains to overseas opportunities.

In so far as they have the means to control and promote social science research it would be in applied research in support of their immediate problems such as the control of AIDS, urban planning, agricultural improvements, corruption and low level selective change. Overall research has sometimes been seen to support a particular oppressive regime and its agenda which is usually controlled by a corrupt national socio-political oligarchy since nationals are not likely to expose themselves and their families to the dangers which would come from the investigation of such practices.

The Factor of Credibility

At any time in the professional world there is a framework of acceptability for ideas, methodology and results which is the basis for research work in the social sciences. This is not static and changes occur slowly as new research work is carried out on new issues and in new environments but there can be violent and radical changes which require an immediate reorientation of methods. The fact that the tsunami in Indonesia killed far more women on land than fishermen at sea and that has caused the 'market' value of women to rise because of their scarcity. This selective mortality has meant that men there have been forced to do their own cooking and laundry so that the whole structure of those coastal societies will have been reorganised in days in ways that could not have been envisaged in any of the existing scenarios for rapid social change and within the gendered dominances of Islamic ideology.

Then there is the work of those such as Castenada (Castenada, 1968) who go beyond these boundaries of existing methodology, thinking entirely inferentially. However 'right' they may be in the long run certainly find their acceptability limited to those on the fringes of academic and mainstream social science. Such thinkers will never have their methods, much less their conclusions, adopted to applied social science requirements. Of course we can say that his publications come from his imaginative reconstructions of what Yaqui Indian intellectuals may have been and religious thinking but these restrictive parameters do exist. The executives who ask for the investigations of projects want the results served up in the factual form related in some way to the other memoranda which they receive in their work; numerical conclusions they may understand but hanging in the air ideas as they do not have any which have no general social science acceptance.

Demographic data is usually based on documented birth data and movements tied to maps so that accurate figures can be produced on the movements of cohorts. But for most populations birth dates are not known except in relation to key events for which dates are known and even if maps exist there is not much use of them in recording movement to and from places which have no relation to village names or streets which have no recorded names. So the recording of movement by direction is as valid a method as any for studying migration but not one acceptable to the current professional ideas of demography. Much of this data comes from church records of dates, sex, address and the recording of names. There is in these records a massive amount of hard data of comparative use particularly in Sweden where the clergy have the legal obligation to keep these records.

However radical the individual researcher may be in their personal views and political affiliations, they are not notably conservative in their thinking except possibly in their own personal theoretical patterning. Their professional standing and future careers rest within the parameters of acceptability which is correlated to this specialised form of credibility.

It has little, if anything, to do with whether these conclusions fit into the understandings of the people about whom the research has been done, indeed in most cases there is no backward consultation or the passing on of their conclusions. Perhaps there is an understanding that it is difficult enough to get professional acceptance without the complication of putting these conclusions into a more popular genre often in another language, but this ignores the fact that any community no matter however 'primitive' it may be materially, has not only sophisticated languages but that there will always be a significant number of intellectuals who will be well able to evaluate new ideas present to them by people who show that they accept some measure of intellectual capacity and mental equality in those with whom they are discussing. It is very difficult for social scientists to accept the intellectual capacity of those who are socially unacceptable and whom they would hesitate to accept into an inter-dining social network. An intellectually acute old Sukuma not particularly clean according to university standards dressed in clothes donated by a Western charity, is not going to be given social equality by a clean social scientist.

In the developed nations the social science parameters of acceptability allow a much wider range of latitude than exist for the harder sciences but they are still laid down by those in senior positions in these fields of enquiry. In what could be described as a profession seeking wider acceptance for its work not much has been done to offset the much quoted Karl Popper's comments that 'the triumph of social anthropology is the triumph of pseudo-observation, pseudo-descriptive and pseudo-inductive generalising methodology and above all makes the triumph of a pretended objectivity and hence an imitation of the methods of natural science' (Banton, 1964).

However social science creditability has no general acceptability according to the predetermined standards of the hard sciences. It is always dependent on what matters and, particularly, for whom. In professional circles credibility is likely to be related to going understandings of evidence and how the whole discourse hangs together and often as sponsoring organisations they will be looking for some assurance from referees, that they are getting a reasonable return on their expenditure from what could be considered an intellectual mortgage. The political power holders will want to be assured that what has been researched and the results available for public use are not contributing to unrest and indeed not overcritical of their regime and, of course, some concern for the people who have been researched who may not wish to know what has been written about them.

Social scientists learn from their university education but if they are to enlighten those who read their publications, their writings have to be more than and indeed qualitatively different from the use of the techniques and ideas which they have received from their academic superiors. Human behaviour is so complex that the understandings of most people are tied to common pragmatism rather than to those of academic analysis. The Tanzanian Sukuma when asked the old English riddle as to why does the chicken cross the road, answer that it wants to get to the other side. Similarly if they are asked why they propitiate their ancestors, the answer will be just as it will be to such difficult questions in all societies and at all levels, this is what we have always done; analytical thought is always a difficult rarity. Too often commonsense is replaced by the satisfying crudities of quantitative science and theoretical complexities. The social scientists, if they want to have influence outside their own profession, have to use their imaginations to link what they see and hear with what those they are observing are thinking (Miller, 1976). The intelligent Sukuma understands perfectly well anthropological theories relating to mother-in-law avoidance and the unity of alternate generations but moving onto more complex ideas such as the Oedipus complex they would think that the enquirer is trying to be funny. It seems likely that the national may be less likely to waste time on issues which both they and their people already know and this makes them possibly more useful in applied social science projects within their own cultures.

The Inaccuracy of Accuracy

Whatever approach is used in discussing applied social science research for secular or religious purposes beyond their own cultural understandings rather than just their behaviour, there are enduring dilemmas. We are seeking to impose standards of scientifically acceptable accuracy on human behaviour when we already know that it is intrinsically and permanently variable and indeed varying as they themselves write their conclusions.

It seems likely that too much attention and effort has been put into the scientific aspirations of the social sciences and the consequent feelings that many researchers have not so much failed but that they could not have succeeded in the first place to achieve any such overall standards of exactness and as accuracy in anything as changeable as human behaviour. Those initiating applied projects for religious organisations should not anticipate exact replies to questions that are probably inexact in the first place.

If we take the opposite aspect we can see how much the exact sciences have to use social science qualitative data in support of their exactnesses. A study of non-smoker mortality from living with smokers (Hill *et al.*, 2004) accepts the data provided by the sample that they had never smoked as believed for which there is no evidence at all, apart from the fact that not much is known about what is involved in second-hand exposure to smoking when much depends on how much time those individuals have spent outside in what may be a polluted or relatively unpolluted environment. Such data obscures the value of Mormon data who in their heartland Utah live in a less polluted environment than New York or Chicago. Much medical research conclusions involve basic data about which there is no authenticated reliability.

Another study of the consequences of public smoking ban on hospital admissions for heart attacks (Sargent *et al.*, 2004) lists among the weaknesses of the study that it did not and indeed could not measure exposure to second hand-smoking. Whether the conclusions will prove to be valid is not our point, only that these researchers had to depend on qualitative assumptions, even if we do not include in these cases that the public opinion on the unpleasant aspects of tobacco smoking may have motivated both the research and its conclusions. Such doubts will always exist unless the hard sciences confine their research work to environments which are scientifically controlled which can only be applied to experiments with animals.

Any current number of the *British Medical Journal* or the *Journal of the American Medical Association* will contain articles on applied medical research which combine factual data from laboratory analyses, standard quantitative information, correlated with qualitative information to which the same principles of pragmatism cannot be applied which are nevertheless treated as important enough to be tied to scientific data.

A high proportion of research articles rely in part on the honesty of informants supplying information and there are no adequate ways of checking on the correctness of varied answers in varied situations. It is not that informants are dishonest but that their memories of what they did or may not have done even a week previously have proved to be almost invariably inaccurate. This is not to suggest that replies are deliberately dishonest although they may well be so, but the assumption that much information is correct is much on the lines of an act of faith that someone looks reliable.

While there are identical twins who are biologically similar, they are nevertheless subject to different environmental pressures when they leave their homes to walk down the street or go to the market. For the rest of society there can never be environmental situations even those of tsunami sea wave disasters which will have similar effects on the individuals involved who are all basically dissimilar. If that recent disaster had occurred at night the demographic profile of deaths would have been different. The Japanese disaster killed a high proportion of elderly because they were at home in communities which had a high proportion who preferred to live where they had been born.

Many social scientists continue to act and research on the assumption that in some way it is possible to group these innumerable and fluctuating differences into fixed categories and to methodologically halt their constantly changing human and environmental interrelationships. This is done so that the data becomes potentially usable by those who usually act from what they consider to be facts rather than inferences, and thus transferable to other situations in which it is assumed to have affinities.

While it is not necessary to go as far as the Buddhist framework of thinking that it is only humans who create the illusion of individual permanency out of constant and varying microscopic units. Perhaps we are still nearer to Malinowski's approach that viewed the Trobriand Island society as a human laboratory. We are usually nearer to the approach that treats those whom we research as 'them', rather than refractions of ourselves. There are few social scientists who approach their understandings of others as there but for the accident of birth and education are themselves.

Since so much social science in both the developed and developing worlds is applied to sorting out immediate problems already defined by political and known social needs, there is at the back of their minds not so much an unconscious wish to know more, but a desire to predict and control. This is not so much because of political pressures but because social scientists may be to some extent mesmerized by the short-term successes of inorganic science.

They inherit the hope rather than the reality of what Auguste Comte's theory that the study of human behaviour could be made into an exact science.

Social scientists are also not happy with the suggestion that they are not only biased in the ways that they collect data as individuals but that they are also subject to fashion in their fields of research and the more social than scientific boundaries that this creates. The study of applied social science projccts which have been published shows that their authors have been influenced by public opinion disguising academic fashions of thought. Those social scientists trained in Western originated styles of method, are biased by what they have culturally inherited. A whole range of metaphysical ideas are discarded before they have been thoroughly researched such as the very commonplace idea that the dead can materially influence the lives of the living and that evil can be created without physical contacts by witches as a barometer of communal social tensions (Marwick, 1964). Social scientists whether Asian, African or European need to recognise more clearly that they view the social world in particular ways which excludes or includes a range of metaphysical ideas which are no part of their cultural inheritance. One can perhaps change one's ideas of good cooking quite easily but metaphysical ideas are always subconsciously adaptive or resistant to adaptation.

This study is an examination of some of the contemporary factors involved in applying social science methods with rather than on people who are disadvantaged in terms of what they are and what the secular and religious power holders hope to achieve within their life-times. There is an immediacy in what social scientists aim to describe and relate to in their conclusions.

There is the need to examine the predominance of Western methodology and understandings in social science research and further the range of influence enabled by the professional predominance of English. Although Mandarin Chinese is spoken and read by far more people than any other language and in which we can assume much valuable research has been written, it is not a language of global influence. There are of course Mandarin readers who are bilingual in English, but they aim to inform the power holders in their own society and do not have much interest or are restricted in how far they can draw attention to themselves by translating their work for extra-territorial readers.

We are examining applied social science between factors restricting and enabling national social science researchers over issues that have a metaphysical basis and the extent to which these are shared between these professionals. We cannot assume that they have an overall advantage since there are internal expatriates, sex and social distance factors which differentiate their access to data and perhaps their interpretations.

Ephemeral Nature of Religious Research

Every study of religious beliefs and behaviour reaches conclusions which are applicable only to that field of enquiry. It is probable that only those researchers believe their hypotheses and that it is not one that would be shared by any of their informants because of the many dimensions of social distance and variable environments.

Unless they are studying the beliefs and practices of a single person there is no reason to suppose that what person *A* does will be duplicated by person *B* even in the same household. All informants are basically different in their personalities and in their experienced social environments. What are being recorded are inferences and rarely facts. What we are left with is that in every society there is something which they regard as sacred and activities which they regard as secular but both these categories are substantially definitionally ephemeral.

There is also the real possibility that the social scientists involved will be influenced by what they feel are exceptional local personalities. Margaret Mead was obviously consciously impressed by the personality of Paliau, the founder of the modernising movement in Manus (Mead. M., 1964).

A Necessary and Influential Inquisitiveness

Social science field work is the exposure of intellectual outsiders, whether nationals or non-nationals, to the realities of social life other than their own which results in a personal broadening of individual understandings. This may be a worthy aim but perhaps not worth the expense of time and effort unless it is privately paid for; it is too personal.

If the field work in developing societies is in any way supported by public funds or foundations dedicated to the public interest, then there should be some close correlation to immediate public needs and understandings. It may become important as the studies of refugees and the epidemiology of newly prevalent diseases. To evaluate subsidised social science field work as contributing new knowledge to any general understandings of human behaviour is a far too general an aim to be justified when so much of contemporary social needs remain without attention from researchers. To push back the frontiers of knowledge into anything anywhere at any time might appear to be a selfish preoccupation of no immediate public value.

There is a need for relevance and there appears to be two processes by which social science could become more related to contemporary needs. Firstly, that research should be related to matters of current concern for the betterment of the lives of people and their descendants. Secondly, this research and its methodologies should link this social relevance to the understandings of the people themselves as far as is reasonably possible; there seems little point in producing research results in forms which can only be understood and appreciated by a professional elite. Every community at whatever level of economic and social development contains an intellectual elite who are well able to understand much of what is being deduced about their society if it is printed in a linguistic code which is understandable to them. Methodologies which exclude this form of social relevance by basing themselves on scientific prototypes may not relate easily to the more immediate aims of social betterment.

On the one hand there is long-term investigative work with an almost journalistic approach to social reality as shown in work relating to the human suffering caused by the Partition of India (Butalia, 1995) and more recent events such as the study of Bombay (Mehta, 2004) and the artisans of Banaras (Kumar, 1988). Whatever language these studies may be written in they would be appreciated by those interested in those matters; there should be a sharing of intellectual understanding and humane concern between the researchers and the researched.

At the other extreme there are studies expressed in statistical terms of information under circumscribed situations which show no more than the betting odds on such behaviour reoccurring in parallel situations which are unlikely to reoccur anyway. It may well be the case that necessarily inaccurate impressions expressed quantitatively are likely to be more influential than qualitative impressionistic accuracy because that is the form with which bureaucracies are more at home; it is both their defensive and offensive currency.

How can social science become more influential because currently in all societies it is only minimally involved when the conditions highlighted by public opinion and the political needs power-holders coincide. We have to start with our own basic professional understandings that there are very few, if any, facts which are not transitory and circumscribed. Unusually a whole academic profession has grown up not so much on the possible value of these transitory inaccuracies but in the hope of being able to achieve accuracy and thus to predict particular types of human behaviour. It evolved in the manipulative traditions of the hard sciences without accepting the limitations and restrictions of the data which they acquired with such care; at best the patchwork nature of whatever accuracies that have been obtained.

Whatever the reasons social scientists from developing nations are under represented on the editorial boards of many international journals and as sole authors of articles published in the major international journals (Saxena *et al.,* 2003). One analyst classified this as a bias against the diseases of poverty (Horton, 2003) This is particularly noticeable in medical articles related to tropical diseases in which only 5 per cent of exclusive authors came from societies classified as having low human development. Ideas may percolate into the minds of power holders who are much less likely to be influenced by documentation which they do not have the time or the inclination to read.

The social sciences have something in the nature of a choice in which direction they should develop in order to be more influential. It does seem that the scientific channel of influence is rarely likely to be available because the information is available too late and to refer to small enclaves in major societies while the human objects of research are in a constant process of changing their behaviour. Finally, the inevitable biases of the researchers are part of the information collected.

The attitude of those in power to the results of social science research are likely to be a combination of what their supporting bureaucrats consider important enough to be given to their political employers in the form of short memos and interviews and the power-holders needs from short-term political expediency. Perhaps also there may be an attitude that avoids any suggestion that what is happening is unavoidable.

The most important aspect of influence is to catch the attention of these power holders by combining research results and their presentation so that they are within the wider range of public opinion needs rather than just getting the approval of professional colleagues who remain on the fringe of decision making or influencing public opinion. Many power holders may feel that they are the victims of factors over which they have no control which may be reinforced by research results.

The difficulty of producing research results which might influence decision making is that this power in any society is diffused. Much of the developing world in which a major proportion of research is done, have oligarchic systems of government whether based on military coups, one party systems, fraudulent ballots or dictatorships; they are in fact almost always nepotic inward looking systems based on tribe, clan, caste, extended families or those who have gone through similar training systems whether educational, religious or military.

The impulse to change does not come from the rational discussion of policy at least partially aimed at the public good. In such situations there is little difference to eighteenth century England in which the political system was described as an oligarchy mitigated by riot. Collective farming in China, Russia and the Pol Pot regime in Indo-China were not the result of carefully researched policy changes any more than that of the villagization mass movement in Tanzania with its consequences of serious declines in agricultural production. These massive changes were the result of applying the rationality of economics and factory production to highly variable and varying human behaviour outside such restricted environments.

The monumentally impressive study of contemporary Mumbai (Mehta, 2004) by an author who should be considered a half and half researcher, puts into exciting prose more information about that city than could be covered by many social scientists. Qualitative results certainly, but the information therein is most certainly already known in general details by those in power and by implication most of those who are experiencing this particular way of living. That information may nudge power holders to initiate effort to solve some disclosed problems.

Of course it is true what Gilbert White, the distinguished English naturalist, who wrote in such detail about his own rural environment that 'the more concentrated the observations, the more accurate will be the recordings'. But this means at the same time that they will be less influential since such data only refers to a few people and will soon have been just part of history if anyone could be bothered to read about it. It lacks the push and stimulus of immediacy.

Most politically inspired major changes start without the social sciences being involved in the planning and in estimating the consequences. Field work concerning decisions which have already been made, make social scientists unwilling partners in political processes for which research is not well designed.

The Restrictions from Terminology

The research worker in social science field work is tied by the professional definitions of those three words. The word 'science' is tied to the pragmatics of cause and effect created by work on inorganic materials, 'social' by any standards is both individual and environmentally variable but the most important word is 'field' which is a concept of a specific area.

Now science deals with veracities of lineal relationships about which there can be little doubt as to what facts are put in and what facts are taken out. There is little allowance for uncontrolled variation. By keeping this word in their job specification social scientists have defined themselves into producing results which are acceptable according to the canons of hard science, but these facts are only pieces on a chess board, in which these pieces can be moved in many different directions. Human variations being what they are, social scientists are perhaps always unable to comply with their own professional expectations.

We have to accept that social factors can never be tied to exact definitions of any type and is incapable of producing any irrefutable conclusions. Even identified diseases may not follow their usual patterns. Any social situation is subject to immense and constant variations in the number and characteristics of those involved. There are in fact no uniformities which can be presupposed to exist in human social behaviour and when no uniformities appear to have been found. This may have been achieved by excluding from this many factors because there are no social science methodologies that can cope lineally with multiple factors.

We have to accept that the characteristics of the researchers are of constant importance who see and hear in individual ways along the basic divide between nationals and non-nationals. They may try to exclude themselves from their observations but they are always the variable centre but constant influence on what is seen, reported on and worked over in final reports.

Then the 'field' in which their observations are made which is substantially varied on a moment to moment basis so that there is a constantly changing amalgam of these three perspectives

It seems that the basic problem may be the lineal demands of the scientific mentality requiring one fact to influence its successors in an identifiable way. No methodology has been developed satisfactorily for relating multiple factors. It has to be accepted that the number of potential factors is innumerable and that quantities always narrowed abstractions.

An individual sees the situations in which they are involved as researchers or as the researched, in an endless series of instant pictures. The wholenesses for which Parallel Distributive Processing is endeavouring to develop into workable methodologies but this has not got much beyond typing.

Anthropologists have always had this workable concept of a field in which they work which has only the vaguest of definitions as to who, what, where and when are involved. Researchers who accept this qualitative approach to their work for which a scientific approach is usually going to be a fruitless endeavour and in which nationals are more likely to have an initial effective understanding as a basis for their efforts and are more likely to produce data on which others can similarly imaginatively work.

Social Scientists as the Weak Link

In our perception of spirituality and well-being related to religious beliefs and practices, the weak link in any understanding of what is happening must be the social scientists themselves who bring to their own understanding a range of personal conscious and unconscious biases as a creatures of particular societies with unavoidable demographic characteristics of age, sex and appearance.

Of course we have cameras and recording machines which will provide us with seemingly hard data but photographs provide no explanations and tapes record only a single sense. Biomedicine has machines that provide information that is finite and short of deliberate deception, they do not lie. Knowing the presence of a particular DNA or a particular virus cannot be invariably causal for particular forms of behaviour so again we are left with inferences.

Thus the social sciences are always looking at human behaviour through a personal viewpoint including doctors. Scientists have developed individual perspectives in what they choose to look at but are rather more able to reconcile particularities through the conventions of inter-subjective agreement, to create what they call an objective account. This has the air of a view from nowhere (Sweeney, 2006).

Social scientists approaching an enquiry linking spirituality with well-being probably have to concede that the correlation exists in the mind. Adam Phillips heading to his review of Spufford's 'Unapologetic' talking about what it feels like is as real as it gets' (Philipps, 2013). PubMed which lists all medical publications globally on a monthly basis provide some 12 thousand references in the last ten years in English possibly connecting spirituality, health and well-being. It is possible to read a majority of these publications for specific or tenuous connections and that would be in addition to specific research allied to such a topic. There would appear to be a surfeit of information awaiting the researcher.

In any research into religion and its connection with well-being there are two connecting themes in the brains of theses researchers. Firstly, there is the topic which they are planning to investigate which may well be their own intellectual and social creation. Secondly, there is the data which they pick up along the way; the accidents of encountering information which cannot be deliberate but founded on chance. The influence of a respected teacher and what might come from casual conversations or the accident of picking up a journal or something that comes up in a computer search.

Social scientists do not have, however much they aspire to having, much hard data from which they can produce hard conclusions. It is not a binding situation in which answer can be either/or or yes/no. Probably if they are honest with themselves conclude no more than the Hollywood film magnate's statement 'I can give you a definite maybe'.

The native's point of view whether in Delhi or Detroit has to predominate in the researcher's thinking and that is the reality with which the social scientists have to deal as their bases even if they are convinced that it involves delusions.

The aim should surely be to see this information as a free as possible from the distortions imposed by the use of Western categories regardless of their material simplicities.

There is always the fact that even the most sensitive social scientists is and will always be an outsider to what he or she is investigating. Even with long association as with Margaret Mead's association with the Trobriand islanders over half a century would certainly lead to unconscious perception but her role there would remain that of an appreciated and valued outsider with no demographic links to them other than the funding of welfare projects.

The Bengali social scientist who has received a prolonged specialised education and socialisation would always be an outsider to the Bengali farmer and his wife, even if he were from the same neighbourhood because of his or her professional training.

Differences in Patterns of Thinking and of History

We have already looked at the spectrum of bias which is built into individual human behaviour by our biological and psychological abilities and from the ways in which we are socialised. In the generally accepted sense it is not 'good' to be biased; it is seen by relatively unknown others as a social and psychological failing and it is not assessed as a form of necessary conformity.

It seems that this is a more individual way of looking at what goes on and does not cover cultural aspects of how we evaluate our own behaviour and that of others. After all the definition of bias (Oxford English Dictionary, 1956; 1175/6) is to swerve from the right line and having a bias is to be unfavourably inclined which covers both individuality as well as cultural predefinitions of what is appropriate.

So bias is deviation from something which is defined as 'right', a moral adjective which has immensely variable meanings so a bias in one social environment might not be one in an adjacent situation. The distaste of the social scientist for bias must come in part from their assumption that there are facts to be unearthed about human behaviour and that bias is a deflection. Freud is reported to have remarked that reality cannot be found. Even rationality can be considered a form of bias as it does not include many factors on which in real life most decisions are made.

It would seem that what facts there are in social behaviour, if they are not physiologically based and in some way inorganic, are more the result of bureaucracy than part of 'normal' social interrelationships. According to statutory law in most societies people are married or not as a result of set procedures and getting a signed certificate to that effect. We can assume that nothing else on the form constitute facts in the same category of exactness.

It may well be that individuals are almost always implicitly concerned with their day to day affairs and another explicitly formulated world inherited from the past and uncritically absorbed (Gramsci, 1971; 337) in which social scientists are over concerned with the latter on the assumption that it dominates the former.

When we come to consider whether bias has any overall meanings rather than being a purely personal tool modifying the possibilities of finding exact realities, we should be considering whether there are any overarching conceptual realities which channel understandings in particular ways independent of more individual social circumstances. It may be more valuable to have this as an idea to explore than to reduce the realities of biases to such factors as age and sex.

Let us examine 'bias' in the context of Gramsci's concept of 'commonsense'. Everyone in every social situation has views and behaviour which are amalgams of common sense in which this is in accordance with time, place and persons with whom they are associating for that particular environment in which there are certain persistent themes which correlate with social and psychological distancing. Thus in the defined sense of bias varying from a norm, there is the snag in attaching a pejorative meaning to that word, is that norms never can have or ever have had any unilateral constant except in some abstract ideological senses.

This is shown in cross-cultural psychological work in which Western forms of categorisation for mental states for which there are no local words, much less diagnostic ones. Even if the states of religious experience are similar with spirit possession in European and African ecstatic cults, there is no reason to suppose that individuals in those cultural environments are interpreting their experiences in the same way beyond the commonplace assertion that this is what we have always done.

If the answer to such questioning is just that, is would seem injudicious not to see that as an important answer and that to probe further into aspects which these people have not seen as important enough to develop further more explicit explanations.

If outsiders interpret the behaviour of cultural 'others' in different ways through culturized cognitive understandings, then surely such conclusions have to be seen at best as peripheral impositions. To paraphrase the analysis of a physician stating that the diagnostic categories of mental states are conceptual decisions coming from committee discussions.

We have to accept that the worlds of religious experience differ both culturally, individually so dramatically that the conclusions based on the thinking of social scientists based on Western professional standards has to be accepted as just one form of explanation among several cultural alternatives and should be viewed with some professional scepticism.

If we accept this commonplace statement that this is what we have always done and as such relying on the simplifications of less significantly educated minds.

In this approach then bias has to be assessed as so individualistic as to be out of agreement with those around them and thus are indeed difficult to assess except in almost pathological terms. In this the views of a hermit, paedophile or door-to-door salesman are not biased in any immediate social environmental sense although clearly biased from the points of view of other levels of social and psychological understandings, we have to consider number of additional factors including their ways of solving individual and communal difficulties. There is overall the unreliability of memory being brought up to date to conform to current social environments.

There would seem to be, therefore, three levels of common sense understandings and related behaviour whether secular or religious. Firstly, that of the individual and their immediate social inter-relationships, primary common-sense. We have to get on with the people with whom we live in the same apartment, house, Hindu joint household or group of huts within a single fence.

Then, secondly, common sense understandings related to the community in which individuals live and finally tertiary ones relating to the overall culture in which individuals and communities are contained.

Thus the ideas of bias should be seen in relationship to these three levels of common sense. The community which is out of functional agreement with the overall culture such as most if not all communities and the individuals and their families who are out of common sense order with both their community and culture such as criminal groups.

So bias in the sense of a non-conformist viewpoint would appear to be a constant in all social situations, but that of both national and non-national researchers have an additional form of bias because in the vast majority of field work situations they are detached from the social situations in which bias and commonsense operate together in socially acceptable ways; they are not by definition at home in primary, secondary or tertiary environments as they are guarded by professional paradigms.

They are isolated not only in the general sense from the three levels of commonsense to which they have been habituated in their own lives but are expected professionally to detach themselves from these ways of thinking and behaving which can only be a theoretical possibility. So there is a fourth professional level of normative and common sense behaviour based on the social impossibility of scientific detachment. This is perhaps the basic and most persistent of role conflicts for researchers, the requirement of objectivity which is paralleled by the persistence of social as much as psychological common sense attachments at all four levels.

If we accept the suggestion that religious behaviour is the simplification of less educated significantly simpler people, we have to look at as number of related factors. Firstly this type of explanation applies much to agricultural systems and ways of solving communal difficulties. Secondly this overall explanation as standard replies to questions which they had never had any reason to think about and much less voice their answers in culturally strange situations.

So it is important that we approach the religious experiences of all cultures including our own using the categories which we accept as appropriate to our own thinking and with which those people use themselves rather than to impose categorisations which degrade their intellectual capacities. The ecumenically tolerant parts of Christianity, Buddhism and Hindu do not use the social science categories of explanationism.

All researchers are burdened by their own liminal and subliminal understandings are inserted into the same tiers of common sense norms. Even the national researcher is only going to be attuned to the cultural levels of common sense but at the individual and communal level they may well be total strangers in terms of their understandings of and acceptance of primary and secondary common sense norms in these field work situations. The abatement of this can only be by the physiological similarities of ethnic appearance, age and sex and possibly biological abnormalities. We have to conclude that in these four senses of common sense both national and non-national researchers are persistently and comprehensively biased as individuals.

Instead of bias being assessed as ethically questionable and professionally unacceptable both national and non-national researchers should initiate their field work by a fundamental understanding that they are seeing their work through biased socially narrow perspectives. These characteristics are minimally at least ten which are accepted as record of channelling thought and behaviour in particular ways; age, sex, religion, education, ethnicity, location, status, occupation, marital status and biological factors limiting participation. These are exterior biases which the researchers bring with them into their work whether they are aware of their extent or not. These will not directly reflect the three levels of biased normalities as they become detached from the social environments in which they normally function.

Then facing them are the same inevitable biases in reverse which exist in all informants which will similarly show their primary individual normative common sense biases and their secondary and tertiary ones according to what information they are providing. Informants are deliberate filters of information rather than reporters of isolatable facts, choosing what he or she repeats or relates. Once a person has become publicly known as an informant he or she may be partially isolated from their own communal roles as they have become allied with outsiders.

2
Researchers

Physiological Factors

Much secular activities are carried out in the open and there are no particular difficulties over the work of social scientist except that they may not be used to physical work when they participate in farming work. Observing religious ceremonies may involve particular strains as they may be prolonged, at night indoors with poor lighting and obscured by smoke from incense and noise. Hinduism despite its involvement in meditation is in its public ceremonies a noisy religion which Western researchers find particularly culturally upsetting.

The sex and age of the researchers are basic problems because they will only be able to get second hand information about the beliefs and activities of the opposite sex and those whose age is markedly different to their own and those with status derived from age may dislike being questioned by a young ethnically different young adult. The unmarried adults are often the object of suspicion. Ethnicity we have already described as a basic block although a Japanese social scientists may look very like an American Indian. It is a culture shock for Westerners to be handicapped by such factors which in their own backgrounds they have felt to have culturally outgrown such restrictions.

While working in another non-natal language in a strange culture will always be tiring, it may be particularly so for researching metaphysical issues. There is also the fact that much discussions on these issues will happen in the evening and it is well known that workers are less alert after midday.

Social scientists areas subject to ageing as other persons and field work in different societies and environment is a tiring occupation. Most have one prolonged fieldwork experience in their early twenties which they may refresh by subsequent short visits as did Margaret Mead so their subsequent professional life is often dominated by theoretical considerations without further fieldwork for which perhaps they no longer have the energy to pursue; grant providers my prefer to support younger men and women who have a longer professional future in front of them. The older social scientists may well be unconsciously dominated by out of date information. This writer's major field work was with the Tanzanian Sukuma and Swahili in the fifties when he was in his late twenties. It was not particularly stressful as he was then living in Tanzania as a bilingual civil servant.

The Roles of the Researcher in Applied Work

To the researchers field work is a perfectly legitimate way of furthering the aims of their profession quite justified by the ethical need to know more about human behaviour for the ultimate betterment of mankind. This is an abstract ideal which is rarely going to be shared by those into whose lives these outsiders intrude in the interests of possibly applied in the interests of applied projects.

The closer those being researched they feel that their lives or the institutions in which they work or administer on logical and indeed to their minds scientific grounds and which they personally value, the less likely they are to accept wholeheartedly these intrusions. American Catholic Bishops contracted a secularly funded study of the Roman Catholic priesthood as an antidote to rumour (Greeley, 1972). The results were in the main reassuring and the conclusions would have been accepted perhaps because although the field work was done by a secular organisation, the final report was the work of a current priest with an established record of scholarly social science research on religious issues.

They are even less likely to accept conclusions which challenge the ways in which they have become used to accepting as best that they can do in the circumstances. There is thus a difference between what can be done in research which has no more than the aim of general understandings and work which is done in applying their enquiries and understandings to particular predefined objectives, like population reductions and enabling women to have more opportunities and domestic authority. The Jesuit superior in a missionary situation on being given the conclusions of a social scientist stated that he would find it difficult to circulate them to the brethren. Employers of social scientists are often surprised as to what they discover by their intrusive and trained perceptions.

There is almost invariably the feeling in the latter case that these researchers will not be able to provide any information of which the initiators of these applied projects think that they are already aware. They will be faced with various forms of obstruction as they disentangle what these people say that they do as opposed to what they actually do. In these situations national researchers may be better able to negotiate themselves round these successive obstacles (Minocha, 1979). Non-national researchers with a more comprehensive understanding of institutions as well as previous experience of working in institutions may be less impeded by these difficulties.

Some Basic Factors in Assessing Religious Practices

In our thinking about the origins and development of religion we restrict ourselves to the written surviving thoughts of those who have reached the pinnacles of particular faiths. There are numerous commentaries on the written thoughts of Saint Augustine but very little is known about the religious habits of the Christianized population from whom he is reacting. There is little supportive evidence of what these people actually did as for that period there are few bureaucratic records and only some artistic and intuitive archaeological evidence.

But these pinnacle occupiers realised that for most of the time, their followers were not following the dictates of official doctrines and that the Middle East in the early centuries of the Christian era was a melting pot of religious ideas (O'Grady, 2012) as travel had introduced some eastern ideas into Christian or proto-Christian thought, such as the Roman trading stations in southern India and the possibility that Egyptian sailors had circumnavigated Africa from Gibraltar to Suez, as well as the knowledge of the shift in direction of wind in the Indian Ocean which would account for Indonesian influences in Madagascar. The people had a sediment of notions shaped by a culture consistently fluctuating, knew what they needed and that the middle grade men and women would never do the religious practices that the pinnacle power occupiers wanted (Brown, 2012).

There are several factors occurring in any analysis of religious experience. Any analysis of social and religious thinking and behaviour, the social scientists will always start with some factors in mind which are either professional or personal and not shared by the people they are studying.

The commonest is the feeling that there is a global process of secularisation in which they have an attitude and shared with modern particularly Protestant theologians that there is at best a religious system of rational theology to which they can accord an intellectual status.

Very few social scientists are active believers and in general they are professional agnostics. Rather like theologians they approach religion in its popular forms with guarded tolerance largely ignoring that it is the commonest form of religious practice and that it has socially useful and reasonable usages which comes from the simple performance of socially approved rituals.

But secularisation is perhaps a more basic difficulty because predominantly they are generally secular professionals; feeling that religious beliefs and practices are intellectually poor and increasing and perhaps decreasing. The social scientists were certainly wrong in thinking and believing or abetting the idea that religions were in the process of fading away as the result of education and modernity.

Could it not be that secularisation has been a basic human characteristic necessary for survival. The following of religious principles would in most cases hasten the extinction of social life like the Christian injunction of give up all and follow me or the Buddhist requirement of secular disengagement. But these doctrines if followed would extinguish social life.

We suggest that human behaviour has of necessity been predominantly secular and that secularisation has not been just a new and modern phenomena; all traditional societies have secularly minded persons. Public worship has declined as has trade union membership but this is probably caused by a series of factors which are not conspicuously religious.

This decline is not confined to the educated or in any increase in radical growth in agnosticism and it is balanced by the growth in the number of people going on pilgrimages and the growth in the number of pilgrimage sites beyond the numbers going on the Hajj to Mecca or Lourdes and the astonishing estimated seventy million who attended the last Kumbh Mela on the Ganges the largest religious gathering ever recorded.

There is also the influence on social sciences of the European Enlightenment which imposed linear thinking on organic problems, which resulted in the predominance of assuming and in terms of linear. While indeed in any human activity there may well be dominant influences but causation involves holistic thinking as there may well be dozens of factors that contribute to any human behaviour. The social sciences find it difficult methodologically to cope with humans behaviour holistically so that linear thinking appears to predominate in their restricting the influences of lateral thinking.

Linear causality would always tend to involve a simplification of social situations. It would seem that linear causality may be more easily recognizable in primary situations which can be isolated socially. But once any behavioural situation is analysed in its environmental and individual complexity, linear causality disappears into the methodological fog of holism. The permutations of lateral attributions that may have contributed something to the situation but in such negligible amounts which may be in fact often be more of an issue of what those social scientists want to illustrate or ignore.

But linear causality will always be a limiting idea in regard to religious experiences which are both ego appreciated and ego evaluated and possibly has little validity outside this personal holistic range. Valuable enough in the evaluations of material change with its definitions but probably impossible for many matters which are abstract and without predefinition as would always be the case with religious experiences.

Social Scientists Researchers

Researchers enter research situations such as a village, school, or institution, it is likely that the people involved there will give them an overall initial role of government spy, plain clothes policeman, inquisitive tourist or interventionist social worker from a non-governmental organisation. The people will always have some idea of what outsiders are doing and there are no longer social environments in which outsiders are unknown.

The earlier social scientists would have approached societies in which there would have been little determinable influences from outside cultures but this will always be speculation and not yet subject to proof. It seems likely that long distance ocean going did occur materially but it would also involve new ideas. Malinowski thought that he was investigating early forms of social life and the Manus islanders had much influence coming from the sea before Margaret Mead arrived. How isolated were the Easter islanders and the sweet potato did not achieve its world wide occurrence by floating. Pumice on East African beaches were from the Indonesian Krakatoa explosion and took some three years to arrive.

They ignore the general way in which traders come into the community from outside and they see researchers as more or less agents of the government which has obviously given them permission to intrude and which in their experience and folklore are more likely to interfere than help them.

But once within such a community a researcher will be given different roles according to the particular interrelationships in which they are engaged. A researcher on the island of Montserrat (Skinner, 1997) with a population of eight thousand people, writes of being a person of ambiguity moving through different communities and social groups in the course of which he related in different ways to tourists, poets, firemen, librarians, boxers, government employees and Rastafarians because he had no single role and was in a constant state of adjustment because no one had any experience of having a researcher in their midst.

These constant adjustments which an applied social scientist is required to make or are forced on them by day-to-day circumstances within which they have to work is wider and more comprehensive than that which an average person would have to undergo in their daily lives even in the most varied of developed communities moving from home to work situation *via* shops, streets and public transport.

No community at whatever level of development is homogeneous and it will have herbalists, diviners, young and old, men and women and those who are influential and those who are not and all will be involved in some way in any applied secular or religious project. The approach and how each will respond to the stranger within their social environments will always be different and subject to constant interpersonal negotiation around particular personalities and evaluations as to whether they are considered to be sympathetic or not.

With any particular roles which these researchers may be able to establish some affinities with the people with whom they are in contact, but this may be difficult as applied research is often short-term and thus difficult to establish any personal relationships. They any significant personal relationships. They may have similar familial relationships and the patrilineal connection make mother-in-law avoidance a shared interest. They may have shared interests in pets, wild animals, fashions and food. The attempt to interrelate in the detached sense required by hard science is clearly impossible in any type of social science research. The youthfulness of most researchers makes them for some the social equivalents of grandchildren, siblings and classificatory children. There is also the fact that in some societies they cannot come within the scope of endogamous frameworks of thinking.

For some of the people in the researched community these intrusive strangers represent social, political and economic opportunities. Wanting to learn about divining or how to carry out particular activities related to farming and house-building turns the researcher into not so much a client but into the status of a pupil building up the status of their teachers. Even outsiders who come to consult local specialists so he must be considered good at his job if even strangers consult him or her. For others these outsiders create opportunities for links with the outside world and they would not provide information out of the goodness of their hearts. These outsiders cannot resist showing that divination does not work which their own sceptics have said in many private discussions in every traditional community.

So all the people with whom researchers relate see them in different roles and the researchers themselves would have to develop chameleon-like almost deceitful characteristics in order to get what they want from real or potential informants. Mascarenhas-Keyes as a native Goan has described the costume and linguistic changes with which she had to conform if she wanted to get information from particular sections of her own society (Mascarenhas-Keyes, 1988). Social scientists are largely oblivious of the importance of costume in their preference for doing their work informally dressed, while power-holders in developing countries pay much attention to costume; anything important requires locally acceptable formal dress.

The Roles Available to Applied Social Science Researchers

These are divided between ascribed roles related to physiology and achieved roles to the extent that the researchers are accepted in some marginal role. The physiological ascriptive roles from which there can be no escape, sex, age and ethnic appearance. However much researchers convince themselves that they have detached investigative understandings the roles related to physiology cannot be escaped. They cannot assume that field work has anything more than rudimentary parallels with experimental work under quasi-laboratory conditions which also has its rituals and costume requirements.

All researchers with their physiological characteristics are working in social environments which have well established rules and roles as to what is to be expected from people with these visible signs of identity. Researchers cannot expect to be able to assume roles for which they are not physiologically entitled. A fecund but not fertile woman is just that and a post-menopausal one has some marginal acceptability into some male dominated social groups. A young man whatever his professional and educational status cannot expect social equality with mature men in another culture however much that this may be disguised by their culturally required politeness to some strangers.

While ageing may be useful in getting additional accesses to information and as does marital status and children, ethnic appearance does not change. This is unique in categorized reactions within a range of sight, an immediate categorizing of the seen individual as someone who is one of 'us' rather than being one of 'them'. The fact that such categorizations may or may not be socially or politically acceptable, does not alter it being the basic reactions to the appearance of any researchers from their first day in the field work area; this perhaps has some ethological groundings. Of course a Sikh with his beard and turban is physiologically outstanding but even if he shaves he still has his visible Asian ethnicity for any research situation.

The Individuation of Religious Importance

There is the important aspect that the social scientists involved in religious research have to select what they consider to be capable of being researched. Whether it is a question of participant observation or the intuitive conclusion from face to face informants, this is very much an individual activity.

Then there is the problem of the extent of cooperation which may be minimal or be whole hearted. But then, we have mass religious celebrations such as the Hindu *Kumbh Mela* with its millions of pilgrims for which any type of sampling would be difficult and subject to methodological criticisms.

It would seem that in any research on metaphysical issues what can be researched can only be carried out in terms of individuals; a basis of individual perceptions and understandings. Whether any concentration of individualism can lead to conclusions which are valid in communal settings is also matter of speculation because the views and practices of each individual may change in the context of the social situation in which it is situated. Metaphysical issues are too shadowy to be extended with any confidence into communal ceremonies and perceptions which change from hour to hour. There is the detailed and lengthy study of Navaho morality which apparently was based on a single lengthy interview (Ladd, 1957).

No Known Role for the Researcher

Unless these researchers are working in a community which has already had substantial experience of social science field workers such as the Coorgs of the Indian Nilgiri Hills, they are social misfits, and the researched have a socially unclassifiable stranger in their midst. All the roles which he or she would have had in their own communities no longer apply. The role of a female social scientist may be particularly difficult coming as she has from a university or professional position in which gender is theoretical but not an obvious problem.

There is a loss of status because of their age as they expect to be able to talk to all on a basis of equality when in most cases they are too young to claim such a right. They are usually unmarried in communities which give little status to the unmarried whether male or female. Materially they are obviously better off than most of those with whom they have come to live and yet they are not prepared to share with those with whom they claim friendship. Finally even if they are nationals they are usually linguistically incompetent in the local dialect and generally behave accidentally in ways that are at best on the fringe of good manners according to local understandings of how visitors should behave. A Brahmin by socialisation may have difficulties from his socialization in relating to people from longstanding culturally inferior Scheduled Castes.

Few researchers carrying out applied research realise much less accept that much of their public persona is dictated by the succession of social environments in which they have lived prior to entering these communities strange to them. They are usually only marginally aware of their own social strangeness to those whom they are now approaching often expecting their cooperation without understanding the reluctance of all communities to the abrupt intrusion of inexplicable strangers. Most if not all people are taught in childhood to be hostile to strangers. Culture shock is certainly bilateral and few will have had any serious experience as to how such strangers behave privately so they are certainly object of interest and entertainment particularly in agricultural community with their rather dull monotonous hardworking lives.

It is not surprising, therefore, that national researchers find themselves confronted with a succession of new social situations for which they are psychologically and socially ill prepared even if they have already some intellectual expectation of differences. Egoism may often make them feel that these differences will be overcome by their own self-evident good-will towards the community and its members on whom they are imposing themselves. Good-will in most communities has to be earned. In the past sociology has always been the field of the national 'native'; Americans and Europeans who have studied people who have at least nominally been members of their own cultures and so anthropology involved non-nationals in foreign environments. Now that African and Asian universities have departments of sociology and anthropology some of which have longstanding and distinguished reputations, we are investigating whether national researchers are experiencing the same problems that sociologists have long experienced in studying their own cultures or do their difficulties reflect those of anthropologists studying a foreign culture; a reduplication of the largely Western problems of the past. We see in Tunisia that social scientist students in doing research practice were treating their informants as social inferiors in much the same way as foreign anthropologists may have done before independence.

The Applied Researchers Initial Ideas as to their Role

We have seen that the roles of field workers which are ascribed to them or to which they may achieve, are a combination of several different aspects; the roles to which the researchers want for their short-term objectives, those which the accepting community impose on them and the roles which eventually develop as a compromise between these contrasting viewpoints. In this there is little difference between secular and religious undertakings, but possibly more extreme as they may not be used to discussing religious matters with anyone.

How will researchers approach their field work and it seems very unlikely that they will approach their work with anything that approaches an open and detached mind. There is the academic requirement of completing the research project, a break from the materialist but long-term routines of their own social environments, wanting to contribute to a better understanding of other peoples and cultures, curiosity about how other peoples lead their lives, putting their own feelings of intellectual superiority to use and possibly having a breathing space in their personal lives. Whatever the hopes for roles may be, they are made to a large extent in ignorance of the social conditions under which they will be working.

The Final Compromises Over the Researcher's Role

If the researchers stay for the full period which they have set aside for their research which must mean that they have achieved roles which enabled them to work adequately on their projects and that the researched people or community have not actively obstructed the researchers' work and their presence there; they have perhaps become unobtrusive and that the research has been largely passively conducted.

What is certain is that the researchers' presence has been to the advantage of certain individuals there who have provided sufficient cooperation to enable each piece of research to be started and to continue but, of course, this is often not what these researchers may have set out to in the first place. What roles have researchers taken on which has enabled their work to be continued ?

Researchers have become paying guests in some households which has provided their hosts with an unexpected income; the role here would be that they are seen as committed to the viewpoints of that particular family with which they are staying. Other researchers set up household on their own with local domestic servants who do the cooking, water fetching and laundry. They are thus employers of locals who profit from being able to retail information into and out of these households.

Then there are those with spare-time either because of age or seasonal or semi-permanent unemployment who find in the researchers a status enhancing way of spending their time over a shared interest in what is going on in their community, a process of professionalizing gossip to their advantage. The researchers interest in the community and what the people do so that they become for their hosts a useful repository of what goes to making them special which they are in their own eyes; they become as it were the community's unofficial historians (Jorgensen, 1981). There are also situations in which the people become sufficiently used to the researchers presence so that they feel and are felt to be sufficiently at home to have more intimate insights than other strangers. All these circumstances may not occur when these social scientists have a contract to report or who have some applied interests which they want to promote in the short time available to them from their official positions. Most social scientists have personal ideological commitments, particular spectacles through which they perceive the religious ideas and practices of other cultures and communities with which they have shared social and national or ethnic identity.

Finally the political tool role. The researchers are seen as useful channels into the outside world from which their informants individually and the community collectively may get some advantages; it is for them an investment of their more or less usual good-will to strangers who might well have connections since they have obviously been paid to do this work by their employers and their presence there anyway means that they must have at least the tacit approval of powerful outsiders.

However the social scientists themselves in accepting an applied project may also be political tools of their employers who want a particular aspect to be promoted or have at least shown their public concern for alternative viewpoints for decisions which may have already been made.

The aim of field work in the social sciences is to take a detached view of what is being observed although it is almost certain that the researchers however well trained and professionally minded, are going to be biased in their approaches, after years of professional training and work, and usually restricted reading within their profession, they will have become unconsciously committed to certain attitudes; this will be particularly so in their religious ideas. An American national undertaking long-term research in a community in which he and his wife were not ostensibly different to those amongst whom they were living, became their own primary informants. It would seem that this may also be the case in most work on religious practices because informants just do not have the linguistic equipment to describe such practices Perhaps it could not be otherwise since he was required to research the educational system in which he could have no undercover role in the five years set aside for this research project; there were just no 'us' and 'them' possibilities in this situation. Here was an altogether pleasant merging of roles but not any practical possibilities of detachment (Hennigh, 1981).

There is also the problem of an underlying lack of cultural sympathy. A psychologists who is professionally agnostic will have difficulty in relating to a patient who has difficulties over their religious understandings; they are not on the same cultural wavelength of accepting the reality of an active spirit world with both benign and malign activities. African and Asian diviners deal with their clients accepting some of their understandings such as the reality of witchcraft. It is not surprising that this cultural sharing increases confidence in their expertise. The cultural alien is not just unsympathetic to the realities of magic or ex opere the utility of ritual performance.

The Impossibility of Social Neutrality

Suspicion of outsiders which is often no more than dislike of one's neighbours in social rivalry and is not easily linked to groups unless they are visibly different by costume or appearance and this has often turned to violence.

Historically Christians have been more violent than Muslims both outwards and with inter-denominational violence in Wilkinson's analysis of deadly quarrels. It would seem that now Islamic violence predominates because of Koranic injunctions in the Lebanon, Sudan and Eastern Russia, as well as almost annual outbreaks of inter-religious violence in India which predates British rule (Richardson, 1980), while they interdependently and amicably for the rest of the year. But not exclusively as with the recent war between predominantly Sunni Iraq and Shia Iran largely confined to desert battlefields.

Muslims have very long term cultural memories and Palestinians may well see their present situation as a continuation of the Crusades with the Israeli's continuing that ancient Western hostility.

On the other hand when violence occurs towards a minority with distinguishing characteristics, it can lead to their greater cohesion.

When Mrs Gandhi was murdered by her Sikh bodyguards, the consequent anti-Sikh riots led to the setting up of closer Sikh communities. After the Mumbai riots the Shia Bohras with their distinctive costume closed ranks into greater communalism (Blank, 2001, 259-268).

There may be general feeling in the West that the belligerent wording of some Christian hymns is now ecumenically inappropriate as would be some phrases ion the *Koran* but Muslims have no central organisation that can alter the reality of the words of God appropriate to a particular historical situation.

No field worker has ever approached applied religious research in a neutral and scientific frame of mind as they are always creatures of their own cultural and religious socialisations. Of course many can recognise and partially counteract their own biases which may be both personal and cultural but much may remain hidden in the subconscious or be the result of both professional and personal socialisation. It is doubtful that anyone can remove from their perspectives the results of their own personal and academic socialisations which will show in the interrelationships with informants.

There are many examples of the ways in which researchers may almost instinctively behave in ways that mark out their outsider status; even a semi-Christian who does not practice may have difficulties in accepting the social and religious implications of Hindu polytheism and blood sacrifices to the Goddess Kali. Most Westerners have a framework of thinking in terms of 'please' and 'thank you' as a form of necessary reciprocity while many societies do not have such semantic usages seeing their actions in a wider framework continuing real and potential obligation so that 'thank you' may be seen as a way of terminating a relationship and 'please' initiating one.

Scientific research in which the object of investigation is inorganic and delimited can only be free of bias insofar as it keeps free of human uses. Once there are psychological, social and biological effects and the factor of choice so in these research situations bias can be more or less satisfactorlly accounted for. Turnbull may have disliked the Ik because it was not the community which he had planned to study so it was chosen for him by the administration.

In field work however value free research is probably not so much a theoretical ambition but a practical impossibility. Researchers are always working within the personal attributes which they already have and socialisation along with their biological compositions has always and already provided them with intellectual assets of likes, dislikes and indifferences which will inevitably guide or restrict them in what is seen and how it is interpreted such as a contemporary Kenyan Christian in a Protestant seminary 'talking in tongues'.

It is important to accept that whatever the project and the methodology the data obtained and its interpretation cannot be value free in the scientific sense and indeed it is a form of bias to even think that it can be. It is not usually the deliberate fault of the researcher but a by-product of the fact that they are individuals outside the topic which they are researching. Even researchers of their own communities can never be free of the tunnelling of vision which comes from particular social and neighbourhood roles and their demographic status which provides them with concepts of normality and deviance.

It is difficult to see how individuality can ever be removed from a social activity such as field work or even allowed to a limited extent. Even if bias is suspected it is more likely to be attributed to informants than to the perspective of the researchers. The mentality with which or through which research is conducted is always tunnelled by biological and social perceptions.

There is always the tunnelling and restrictions imposed by natal language and the fact that the researchers are men or women, of a certain age and ethnicity who use it in specialised ways. They are socialised into caste or class status and specialised in their perceptions by professional training. All have likes and dislikes and all react in their individual ways to the unexpected. Agnosticism comes with the social science's professionalism and it is a pervasive ideology.

It is from this biased and biasing diversity that applied social research whether it is done by nationals or non-nationals are an important part of the dialectic by which human behaviour and sociality is always in the process of changing and being changed.

National and Non-national Researchers in Context of Developing Nations

In comparing national and non-national researchers in the context of developing nations, this ends up as an assessment of social science research by Westerners or non-Western societies. As we have seen few non-Westerners have done research in Western societies, except in the context of white Americans working on American Indians, while there are few, if any, non-Western societies which have not been visited by Westerners for research purposes. It would be incorrect to see this in racist terms, but research by Westerners in non-Western societies is almost always a necessary and expensive step for academic advancement; their use for research could be seen as an export which does not figure in their balance of payments.

We can assume in the absence of any conclusive evidence to the contrary that every society has a proportion of intellectuals not to be confused with educated literates, capable of fulfilling the demands of social science research. So can we not assume that if the United Kingdom has '*x*' number of researchers, the United States might well have '4*x*' and China with a population of over a billion might well have '16*x*'. This is just to tentatively suggest that in marketing terms that Asia, rather more than Africa, is the field in which social science fieldwork may well develop. Very few social scientists working in developing countries have not encountered men and women with intellectual capacities parallel to their own.

But of course the numbers of social science practitioners does not depend on the factor of intelligence in isolation, but on other prevalent issues principally cost and socio-political access.

It seems likely that the majority of social scientists publishing in a major international language about research in developing nations are non-nationals. These people can be described as primary since they instigated the research projects and arranged for the financial support.

However in a growing number of projects, particularly those that are more narrowly scientific, there are trained and active nationals as secondary researchers co-equals in authorship with the primary ones.

Beneath these qualified and aspiring national and non-national predefined leaders of any research project there are large numbers of tertiary nationals without whom no research anywhere can be carried out. Even if we accept that these people were helping primary and secondary researchers for entirely personal ends, they remain the building blocks on which research is constructed. More particularly if we discredit them for their economic and other motives, in what ways are they different to the primary and secondary researchers who are not exactly working for disinterested motives.

We know little about these essential people since the acknowledgements prefacing publications they are often grouped rather than given names. It would seem reasonable that anyone who spends more than a few hours in providing negative or positive information for a researcher should be acknowledged somewhere as a contributor whether they have been paid or not. There are usually fulsome acknowledgements to other academics who may have spend far less time on reading a draft than some distant elder or specialist who may have spent days in discussions with these researchers.

Very few non-nationals can afford to have another non-national in the field as a research assistant unless they are long-term partners who in effect work for nothing as was the case with Colin Turnbull and his companion in his Uganda work. There have been certain partnerships in which both worked on interrelated projects such as the Bohannans and Margaret Mead's second marriage but still there are the rings of tertiary helpers without which they would have achieved little. Very little social science research has involved the primary researcher finding their own data without the help of secondary and tertiary nationals.

3
Culture Shock

The national social scientists working in their own country unless it is in their own social environment and amongst those with similar social understandings of themselves, are social and psychological migrants. The only difference to those who migrate in the usual sense of the term, is that they are committed to getting on with the people needed as their necessary informants for their applied projects as quickly as possible on whom they are dependent without being employed by them. Culture shock can occur as the result of very personal experiences as the middle class Brahmin researcher collapsing in the street and coming to in the slum hut of a sympathetic untouchable family which resulted in him choosing this area for his research (Varadachar, 1979). The social scientists unless they are particularly insensitive are going to be confronted by a range of cultural surprises; shocks as they could not be anticipated; realities which contradict their own socialised conceptions.

Every social scientists in his or her field work comes from a different cultural background both ethnically and because of their professional training and the possible influence of charismatic teachers opening up new patterns of thought and understanding.

Most will try and alter their own behaviour so that some aspects of the body language does not upset their hosts but there are limits as to how far these changes can go because much of human behaviour is semi-conscious outside deliberate conscious causation.

It would seem that the interpretation of religious ceremonies by social scientists will inevitably be individual possibly modified by recent largely dialectically unrecognised influences. They are obviously conscious of the fact that they are different metaphysically and socially to the people they are observing.

This is a peculiar form of dependency which is much more inclusive than that of other forms of migration in which migrants keep or are kept to themselves except for those marrying into another culture or who move there for some form of missionary commitment. These social scientists have to force themselves to be extroverts and push themselves into social relationships which they would not otherwise have entered.

However well-equipped and intellectually ready researchers may be for the experience of a particular piece of applied research, it is always a personal experience. Whether the researchers move from Belgaum to Banaras or from Berlin to Birmingham it is inevitably filled with surprises that they can accept intellectually but nevertheless impinge on them personally in ways that cannot be avoided; they are professionally committed to include their own reactions in balanced perceptions of what they have set out to do and record. A left-handed male Christian social scientist would prefer to sit on the left side of an Indian church and would be shocked to discover that he is sitting on the women's side and that since he crossed himself with his left hand some viewers doubted that he could be a Christian.

But it is in metaphysics that the differences are most extreme. The belief in the reality of witchcraft in the sending of evil without human contact is almost universal in south of Sahara in contemporary Africa. The contemporary Hindus are rational enough in today's India but how can they believe that the worship of an elephant headed God can have a benign effect on business prospects.

This problem of rationally absurd metaphysical beliefs exist in a world that is predominantly governed by rational considerations. So it appears that humans have at least two sets of beliefs; the limited rationality needed for agriculture and a metaphysical myth based system. One can see this in the development in the Western world of rational theology free of myths. That the linear approach to human causation cannot apply to metaphysical thinking.

A distinguished German social scientist has proposed (Schutz, 1962) the need to develop sub universes of reality and that humans find no difficulty in believing two sets of reality where rationalities clash which solves the problem of the ambiguity of many metaphysical concepts.

In the research situation there is not really anyone who is so open-minded as never to be shocked by the behaviour of others they encounter but in applied work they have limited ways of manipulating them. It is theoretically possible to take every experience as paralleling writing on a blank slate but in reality this is impossible even for the most imaginative and sensitive researchers. In such contexts even imagination may be a form of bias because it leaps over the boundaries of the available and perceived data. Few recognise in themselves the extent that they are programmed by socialisation and how this influences their attitudes to people different to themselves.

Culture shock may be dyadic as was the case with Zigua adolescents in Tanzania who were shocked by the way that Europeans cleaned their teeth with water which they were thought to drink. Personal hygiene is inevitably a matter of disturbing realities whether it concerns bathing, excreting or menstruating. Some field workers find their situation so personally difficult or distasteful that they give up and retire to do their field work from within the social safety of a university campus or hotel. Most make some sort of a showing in at least attempting what they set out to do but in applied research they may not have the personal ability to adjust their thinking or indeed the personal time to adjust.

In this they will be shocked by some aspects of their experiences as their hosts acceptance of strangers which they interpret in a personal way or malignly so boycotting others because of the noise, lack of privacy and dirt. No researchers feel totally at home because they have always been socialised into other patterns of personal behaviour to which they are socially and psychologically committed; 'clean' and dirty are social not medical concepts.

Even the national researcher may feel the greatest range of culture shock because they know themselves to be cultural aliens when they move from the south of China or India to the north and they are always ready to be surprised ideologically by matters which are in practice on the fringes of everyday life. They are much less prepared for the intricacies of inter-personal experience in how they use their hands, eyes and mouth for which there are no internationally acceptable ways of behaviour; to be left-handed may be a grave disadvantage since it is too deep set in the mind to be turned overnight into right-handedness and that the Western practice of shaking hands may be instinctively polluting for even the most modernised Hindus.

In much the same way non-nationals maybe delighted and indeed overbalanced. This writer once experienced a fortnight of continuous rain in north Burma by the freshness of their experience. Blue skies and starlight can be confusing after the miseries of the European or north American winter until they have experienced the monsoon and the extreme heat of a northern Indian summer.

Of course culture shock can be a matter of extremes, an agnostic national can be revolted by the blood sacrifice practices involved in the worship of *Kali*, in the overwhelming poverty of a Dakar or a Lima urban slum and the treatment of women whom the male researcher from an upper class educated family may have never met. The culture shocks are certainly more intrusive and much more continuous in emotional matters. National social scientists can have an uplifting excitement from seeing Sonjo men dancing in honour of and becoming possessed by the spirit of *Hambagau*, their tutelary spirit, of being in a Kachin long house for the dancing and drinking in honour of the dead house-holder and appreciating the many ways in which the Sukuma of Tanzania circumvent their inevitable miseries. The overall shock that so many people in other cultures within a single nation seem better able by design to cope with their difficulties without intellectuals and bureaucracies telling them what they should do.

To what extent is the national researcher liable to experience culture shock and to be affected by it. Almost certainly they are in the sense that they cannot explain it away quite so easily as the non-national who is able by definition to explain these issues in terms of 'us' and 'them'. The national cannot so easily bracket off such issues because they are by political socialisation not so clearly divided off from 'them'. From socialisation they are far more committed to the intricacies of their own societies and are less able to circumvent them by design or social ignorance. Since these national social scientists have become in some ways a self-recruited intellectual elite, it may also be more difficult for them to excuse activities which in terms of their national image or social progress may shock their sensibilities as 'feudal survivals' in the propaganda of the Chinese and Vietnamese communist political directorates.

The stimulus to research and the excitement which comes from this work will usually lie in the differences that researchers find between their own life styles and understandings and what they encounter in their applied work. Whatever form it takes there is bound to be some culture shock 'the personal disorientation that may accompany entry into unfamiliar social worlds' (Macionis, 1989; 62) which is perhaps inevitable particularly in applied religious work.

This disorientation is obvious enough when anyone moves so far out of their own social environment that they are deeply shocked by what they encounter for which they have had no previous social warning. Few social science field workers are likely to have anything approaching Chagnon's first encounter with the Yanomamo 'I looked up and gasped when I saw a dozen burly, naked, sweaty, hideous men staring down at us down the shafts of their drawn arrows. Immense wads of green tobacco were stuck between their lower teeth and lips making them look even more hideous and strands of dark green slime dropped or hung from their nostrils-strands so long that they clung to their chests or drizzled down their chins. Then the stench of decaying vegetables and filth hit me and I almost got sick. I was horrified. What kind of welcome was this for the person who came here to live with you and learn your way of life, to become friends with you' (Chagnon, 1983;10). Indeed we must also notice the use of the term 'friend' which the non-national researcher often uses in relationships which has no parallels in their societies which is based on networks of reciprocities. If he or she acted in accordance with traditional concepts they would soon run out of petrol, patent medicines and ball-point pens. But this surely will be the type of reaction that social scientists may feel in their obligatory encounters in applied research with deviants such as transvestites, homosexual prostitutes and extreme forms of mental illness and physical violence.

Of course this is an extreme case with a North American academic going to do field work with an Amazonian tribe which had had little contact with the outside world and did not want to increase any such relationships into personal intimacy. Any individual going to a locality with which they have not been in regular relationship before must experience some mental stimulation because these people are behaving in ways which are strange and at the first glance inexplicable. A woman social scientist going from a university in Mumbai to work in Manipur will be struck at once by innumerable differences, just as a graduate man who moves from Belgaum to Banaras to do research.

It is one of the truisms of research that national researchers have a social nearness which enables them to have particular insights which are not automatically available to non-nationals. It is certainly true that a Hindu or whatever socialised with their particular social environments will have many insights into another Hindu community almost automatically because Hinduism is so institutionally pervasive.

Such socialisation enables national researchers to avoid the long working-in period when non-nationals attempt to become acculturated to the new communities in which they come to do research on some previously unknown aspect of their lives. The snag here is that such people may feel that they already have some natal insights into this community and thus they are lulled into not recognising the importance of the stimulus which must come to them from culture shock. However this shock is always bilateral in that it is experienced both by the researchers and by the researched.

All researchers whether nationals or non-nationals go through a process of being initially liminalised in ways that parallel the patient entering a hospital; the individual is defined in terms of the receiving institution and community. In the research situation much of the social scientists' social features are stripped away and redefined by the people whom they are forced to encounter by the necessities of the applied topic. If the researcher is asked to assess the work of a particular church, it is no part of that requirement to make assessments or comments on metaphysical issues about witchcraft and ancestor propitiation.

Shock of course is a loaded word and to change it to a confrontations with the unexpected may diminish its realities. Bob Geldorf who started the global charity Band Aid has spoken of being anaesthetized by mass misery. The abrupt realisation that 'the other' is different and this is so obvious that social scientists are inclined to neglect its significance; not the odd strangeness but the totality of 'otherness'. Hence the importance of the researchers accepting their liminal status.

The Advantages of Culture Shock

Social scientists must usually approach their field work with some conception of the philosophical unity of mankind and yet this is contradicted by their applied injection into communities which are not only different but prefer their differences to their inclusion in the larger world beyond their own social and psychological horizons. There is always an element of cultural self-satisfaction.

Of course we are always surrounded by the 'other' but social scientists remain ego-centred throughout their lives and as much as they can avoid adjusting this to the relationships which they encounter. The more striking the contrast with the 'other' in terms of culture shock, the more likely they are to resist these influences and to avoid the nibbling away of their personal identities by enforced change. So culture shock can be an essential element in stimulating the researchers to approach their applied projects with some appreciation of their own ignorance. The nearness in terms of social distance to the 'other', the greater the researchers' difficulties in practising detachment.

The importance of culture shock is the recognition by social scientists that they cannot be detached even in experimental situations from those whom they are working on. In practice there is little hope of human social life being successfully studied under the canons of Western scientific detachment initiated by the European Enlightenment. Working on an applied project is usually a combination of existing social situations in which power-holders have already laid down their positions whether they are politicians, priests, farmers or manufacturers. It may be a severe shock, to find that people of intellectual status similar to their own hold views diametrically opposed to those held by the social scientists, particularly in relationship to non-Western religious matters. It would be difficult for them to accept the pervasive Asian concept of 'hungry ghosts' of those improperly buried, witchcraft or socially active ancestors.

So accepting that social science fieldwork in all its aspects is a social relationship from start to finish between the researcher and the researched with hidden third parties in the background, its most important component is culture shock. The immediate and important reactions to total differences. The value to the potentially enquiring mind at its most obvious would be those who move over the East-West divide such as Nirad Chaudhuri (Chaudhuri, 1959) preferring England to India and Lafcadio Hearn (Hearn, 1894) preferring Japan to the West. Social scientists working on applied projects will have to accept that they are working within an existing social system and that the projects exist in a short-term framework of thought and action in which there is no place for grandiose cultural dissatisfactions. 'Hungry ghosts exist and that is why it is not a debatable issue. The shock which we can anticipate in mind of the African Christian who stated that she was looking forward to visiting 'your great Christian London'.

The Cumulative Importance of Culture Shock

It would seem obvious that social scientists working within their own country and having legal status as citizens there, would automatically have advantages over non-national ones but their overall position as researchers is divided over a number of complex issues.

The researcher working in the field is always at a disadvantage; however well-prepared they are and committed to their projects, as they are outsiders by almost every social and demographic category used. Except under very specific predefined and onerous conditions, can they ever become participants rather than observers; in Western experience the results have often been personally disastrous in personal relationships and health. Possibly so in the use of tools but not in the administration of social and religious ideas.

In the main they are outsiders for reasons which have little to do with their personalities and professional competence A major and growing distinction is between researchers who are working in their own social environments and those who come from elsewhere. There are internal as well as external expatriates in countries as culturally diverse as China and India in which there is no more than a legal unity between those living in the north a thousand miles from those living in the south in a totally different social and climatic environments. Social behaviour is at least in part dictated by climate as stopped by persistent rain or heat. One can only admire the strength of character of the Canadian woman researcher who stayed in a single shared Eskimo hut throughout the Canadian bitter winter.

We need to examine their ability to work effectively according to a number of factors; the value and extent of legal status, academic relationships, grant support, self-imposed and legal censorship, political issues, shared language, religious background and social status in terms of national and sub-national identities. It may well be doubtful whether we can accept that social scientists in these two groups are dedicated to finding out and using the same range of facts even when working in the same fields of enquiry. Their viewpoints, even their biases are likely to be different as reflections from a range of direct and indirect factors which may have little to do with personal choices.

The Individualization of Important Religious Thinking and Practices

There is also the factor that researchers into religion have to choose the localities on which they will focus and to decide what aspects of religious belief and practice are essential to their project and what information on private prayer is at best always second hand while public prayer can always be visually substantiated by witnesses more important these aspects are capable of being researched. It seems probable that the beliefs and practices of high status people will rarely be available to researchers.

The difference between religious activities in which the researchers can genuinely participate such as the recent *Kumbh Mela*, but non-Muslims cannot enter the Mecca area and those who are not Mormons cannot enter the Latter Day Saints central temple in Salt Lake city. There aıe many religious sites which are barred to unbelievers and certainly researchers.

4
National and Non-national Researchers

Citizen and Foreign Researchers as a Legal Distinction

The distinction between the citizen and non-citizen is a legal one and although it has many social consequences, it is an abstract classification which is not aimed at any particular person beyond some idealistic conception of the impersonal obligation of citizens to the state and the state to its citizens; in terms of Orwell all the animals are equal but some are more equal than others (Orwell, 1946). The value of this legal status will allow researchers to do certain things while at the same time restrict them in others. In this respect citizens are not equal.

The citizen as a researcher involves a further category as an individual. Any group element is likely to be circumstantial so that their personal contribution to any situation will be a combination of what they bring to the situation as individual personality and the particular circumstances of the research with which they are involved. The situations from which they come may be circumstantially irrelevant. Social importance in one society cannot and professional importance cannot be transferred to another social setting.

Outside this legal definition, the social constituents of citizen even in an ostensibly homogeneous state can never be uniform. An individual doing research may state that he or she is a citizen of Zimbabwe, but this person turns out to be a member of the white minority whose influence and indeed ability to be heard is both marginal and probably suspect in the minds of the dominant black majority. This is not an extreme case since parallel examples can be found in many contemporary states, such as Verrier Elwin, an Englishman who became an Indian citizen, with his nationally accepted work among Indian tribal peoples and having an Indian wife and family.

The importance of citizenship is only in theory a static value and much will depend on the circumstances in which individual researchers are involved and what politicians and officials want to utilise at any particular time. Citizenship is just a card in the pack which has a theoretically defined value but its power will always depend on what other cards are being played.

Leaving aside issues of academic intellectual immunity there is a somewhat instinctive assumption on both sides of this national divide that the citizen has research advantages over the non-citizen. The latter feels that the citizen has numerous automatic advantages in the sympathetic biases of those in political and social authority, language, social understandings, ease of acceptance and access and less likely to be the subject of police surveillance. We will see that this in fact is no more than an idealistic hope.

The citizen researcher in every state and not just in non-western ones with a long history of academic independence, may have a somewhat instinctive assumption that they should have some sorts of priority based on various academic and political considerations. A refraction of the modern political obsession with nationalism which those in authority expect to be supported by state supported or tolerated intellectuals. Power holders in both the secular and religious communities see that detachment is a poorly disguised opposition which only makes their work more difficult.

The need to support the intellectual aspirations of these newer states whose academics may feel that these should have priority since they as citizens have a more natural and automatic understanding of their own people. The need to oppose the supremacy of the outsider academic establishment dominating grants and publications in a dominant language to which they do not have any proprietary rights.

The formalisation of an almost ethological 'us' and 'them', the need to exclude outsiders from unformed ideological separation in which the 'others' are using national data for their own advancement. Finally some conception that specialised knowledge is both private and individual and thus marketable and as part of the national stock which should not be used and not taken away by non-citizens which is a popular and widespread feeling.

In religious research much depends upon the researcher gaining access. Non-Muslims are not allowed to enter the Mecca area. In Salt Lake City the Mormon central temple is barred to non-Mormons. Prior to constitutional changes Indian Hindu temples often had a notice barring entry not only to non-Hindus but to various caste categories within Hinduism. This accounts for much of the preference for urban temples as there is no way that caste categories can be established before entry. Going into a village temple to which their caste debarred them has often been the occasion for lethal violence.

The Intra and Extra National Field Worker

Has there been any change in the field workers experience when they are of the same nationality, religion and ethnicity as the people with whom they work in applied projects and into whose communities they are injecting themselves. The word 'injecting' is used advisedly as even if the researcher is studying her or his own community or work situation, there are always methodological problems. Few undertake such introspective research because of the personal and moral conflicts involved as they have to live socially with their results.

In the earlier situation of Westerners researching non-Westerners, the dichotomous situation was so obvious and all-embracing that no one was under any illusions as to the degree to which they might become participant observers apart from the fact that they were seen as operating under colonial sponsorship. The personal relationship aspects were more or less ignored and only gradually did this become a factor with the expressions of gratitude to those researched and reference to key informants as 'friends' which in Western social environmental terms they were not.

However well researchers get on with the researched community, they are and will always remain social outsiders; they probably look different for a start in how they dress, talk differently, eat different food whenever they can and in their treatment by the receiving community, there is always the initial ethologically reasonable based hostility.

However, when the national researcher comes onto the scene to what extent can they expect to be seen and treated as people who have by definition reduced the social distance between the researcher and the researched. The national researcher working with nationals may well be experiencing a much more refined and difficult situation than that of their non-national professional colleagues but there is always the factor of social distance, particularly when the new state has an ideological basis for its policies.

The first difficulty must be the overcoming of any feeling of 'spiritual affinity' and that the 'us' and 'them' environment of the colonial era has been eliminated by political independence; the experiences of Indian social scientists such as Srinivas are illustrative of this. Further that their dominance in and control of national institutions of higher education and research endorsing committees insures that there are known and also have largely unexpressed shared national interests.

The Internal Expatriate

The expatriate 'white' classification starting in the colonial era and now applied to a much larger number of foreigners working in nationally independent states, is based on an obvious ethnic division. Now it is a much more complex division with Chinese, Egyptian, Japanese, Pakistani, Palestinian and Philippine professionals working 'abroad' in large numbers but not in applied research. Political independence may result in an increase number of expatriates there overseeing their aid donations. The Chinese in Zimbabwe and their role in constructing and running the railway from Tanzania to Zambia.

In terms of what nationals understood to be their community, there was a further classification from the earlier period of internal expatriate, when nationals entered the colonial civil services. Individuals serving in areas where the people regarded them as social foreigners such as a northerner working in the southern Sudan, a Shona in an Ndebele area of Zimbabwe, a Burmese in a Shan or Kachin area of Myanmar, a Han in south-western or north-eastern China. These intrusions praise folk memories of previous dominances controlled in the colonial period but in contemporary Myanmar this has erupted into prolonged guerrilla activity in the tribal areas surrounding the Burmese heartland.

The complexity of the cultural situation is perhaps at its most detailed in India where, except in terms of nationality and national pride, there is little in common between Assamese, Bengalis, Rajputs and Tamils; they are distinct by whatever social category is used in addition to which there is the complication of caste over a much wider social arena than Hinduism involving Muslim converts and Roman Catholic Goanese.

The situation of the internal expatriate is compounded by the fact that they may consider themselves to be working under handicaps which they feel should not occur from their shared national identities. In fact this classification augments the other distinctions between nationals and non-nationals in their ability to function as efficiently as they would like as social scientists.

The Foreign Researcher and his Social Competence

Foreign researchers are often accepted into their field of research by those involved as socially incompetent however well intentioned they may be and however much their good intentions are accepted. Basically they do not know practically how to behave according to their perceived status in the research environment according to their age and sex and whatever role is attributed to them, despite their theoretical and carefully learnt sensitivities. Most Westerners shake hands with strangers almost compulsively which is disconcerting for many in other cultures.

Almost certainly the biggest area of social mistakes has to be in the use of language in which they will have either learnt scholastically probably as a national state supported language or taught to them by locals in terms of their own social roles. Every language is sophisticated in its own structure and even more so in its semantics.

The lack of missionary success in China has been attributed in part to the lower class nature of their spoken and written Mandarin while the Jesuits learnt its upper class variety of the elite; no doubt a feature of all foreign learning of non-alphabetical languages.

Then there are the permutations of age and sex correlated behaviour which is so much a part of socialisation so that the actions of the researchers may be triggered off by quite appropriate responses in their own cultures, but quite wrong elsewhere, particularly in relationships between the sexes; eating behaviour, joking relationships, mother-in-law avoidances, body language and particularly clothing. An Indian woman researching in Goa used four different styles of clothing according to the situations in which she found herself (Mascarenhas-Keyes, 1988).

One suspects that foreign researchers not only provide a source of gossip and anecdotes in the communities involved in which they have been inserted as foreign experts but also provide these people with their first personalised expansion of scale; close contact with someone from the outside world. Much more than objects on sale in markets, mass media advertisements and the irregular presence of government officials and soliciting politicians, their role as resident outsiders with an applied objective provides their hosts with the opportunity for the continuous observance of the overall accidental rather deliberate weirdness of social outsiders and what they talk about.

These foreign researchers are perhaps tolerated because they provide entertainment, commercial opportunities and mental stimulus for a few and a feeling that it would be politically unwise to reject their presence as pawns or spies for the government which has allowed them to come there in the first place.

National Social Distance Factors

The instituting of democratic voting procedures has increased the importance in every state of the numbers of people who have shared interests and power. It is not just a question of whether 'tribalism' is a new phenomenon attributable to colonial machinations but its combination with ethnicity, religion and caste has insured that national researchers will have particular difficulties because of whom they are before any professional status comes into play.

Thus there are very strong antipathies made worse by the creation of permanent voting minorities of people who see themselves primarily as belonging to a certain type of communalism. Sometimes these are clear dichotomies as in India between Hindus and Muslims or between native Pakistanis and refugee Pakistanis from India. But almost everywhere researchers will be out of place in most of their national communities; they are not readily acceptable because they represent outsider classifications as with Outcastes researching Brahmins and *vice versa* and a Bengali researching Biharis.

The Internal Expatriate

The smaller the nation the greater the possible coincidence between individual social science researchers and what might be called national averages of social understandings and behaviour. This would appear to be the case in Bhutan and Luxembourg, but this cannot be so in nations of many millions of people and enormous geographical size. People from northern India and northern China have little in common other than nationality with their southern compatriots in language, social behaviour and their equally important geographical environment. They share a political identity under a single flag and a sense of pride in their nation when its status is challenged by outsiders. Beyond this there may be little that is sufficiently shared to make a marked difference to what researchers may discover; political and religious ideology may have little influence on behaviour at lower levels.

Sometimes these differences are so extreme as in the case of Kenya in which the two largest tribal groups, the Luo and the Kikuyu dominate the political structure, they do not have their languages within the same linguistic group as well as the pastoral Karamajong and Maasai who are outside this binary political structure altogether.

So we have here categories of researchers who are nationals but in terms of their areas of field work may be in practical terms 'internal expatriates'. There is nothing in common between the researchers and the researched except perhaps physical appearance as well as possibly some measure of acceptance simply because they are all nationals and are people of status with whom the researched community have regular dealings which will have confirmed the researchers' national status and thus removed a potential source of difficulty.

Beyond some primary feelings for their acceptance these researchers may have to go through the same prolonged processes of filtering themselves into the community of their choice as if they were non-nationals. There would be a tendency for nationals belonging to well defined segments of the national population to carry out research within that group for Punjabis and Baluchis to work on their own kind just as it would be for the northern Han to research north of the Yellow River in China.

But these could be classified as soft options so that researchers with different intellectual ambitions and divergent topics of research will go into communities with which they have no natal affinities at all. An example of this internal expatriate research would be the work of someone from West Bengal researching the feeding habits of Tibetan women refugees in northern India (Be a, 2004) who might well have felt that this enquirer was some type of government official.

The National Researcher

I am one of them, therefore, I know them.

This is certainly the basic feeling of a national social science researcher. Anyone in their own social environment has the same field work status as an informant modified by social distance factors. They may be well informed about their own community and their own part in it or they may be singularly unaware of the social conditions within which they live and work because of socialisation and the fact that their education is likely to have dealt with the 'other' rather more than 'us'. But they cease to be one of 'us' by the fact that they are now researchers as they have been set apart. By claiming special insights they are in fact attempting to reoccupy roles which they have probably vacated some years previously; they now occupy special roles indeed but not that of anything approaching current memberships of these communities in which they may have had at some time close relationships.

In fact it may be almost fallacious to suggest that they have a particular insider form of social knowledge other than that which comes with the ascribed and achieved roles which they currently occupy. The value of such national researchers may be in their contributions to wider ranging studies about particular roles; they have no automatic understandings of how their society may be functioning now.

To what extent then do nationals know 'them' in the general sense of sharing not just the generalities of their culture but its particularities and practicalities involved in field work; they have roles which have to be explained and detailed since this will be a form of bias as in the anthropologist in Papua New Guinea to whom was attached the role of the ghost of a dead child. On top of this can we be automatically assure that they do have a theme of sympathy in their minds for their fellow nationals apart from some shared parts of nationality and language which gives them significant advantages over non-nationals but not to the extent implied by this heading they may have useful knowledge of the ways in which it is possible to get through the intricacies of local bureaucracy.

A Chinese anthropologist from a by-gone era (Fei Hsiao Tong, 1939; xiii) wrote 'if it is true that self-knowledge is the most difficult to gain, then undoubtedly the anthropology of one's own people is the most arduous, but also the most valuable achievement of a field worker'. An Afro-American (Szwed, 1969; 170) wrote 'it is naïve to believe that native anthropologists necessarily will do more satisfactory work than non-natives since the United States black social scientists have brought the same methods and conceptual approaches which rendered their white brothers incapable of dealing with a major portion of lower class Afro-American life and culture'. It is perhaps impossible to use the linguistic codes of other cultures correctly.

It is also naïve (Sobro, 1982) not only because the insider's view is only a partial approximation of understanding but also because comparison is the social science's methodological equivalent to experiment and allows them to expose analytical parallels and to falsify hypotheses.

But he is motivated by a profound desire to improve the life situation of his country's population by academic ambition and monetary reward, but is continuously frustrated by the overwhelming reality of underdevelopment, the policy decisions of his own government and by the fact that he himself is rarely given any power to use his critical powers for the public benefit. They come under attack in their own countries from the people they study for their hidden motives or for their inferred role as do-gooders and scientists in the service of government. In applied work there is often the presence of pervasive corruption which may involve the power holders who initiated this enquiry.

There is probably no such thing as an isolatable indigenous pattern of thought and behaviour; some identifiable paradigm which is exclusive to some social group. Just as demographically and linguistically they are an amalgam of features which come in from many other outside sources, so will their ideas. The Sukuma quasi-traditional diviners who used fire-walking and Coca Cola bottle tops for their diagnoses in which of course there is the possibility of originality. It is more likely that their thinking mixes the remainders of tradition with cinema scenarios, advertising pictures and ideas that come from the fringes of all the religions available locally, traditional Christianity, Hinduism and Islam. Some viewers of a Oliver and Hardy comedy saw parts of it as a documentary of Western life involving road repairs.

There is no evolutionary change from backwardness to capitalist oppression (Warman, 1982) but a zigzag between the physical forms which are taken on by literate and non-literate ideologies. Indigenous thought and practice in Birmingham, Banaras and Bamako are always going to be an amalgam and their model of the nation is unlikely to be that of the elite group in power but one much more local and personal.

Their current thinking is always going to be dominantly contemporary however much we may be conscious of genetic and ethological factors. What is called traditional thinking is just the framework within which their current lives are working; an Indian thinker in a village preoccupied with caste issues, not because of some ancient continuing paradigm but because that is how this community works now; this existential reality does not need any other explanation. A social scientist working on some applied problem may intuitively think that much of contemporary beliefs and practices have a traditional elements within it but to prove this is probably impossible and unwise to suggest such backward looking explanations.

Although it is physiologically possible that nationals may have some immunities to local diseases such as the presence of the cycle cell immunity to malaria in West Africans, from malaria among some West Africans they are just as liable as non-nationals to catch others. This is particularly so as their current domestic living conditions are as likely to be different to that of their area of research as might be the case with non-nationals. It is rare for field workers to detail the handicaps which they have undergone and its absence allies itself to the hopes of social scientists that their work would be considered scientific. Professor Srinivas details some of the difficulties which he encountered in his field work (Srinivas, 1979). Far from choosing a village on account of its suitability for his research, he ended up in one village because it was the only one in which he could find a place to live, ending up in a cowshed which he shared with these animals and a Muslim client of the headman and his family. He was one of the few field workers who have detailed the problems of excreting, writing that the headman's son had showed him in which field he could defecate; he commented that this was preferable to the indoor lavatories of the few rich people and to defecate only at night.

The Ease of Access for the National Researcher

A citizen has the legal right to be in the area chosen for research and they do not have to go through any existing procedures to enable research to be started and applications for visas which would apply to non-nationals. They cannot come into a country on a tourist visa as research must usually involve long periods of residence. This comparative simplicity is probably an illusion.

The suspicion of the foreign researcher does not mean that there is no suspicion of national researchers in the eyes of governments and in the perceptions of those researched and their communities. They are likely to be seen as working directly or indirectly for or against the government. The ease or difficulty of access must depend on the type of government, the size of the country, the type of research and related cultural and locality issues.

Most countries are only nominally unitary and access for anything more than covert personal projects may require the agreement of different layers of authority; the bishop may agree to a project but that does not mean that parish priests have agreed enough to participate whole heartedly. Some nations are federal and whether this is so or not, there are likely to be provincial and even lesser local authorities which would have to be in agreement over anything more than a single small community study.

There are often frontier areas closed to non-residents and civil disorder limitations in which governments do not want the additional responsibilities over the safety of a well known national researcher from even the most prestigious national university; a researcher whether Hindu or Muslim is not likely to be given access to the India controlled part of Kashmir. Some countries do not have governments which are in control of their own territory whatever their legal status may be. During civil disorders in Uganda, the police returned national researchers to the university for their own safety.

Some countries are so huge that in terms of their characteristics, they have an almost continental variety. Countries such as land bound China, India and Russia are so huge as well as the string of islands comprising Indonesia. Access to one part may involve as many cultural changes in understandings as might be the case for such researchers moving to Germany or Canada. In these circumstances they are in effect internal expatriates. The study of a Yunnanese community by a Han Chinese researcher would have more or less the same problems as he might have had in going to study a community in urban America (Hua, 2001) in fact it would be cheaper, easier and less bureaucratically restricted had he gone to the United States and picked any community from a map of the environments of Arizona or Utah.

It is unlikely that any national researcher is going to work without the support of some national university and in the background some non-national body which is prepared to provide finance for some projects. The national university will be thinking in wider possible political terms in supporting a particular piece of research by a national; they will not want to be involved in any activities which the national government might consider disruptive. How Hua got permission to study a Chinese tribal community in a political climate against any sub-divisions of national unity must have been a marvel of negotiation and covert intentions and indeed ultimately involving his emigration since this study was written up and published in French; he will do no more research in the People's Republic of China.

Some research by a respected national will involve enormous amounts of preparatory negotiation with those whose cooperation was necessary. Kochar's study of the excretory habits of rural Bengalis (Kochar, 1977, 1978. Kochar *et al.*, 1976), remains the only scientifically acceptable study of this universal behaviour, if only because of the enormous difficulties of getting the cooperation of sufficient numbers of people to make the study valid. One can only marvel at the dedication and persistence of Kochar in this field work on excreting which a non-national would never have undertaken in the first place or persisted in the face of so many methodological difficulties in obtaining this degree of accuracy on a very private and personal activity about which the social sciences know very little.

It seems likely that national researchers will always be able to keep in touch with their field work areas of study over much longer periods than most non-nationals; they may be only a bus ride or rail trip away and thus can keep in touch without the difficulties of writing, indeed they can plan on researching these people in the same community over ten years or more without much expense or the endless search for grants to enable overseas work to be even started. One group of Chinese researchers made a longitudinal study of the social adjustments and functions of Shanghai children (Chen *et al.*, 1995) and a Tanzanian made a long term study of the adjustments to change and poverty particularly over the poor water supply in the informal sector of the capital Dares Salaam (Lugalla, 1997) on the doorstep of the national university.

The National Researching in their Own Country

We have to consider the assumed advantages that may lie with social scientists doing field work in their own country while remaining resident there. Until recently the number of nationals doing such work has been small in terms of published results but now there are large numbers researching their own cultures for a combination of the demands of personal advancement and national needs and as fulfilment of some part of a degree course.

The relationship with informants will not necessarily be simplified by what might be called the nationalisation of social science research since it not only involved the same problems as will be experienced by non-national researchers, but will have new ones added, probably because social distance factors are just as important but not regarded as a political and moral issue. It is just part of that contemporary culture.

The assumption in the minds of some national researchers that they have an automatic advantage over the non-national is of course questionable since much must depend on the circumstances and topic. The concept of national identity overriding tribal paradigms of thought and bias, new but obvious social class differences and the use of a lingua franca as well as the possibility of the research involving second or even third languages. Strangers are always in all societies suspect. While the non-national is always an outsider, national ones have always to work themselves into the researched community so that they can become to be treated there as privileged and useful citizens rather than as suspicious outsiders and potentially enemies (Naderi, 1962).

National identification is new in Third World practice. It may have been a creation of the struggle for political independence and for use in foreign affairs. In general post-independence has not been a steady progress towards the development of functionally distinct nations with the population thinking and acting in national terms. Most of these new nations have had a continuous and continue to have serious tribal, religious and linguistically based political conflicts and attempts for parts of a legally defined nation to be subdivided by independent units as in India, Indonesia, the Sudan and Somalia. The elder who when asked who he was and replied that he was a Somali was laughed at as everyone knew that he always acted in the interests of his clan.

The national researcher is not only primarily a member of such groups or under their influence unless he or she has emigrated from which it might be virtually impossible not to be mentally if not socially associated. So much so that they might prefer not to do field work in an area or on any topic with which they might have some prior personal connections, but to retain a national identity and for research purposes become an internal expatriate. Even Western social scientists are unaware of the extent to which they think as monotheistic Europeans, unsympathetic to Hindu polytheism and the existence of hungry ghosts in Indo-China.

This is what may be happening in practice since student researchers may start their field work within the social environment of their university rather than expensively farther away or confine their research to the university library detached from any serious personal exposure to the political, social and possibly dangerous problems of working elsewhere.

Status factors are bound to intrude since university education leads to a real sense of elitism which intrudes on the satisfactory performance of field work. This is no more than a reflection of the non-nationals' built-in sense of superiority which comes from a combination of educational, ethnic and social factors which in their own cultures have a very long history.

On the other hand in the Western and North American environments the social sciences in the field of sociology, have always been in the hands of nationals with Americans studying American life and indeed in a growing number of cases urban Americans have been cooperating with tribal Americans on joint projects (Chrisman *et al.,* 1999; Finlinson *et al.*, 1999). Anthropology has always been seen more as a field of research beyond national boundaries with American Indians being seen as legally included foreigners and thus targets of much research.

We can conclude that researchers from both African and Asian universities with social science departments, some of which have had long standing and distinguished reputations, may well be experiencing much the same problems as their Western colleagues who have long undergone training in studying their own cultures as well as those that anthropologists have also experienced in studying foreign and distant cultures, made worse by limited funding and explicit restrictions on intellectual freedom.

The main problem is likely to be that of social distance which is almost inevitable when the national as much as non-national researcher come from another cultural environment and are usually very obviously at a higher educational level with personal habits learnt in another cultural environment. The difficulty lies in crossing invisible but very patently existing boundaries which cover every aspect of the researchers and the researched lives.

The national researchers are usually ethnically similar to those researched and thus the first and obvious hurdle of biologically visible difference does not exist in most cases. Nevertheless this does remain a difficulty when physical appearance is allied to the nuances of behaviour which may distinguish a Brahmin from a member of a lower caste. There are also differences in appearance of southern and northern Indians and similar ones between Chinese from their north and the south. There can be no assumption that physical appearance allows some form of automatic entry into ostensibly ethnically similar communities, apart from the half and half researchers who have returned from long periods overseas.

There is nevertheless the feeling of the national researchers that they are one of 'us' rather than one of 'them', some underlying feeling of affinity. This besides the persistent illusion of social scientists that they will always be able to lessen social distance by long-term amicable association. What is certain is that the nationals researching within their own country will not have the same frisson of excitement which non-nationals have in entering as totally strange cultural environment. Here it is not the same level of suspicion that would greet an expatriate researcher.

The non-national knows that he or she is irrevocably different to those that they are researching. It seems likely that the highly educated Dinka may have more of a problem understanding his own culture than a similarly educated Englishman would have in studying a Gipsy encampment in Hampshire The differences in their current experiences are more extreme in the former than in the latter. One can only wonder at the mental convolutions of a Nuer in a restaurant in Syracuse who has a series of tribal cuts round his head testifying to his adulthood in that far away Sudanese culture. Deng (Deng, 1971) writes from his 'half and half' and retrospective situation rather than from any field work since he does not mention any difficulties nor that he had the advantage of conducting his research in his own language.

The non-national social science researchers are often looking at their work in terms of broad long term theoretical issues in the context of a global environment with the aid of a grant from a non-national source. In doing so they may to some extent avoid the realities of social existence for many people whom they assume are much like themselves.

When national researchers look at their own people whose preoccupation is survival in a hostile and overcrowded social and physical environment, then they are more likely to relate their work to these realities; it becomes an ethical obligation for them to react as citizens (Dube, 1973; 21-2) rather than as researchers.

However, the path of the applied social scientist is usually one which has already been marked out by technicians and politicians; it is rarely a situation in which these professionals are asked what might be the best way to improve the standard of living of the people involved about which they might have as tunnelled vision as any power holder. Theological conclusions are not actually explanations of what people actually do but what they should do in terms of orthodoxy. It is not only that intervention has already been decided upon as both political dogma and slogan but its form has already been laid down. Ideology supported by an efficient bureaucracy and a system of enforcement has terrible destructive force as in the millions killed by the Chinese great leap forward. Almost inevitably they are asked how the proposed intervention can become institutionalised while making the minimum disruption to the lives of those involved (Cernea, 1982).

Unless these changes are entirely staffed with nationals, these technicians will always prefer to work with one of their own kind with whom they can relate on some basis of professional equality. Social scientists are not powerful members of any management committee and they do not usually have their own power base from which to negotiate and the recognition of the possible short term effects of change.

If they ally themselves too closely or too obviously by inference with the nationals who are going to be affected, their suggestions are likely to be seen as challenging the power holders who have assumed the political role of working for the benefit of their constituents of whom those affected will be a small minority. We see how the Egyptian sociologist working with Nubians displaced by the Nasser High Dam became disillusioned by their failure to recognise the efforts made on their behalf by a government with little financial surpluses. So it would seem the side of the national government rather than that of the Nubians who had lost their homes and the graves of their ancestors to a far away civil power and not from war or famine which they could have understood.

National researchers work from a broader and more knowledgeable background than might be achieved by a non-national imported on the basis of a well-earned reputation for advice from applied work in another country with different social and geographical environments. They may even be mistrusted on this account as it is usually a situation in which 'us' and 'them' are clearly in opposition on many accounts.

The Limitations Imposed by Citizenship

National researchers can be considered to belong to only one exact social category and that is their citizenship, but beyond that legal one both national and non-national researchers may belong to as many different categories as may be created in their descriptions.

We have seen that in many cases the national researcher may be considered an internal expatriate, a sort of quasi-foreigner quasi-native who might be considered to be one of them in certain situations but not overall. A Han Chinese researching Cantonese family life, a Kikuyu researching the predominantly Luo port workers in Mombasa, Kenya and a Tamil researching Gujarati Patidars in their trading networks in India and East Africa are to all intents and purposes internal foreigners.

An internal expatriate may have even more trouble in getting accepted as they may be seen as agents of the dominant government in a distant part of the one country. The Lapps of Norway waging a campaign for greater legal and ethnic autonomy, saw anthropological researchers as 'foreign interference' providing information to enable their continuing dominance by Norwegian society based in very distant Oslo (Keskitalo, 1976). In Spanish speaking America the bureaucratic processes of the state as part of their colonization made both the Aymara and Quechwa wary of providing any information at all to outsiders which might relate to their disadvantage and answers to questionnaires and tests would be part of this native ethic of subterfuge (Ortiz, 1982). The national field worker has a difficult job to break free from this blanket of mistrust even though freedom from Spain was achieved generations ago. This may be much more so in British and French ex-colonial territories which involved far higher and more persistent rates of interference in the lives of their citizens.

So at one extreme there are issues of great social distance between nationals who are researching and nationals who are being researched. The issues are entirely different when there is some degree of social closeness A non-national can always pretend that there is some neutrality in how they look on what they are doing in their fieldwork, but a national can never pretend to be quite so neutral. They are ethnically and linguistically committed to a particular culture rather than another because of their socialisation in childhood.

There is however a sense in which they are no longer natives unless of course they are researching the academic or professional community in which they work; they have left their natal environments for good and they do not really believe that they will return. They have become different by the nature of their professionalism. A long period of intellectually alienating education which is not based on natal needs.

Away from this restricted environment they will always have limited social freedom as the nearer they come socially to their natal environments the more their social position becomes related to caste, religion and land holding as well as their membership of a particular family.

Another factor is that they cannot easily escape from the consequences of what they report which is easier for the non-national who has by then left the country and may not wish to return. So that the national researchers are likely to work on matters which have no direct political implications or impose on themselves self-censorship in which they do not publicise matters which reflect on the dignity of their nation or draw attention to criminal or immoral matters connected to powerful individuals.

Objections to the 'Native' Studying 'Natives'

There have always been methodological objections to social scientists studying their own societies. This may well belong to a previous era in which it was assumed that an undeveloped society had a social homogeneity so it was assumed that a 'native' was always intimately involved in some part of the community which was being observed. This overlooks the fact that in most social science university courses whether they are in Birmingham or Banaras, the only field work practice that is possible for most students is in the surrounding society; cheap, convenient and involves no prior requirements of language or particularised social training. So it seems that most social science researchers start their field work experience in communities which are part of their own existing lives with no large dissimilarities in their mutual understandings. It was this assumed closeness of one to the other regardless of circumstances that made Western social scientists ass'ıme would inevitably lead to loss of objectivity.

This is not a particularly logical objection because every researcher is aware of themselves as the centres of their field work, just as every research report has to clear away any suggestion of avoidable biases. It is not even sensible to suggest that these possibilities of bias override the economic cost and time wasting needs for learning another language or linguistic code, as well as having to travel long distances in order to ensure that pre-defined biases are as far as possible excluded apart from the fact that other less ostensible but possibly more pervasive biases creep in.

It seems likely that these earlier grounds for objection which were specifically disallowed by Malinowski who asked why it should be necessary to justify the claims of an African to write about his own tribe when a European's competence to study his own society is not questioned (Malinowski, 1938), may have been a combination of Western biases against 'natives' tasking over their profession by socialized means with which they could not compete.

In any case what does a project being run by a 'native' actually mean. By reason of their training and almost certainly many years away from their natal community, what is the area of research from which they should be excluded because of professionally defined and personal biases. It probably comes down that they should not undertake research involving their own university department.

There are numerous examples of research workers moving short geographical distances and finding themselves in situations in which social distance factors make for intellectual stimulation; as stimulatingly different as if they had crossed national boundaries and indeed moved to another continent. On the grounds of language alone the advantages of researching within their own linguistic group are overwhelming, probably reducing the lead-in period by at least a year and avoiding the inevitable biases which come from the use of interpreters and language teachers. Just as observers will anthropomorphize the behaviour of primates, no researcher can put into the religious behaviour of others emotions and beliefs from their own socialization.

One suspects also that there is an element of jealousy at the ease with which a 'native' can slip into a research environment within their own country without the inevitable problems of visas, permissions to do this or that and the costs.

The social sciences have some notable examples of economically costless research and there appear to be no sustainable objections to research by 'natives' whether in developed or developing countries which have not been bypassed by the huge growth in national research by nationals apart from the surrounding political and educational realities. The objections may be better founded in the dominances which many national governments have on who researches what, where and when.

The Dilemmas of National Researchers

Research styles vary with the social settings in which they occur and in the middle of each is the research worker. The polarities of this are between the researchers who to some extent work within their 'home' environment and those for whom these understandings are exotic (Welcott, 1981).

While in a Western urban environment researchers are going to come across minority communities which are visibly different to themselves in clothing and ethnicity but shows members are attempting to become assimilated to most aspects of the surrounding major culture, this is not so in other societies. In India researchers are going to be confronted with differences between Hindus and Muslims and as Hindus differences between castes, sub-castes and untouchables; no amount of manoeuvring by researchers there is going to prevent attachment to some and exclusion from others.

Researchers can be 'at home' studying aspects of the universities in which they have spent most of their adult lives and another may have similar feelings in the social context of a Hindu joint family in which similarly they may have spent the earlier part of their lives. They will at least have some paraphrased understandings of prostitution and other social issues in Manila and Mombasa if they have lived there.

The 'away' setting can involve research which is not only different from what they may have experienced but completely different to anything which they may have experienced at 'home'; cattle thieving in Tanganyika, double cousin marriage in Mombasa or strippers in New York. There will always be aspects of the religious beliefs and activities of 'others' which the researchers view with sympathy and others which revolt them morally.

Of course the converse would be equally true for researchers brought up in so-called isolated nuclear families in the suburbs of

Paris or Strasburg confronted with the Hindu joint family or the barrack-like life of the Hutterites in Canada, just as the Muslims who marry their cousins for reasons of retaining property within the family and avoiding the difficulties of divorce as in-laws would also be uncles and aunts, and the couple would be classificatory siblings to each other, who would find free choice not only exotic but rather stupid with the socially unknown marrying each other.

When nationals study some area of research within their own cultures with which they are conversant through socialisation and long-term adult commitment to some particular field of study, the dilemma is over the extent to which they can use themselves as informants and indeed their own reliability in this context. Such researchers are in some ways keen to control of their subjects and in broad terms they will have difficulties in deciding what is within and without their topic.

In this context, rightly or wrongly, the nationals in their 'home' environment start with an enormous amount of accumulated information which gives them personal satisfactions and confidence. They do not have to learn and write down too much as it is already in their memories Thus note books are not filled with data which may only be peripheral to the main topic.

In exotic settings confronting the non-national so much is unknown that their impulse is to try and record too much and then have to cut back probably missing much that is important. This again turns on the length of time that the non-national can stay away from their homes which is not such a constraint on national researchers. The more exotic the setting of research, the greater the personal and material handicaps facing the researchers.

The nationals in the 'home' setting of the environment of which they know much about its social foundations, do not have to be so careful in what they research as they already know the dimensions of acceptable behaviour. They can push and shove themselves into situations which would be impossible for non-nationals who would find themselves almost by definition permanently in exotic settings.

National researchers must have greater confidence in their knowledge of their 'home' environment but there are still the dilemmas of acceptance and understanding within such broad acceptances. The Brahmin researcher is not at 'home' in wc king with a Harijan community in Banaras any more than he would be in studying the Nagas in Assam despite Gandhi calling 'untouchables' beloved of

God. They will always have the linguistic advantages over the non-national but it will be the linguistic code of the educated and probably sexually defined so that there is no social science neutrality in how they use their own languages.

Nevertheless 'only here I feel, do I observe, participate and write under conditions in which I am most likely to understand most of what is going on, as knowing nuances, double entendres, conflicting explanations and so forth all apt to go noticed rather than unnoticed' (Wolcott, 1981).

The home and away distinction between national and non-national researchers may have clear cut implications in which the competence of the former is easier to assess because of their ability to function from a less handicapped starting point. They do not have their thinking challenged by the complications of coming from an environment with other cultural understandings but then there is the dilemma that these are challenges to the partial *status quo* of their own thinking from what comes in from other cultures. The cultural complacency and possible conceit of national researchers over the adequacies of their own social institutions and systems, can be modified by cross-cultural contacts. The overriding anthropological concern for culture and for the relevance of that concern in helping us understand not only the lives of others but our own lives as well'. (Wolcott, 1981).

Social science researchers, except in unusual and rare individual circumstances, are not often similar to those they research or their communities. Their social base is elsewhere and they are not permanent members of the communities in which they work. Their level of education is usually above that of the people with whom they work, their research speech is a specialised linguistic code and their material life is above theirs. This is apart from their personal practices and ideas which come from prolonged higher education. They are not as one with those they research and they do not feel that they are however much they attempt to disguise these differences.

Few social scientists record their personal views of the people which they are researching. Turnbull certainly came to dislike the Ugandan Ik because of their lack of charity to their own people but it may also have been because to research this small 'insignificant' tribe was not his first choice.

However, it must be admitted that researchers do develop an affection for the people they study, a mixture of admiration and gratitude. Southwold (Southwold, 1978) in his study of Sri Lankan

Buddhist concentrating on the debate as if it as a religion or not. Intellectually he states that there is no evidence either way as to the existence or not of serial reincarnation. But then he goes on to argue that the assumption of its existence depends on social factors and as his relationship develops in appreciating the qualities of the people with whom he is dealing, he seems to have began to doubt the validity of his detached intellectual and western rationality. He seems to have, in the end, accepted its reality as that was the framework in which these people thought and acted at least partially because of the respect which he had developed for these people with whom he had associated so deeply.

Although to the observant the social distances between the top and bottom of developed societies may seem extreme, the majority of people are in the middle where the average standard of living in comparison to the averages in less developed societies makes them on the wealthy side of any dividing line between those who are subsistence farmers and workers and those who are not.

The non-national researcher are by definition socially distant from whatever they chose to investigate and thus their connections are the tenuous ones of theoretical training which will be reduced by the feelings which they develop for those they have come to know more intimately; they are always somewhere within the category of 'honorary foreigners', and this may make the detachment which is so much a part of social science field work ideology, a slightly more realistic possibility. In the developed world the social distance of most social scientists from the communities into which they were born and in which they are now researching may be less than in developing societies.

A national researcher does not have this automatic almost overwhelming distancing which may well make the research of the non-national free from the dilemmas which are part and parcel of the former's existence once they start research. There are many similarities in their ways of thinking and behaviour and indeed what they expect to find, may not be all that different. Most social scientists involved in field work may have some years exposure to theoretical sociology. Even though they may be internal-expatriates, they are less foreign by most categories of common acceptance.

Nevertheless a factor in the national researchers' involvement in this work must be ambition and the hope of bettering their status, in fact it would be ridiculous to suggest that this is less the case than might have been their situation in business or politics; the abstract idea of seeking the truth or whatever can only apply to a few and even then for only a part of their work. The contexts in which national researchers work have been set by Western professionals both for orthodoxy and the need for publication. Their political ideologies are probably not too far distant from those of national power-holders and there will also be trends towards theological independence.

As nationals from less developed societies come into the international professional market by reason of their competence and the fact they provide Western academic life with high quality thinking and who by reason of their origins provide different approaches to social science issues. But these non-national posts may no longer be available and the national researchers may be left with the avenue of publication as the only one available for career advancement, in which the standards have been set by Western scientific professionalism.

The comments of the distinguished Chinese social scientist Fei Xiaotong who suffered extraordinary persecution during the Cultural Revolution are relevant in this context (Pasternak, 1985) when he said that 'knowing for the sake of knowing is playing games and more importantly that for the future the basis of control must be factual knowledge not 'isms''.

Once it may have become generally understood by national social scientists that their professional futures cannot lie in Western developed societies, there will be a growth in their commitment to work within their own societies within the constraints of globally accept standards of professionalism. The blocking off of extra-territorial opportunities may have coincided with the recognition of national and local for which their own ambitions, understandings and natal abilities are important qualifications.

If it is considered essential that aspiring national field workers should be able to evaluate, expose and exploit their knowledge of their own societies whether in Banaras, Shanghai or Abidjan they are going to be faced with enormous divergences of behaviour from their own understandings which may be both a shock and a stimulus (Hughes, 1960; vi). In this there is often anecdotal evidence of peculiar beliefs and usages, as in Ethiopian theological students studying in Britain believing that the world was flat.

On the other hand in these situations of wide social distance national researchers are just as liable as non-national ones, to feel uncomfortable in the research environment as well as to develop ethical worries which may start to handicap their efforts to be detached. Extreme poverty, unhygienic behaviour, catastrophic illness and horrendous accidents amongst those to whom these researchers are personally committed can be unbalancing to them despite the social distances involved.

But it is not the problems of collecting data which after all is only the primary stage of any field work research, but the next stage. What happens then is the impact on the research data of what is already in the minds of these national researchers because of their socialisation.

One thing is certain is that the non-national shares very little with the national researcher except the abstract interest in acquiring new knowledge from their field work. They may have read the same text books and ostensibly taken courses with the same titles and same objectives, but there are always the underlying factors of what they are bringing to their work from the social environments in which they have been brought up and worked.

The national much more than the non-national in coping with research data is dealing with recent history even though this is masquerading as contemporary social science data. An Indian who had researched the views of nationals born after 1980 stated (Kumar, 2001), 'the problem for historians arises in the impossibility of distancing themselves from a judgemental involvement in the historical process. What we say will suggest partly by implication, whether we are personally wedded to a one-nation, a two-nation or multi-nation theory, whether we believe in the continuity of history or a nationalistic historiography or not, what content this nationalistic historiography to have and whether we celebrate the efforts of communities to reproduce these local identities at the expense of a national one or consider it a regrettable attribute of their marginalization'. The national researchers will always be looking at their work through spectacles which are part of their local and personal position. A Tanzanian researching the Sukuma might point out that their widespread beliefs in the reality of witchcraft and the need for ancestor propitiation are sustained by their own language. The national lingua franca probably does not yet have any emotional appeal beyond the coastal fringe of natal Swahili speakers.

We can perhaps assume that national researchers may have a degree of objectivity about the work that they have undertaken since they are from the start a functional part of what they are studying and can be less intrusive than a non-national. However, it is from this closeness of any dilemmas arise.

How far can a national researcher go outside their national identity and what it involves. In many new nations tribalism in politics and social science research is likely to be seen as antinationalism. These researchers, unless they can be assured of having a future outside their own countries, have to think ahead in terms of their hope for careers; they and their families remain within their society and this is certainly a restraint on what they research and what they publish afterwards.

Researchers in India collect what they accept as facts such as dowry extortion and the suicide of wives, corruption in local government and so on. Almost all social science field work results in the researchers learning much about the underside of communal life. How far can nationals publish what are certainly facts without endangering themselves and perhaps their families as well as handicapping their future careers. There is certainly much self-censorship in what is published. It is safer to research agricultural methods or the domestic economy of those that live on the streets of Kolkata and Mumbai The non-national does not have these worries as he can publish in the safety of his own country particularly as he may not have to consider whether he needs, much less wants, to go there again (Green, 1981; Scott, 1969).

There is another aspect which may separate the involved national from the uninvolved non-national researcher and that is the blandness of much social science writing. Since the latter may not spend as much time as the national in their research areas, it may be difficult for them to fully appreciate that for most of those in developing societies life indeed is nasty, brutish and short for which they can only have an imagined understanding. In Western societies much distress and deviance is hidden in special institutions and in the provisions of the social welfare system. Disclosure is not often thought to reflect on national character and status.

If we start from this assumption that for most of the world their lives are more than occasionally violent and often oppressed and that they live under conditions of periodic privation and persistent shortages, it seems likely that the national researcher must have a more real understanding of these realities. The feelings of the surviving family members of Hutus who killed or were killed by other Hutus in Ruanda, of women who were abducted or raped during the Partition of India, of the surviving men in families without women after the recent south Asian tsunami and of the Nuba surviving in refugee camps after the destruction of their homes in the Sudan as well as the Sikhs who became refugees within India after the assassination of Indira Gandhi by her Sikh bodyguards in 1984.

Being Closed to Home and the Fading of Detachment

It is often suggested that the nearer the researchers are to their native environments, the more insights they are likely to have about what is going on and the thought behind behaviour. There may be a sense of shame by researchers discovering that the extent of witchcraft and other traditional beliefs is more extreme than hitherto suspected. This may well be true but what influence do these insights have on the researchers own conceptions is the job of researchers to duplicate what they see and hear and leave their analysis to others or are they competent commentators on what is virtually their own behaviour. It is not just the researchers returning to a generalised environment in which they were raised at least a decade before their present return. Is it just a return paralleling that of a concerned visitor to some part of their past and to what extent do the cultural origins of the researchers take over their perceptions and what is the consequent relationship to what is called truth.

However, researchers who return to do field work within the communities in which they were born and had their earliest years are in fact half and half people because they have left their natal communities and in fact they have no intention of ever coming back to live there again even if they are nationals still living in their country of birth; they live and work elsewhere and almost certainly they have not married according to the dictates of these localised cultures.

National researchers more than the non-national have difficulties in putting themselves into a detached framework of thinking when working in their own societies because of their own 'bourgeois' sense of superiority to those beneath them in social ranking. Of course in their own eyes and in those of their families they have deservedly succeeded in becoming upwardly mobile. In doing field work with farmers. Tunisian students treated them as their land-owning fathers would have done, as magistrates conducting an enquiry and at worst as representatives of the Governor on a tour of inspection (Cuienier, 1982). A personal sense of sympathetic understanding for those who are not as fortunate as themselves is difficult to acquire without some imposed introspection.

The Covert Nature of Research by Nationals

It is obvious that research by non-nationals can rarely be covert since they are different by sight and by sound and also very probably by their behaviour not fitting into that of the community in which they have come to work; they are strangers doing strange things for strange reasons.

The national field workers theoretically can fit in much more easily into the communities in which they are trying to work. Except in situations when they are specifically asked to research a particular problem of which those involved are aware; factory production problems involving workers, management and union officials or communities which are about to be flooded by a new dam, which will always involve religious issues in the destruction of shrines and the disappearance of graves. There is always going to be a covert aspect.

It is difficult to see how any research can be carried out without some degree of deception even if this unfortunate word is rephrased as covert behaviour. The fact that such research is being carried within professionally accepted guide lines is no more than an acceptance of the fact that researchers will always have to act in terms of their professional standards or suffer professional censure. The 'I' is primarily part of the professional 'us' which usually has priority over 'them' who are the objects of research. Even if the research is done for the highest of moral objectives by researchers of great sincerity, this may not be shared with those at whom this research is aimed.

For research to be without deceit, its covert objectives which may indeed be entirely selfish for career gains, there would have to be a shared identity of interests covering the objectives of both 'I' and 'them'. This is virtually impossible since it is rather like suggesting that in ostensibly ideal marriages that husbands and wives have the same interests.

In theory the most potentially accurate research would be when the researchers become part of or already are part of the community in which they are proposing to do research but there are a number of dilemmas in any such positioning. It should be possible to discuss possible biases as the sex of the researchers and their status. Primarily, if the researcher is doing research in this hidden way, it is rather like spying with parallels to the police informer. Is it morally correct to take advantage of people in this way not just over a single issue but over many months. Most researchers will have solved their moral scruples before accepting a project which will often be override by professional needs.

The obvious point must be that in such covert work they may well find out matters which these communities keep secret from the authorities and indeed their employers. Superiors in both religious and secular institutions often have difficulty in accepting the fact that usually its members have created a secondary system within the official ones, which helps the organisation to continue. In the former case there are legal issues since in knowing about serious crimes and not reporting it they are accessories after the fact; being a care worker and not reporting the abuse of children, and being a member of a gang intending to commit armed robberies or cattle thefts from a neighbouring community.

It would be likely that in any research whether within an institution, company or village there will always be those who are breaking the law to some degree since it would be virtually impossible not to do so when it is a basic point in law that not knowing about a particular law is not regarded as any excuse for an offence but it would be a factor in the sentence after the finding of guilt. This of course would not occur in customary law issues and only when government is largely known through its bureaucratic tentacles.

Perhaps the moral issue here is the magnitude of the deception and whether the assumed moral rightness of the ends justifies the means by which data was obtained. To become a casual worker to expose the degree of servitude and indebtedness of such workers but there are always such factors and whether it might result in the closing down of that work and the workers returning to unemployment. It is widely known that underage children work in large numbers in many industries in India and Indonesia and that this is contrary to national law passed in many such countries as part of their alignment with largely Western trends in social and political thinking. Researchers who disclose these practices do not accept that it is justified by the fact that those people are providing an income for people who would not otherwise have any other social support. Without their contribution to the whole family income, the family would breakdown.

There is another dilemma connected to the degree of covert involvement with which there will be a corresponding decline in the degree of detachment with which social science researchers should observe their fields of enquiry. They may well identify with those with whom they are now living and see themselves as part of their 'us' and in opposition to outsiders. Even when researchers are overt in their fieldwork it is hard for them not to prefer that community to other ones and to see their own researched community in very personal terms. Margaret Mead's long association with the Manus islanders must have made her think of them in such personal terms.

In field work in which there is a prolonged and major deception, there would always be a parallel continuous strain on the researcher to maintain identities which are not their own. This is certainly difficult for anyone who is not a professional and well trained actor and indeed in the fact that this deception is not just for an afternoon's performance it may well have the characteristics of schizophrenia. Such researchers have to be prepared to separate themselves from their private personalities and domestic roles. It would seem unlikely that any Indian social scientist would be prepared to take on the public role of as an itinerant *sadhu*, prostitute or casual worker in and around major cities although such work would be of exceptional value. Research workers who have almost totally accepted an impersonation of another role such as a mental patient or a criminal or a homeless destitute face the possibility of the destruction of their own original identity.

There are, however, other covert research field work which does not involve any deceit although these researchers are fully involved in what they are observing. It is easy for researchers to do field work on rush hour behaviour in Mumbai, pilgrim behaviour in Banaras or one of the four major mountains used for pilgrimages in China, market behaviour in Accra and how restaurants work in Massawa. No one knows that they are being researched and their work might be more valuable because it is qualitative rather than the inevitable inaccuracies of quantitative work.

Covert behaviour and more certainly covert thinking is certainly part of all research which is not narrowly experimental. No fieldworkers are likely to expose themselves to the communities in which they are working by explaining their tentative hypotheses in matters which would be likely to upset their informants. The researchers would not want to upset the working relationships which they have achieved from a considerable investment of time and effort.

The hooded nature of all personal rather than just professional relationships is surely part of all social life. This is not very different from the ways in which these informants conduct their own relationships. The villager does not disclose what he thinks of his neighbours and both men and women practice a necessary continuum of deception because that is how village life is maintained between people who have to live closely together for many years. Surely this occurs in most marriages and within families quarrels may occur when the practice of deception has been broken down.

So except in extreme cases in which national researchers take on the roles and persona of people other than their own in which there is total deception, some degree of deception is likely to occur in all field work, because the outsider will always have intellectual and economic advantages over most of their informants. The point may be that this is not seen as deception as their field work practices are not according to some job specification but rather within the normalities of research as something which helps their work along. It is perhaps not rational to expect them to be straightforward about what they are doing as they may not know themselves what they have done until they start to write up their field work.

Although almost all researchers both national and non-national are by their nature outsiders the former have a far better chance of becoming, as far as possible, insiders; the degree to which the national researchers manage to achieve this may be the degree to which they have been able to manage to role conflicts over being professionally one being and socially another. In other words the control of deception within a framework of immediate social acceptability.

The Advantages of Being a National Researcher

Anyone from China, India or Malaysia who comes to do research within their own country has the advantage of knowing so much about the overall cultural background before they start, of course, this could be also seen as having some factors in common with the enclosed mind, but surely this does not overlay the advantages (Hennigh, 1981).

Such researchers start with some comprehension of the entire system in understanding something of the national culture and what are the points of tension. Many matters which come up in field work would not have to be explained to such researchers. But my (New Guinea) friends, who spent their childhood years away from their village in pursuit of an education, found on returning to their village, that they were incompetent at farming their family gardens because they had missed out on mastering a large body of complex knowledge (Diamond, 2005;281). Malinowski wrote long ago that a man who lives in a polyandrous community cannot experience the same feelings of jealousy as a strict monogamist, though he might have the same elements of them (Malinowski, 1961; 23).

The non-national apart from their theoretical understandings which come from their training, have to work out the feasibility of any hypotheses with which they may want to work. The national researcher is better able to see the feasibility or not of many hypotheses in particular situations.

The national researcher has local commitments from which they are not separated by distance and international law and these remain however much these researchers change their status or domicile. This is bilateral, their communities retain an interest in them as they do in them; there are always exchanges of visits and presents and perhaps even for generations there are long standing reciprocities.

They may have connections in their research area before they start work although it may be easier to carry on research work without disclosing what they are doing but that is not sensible as they will always have to live with and explain what they have written should it be published and even if this is done in as major language not directly known to these people they will find out soon enough what has allegedly been written about them according to the communities' network of gossip. We know that the very public protests about the novels written in English by Salmon Rushdie came from many who had not read those works.

There may also be clashes between what these researchers see and experience as insiders and put into print may lead to difficulties with the authorities who are administratively and politically responsible for such situations. It is usually assumed that their conclusions are partisan because there is no such thing as a neutral position in community life; goodness or badness and indeed everything else is always referred to in the context of personal pronouns.

But then there is always the difficulty as to whether someone who is a natal member of a community or social group can ever have the necessary detachment to research their own communities. Then this coincides with the whole issue of bias and probably ends up with the acceptance of such data with what can be assumed to be their known biases is likely to be nearer social reality than the observations of others whose connections with these same communities is both partial and periodic.

National Researchers Role Ambiguities and Adjustments

National researchers can only expect to slide into fieldwork situation without serious problems if there is some elision between who they are in reality and in the situations in which they have placed themselves. This is rarely the case although the problems are not likely to be as severe as those experienced by the non-national.

A Bolivian born social scientist with Spanish as his natal language despite being a national was always looked as a foreigner by Bolivian Indians and indeed came to accept this role (Buechler, 1969). He and his wife had decided to research the new land-holders of a former estate which had been redistributed to their former tenants and employees, but neither spoke Aymara and so were dependent on interpreters which cancelled out the fact that they were Bolivians by birth so they were seen as descendants of former Spanish colonial officials.

Whatever the status of the researchers who may consider themselves to be insiders in the situation which they are going to research, they are either too close so as to undercut the detachment necessary for valid research or no more than some personal understanding of their own role which may have no bearing at all on how those being researched see them. They have to work out for themselves the type of status role they can achieve which will further their research objectives.

The Bolivian researcher decided that in the circumstances of these people occupying their newly acquired land, his best role would be for him to act as an interpreter to them of the outside political and social world with which they were having primary dealings for the first time in which the interrelationship was not weighted against them. In this his nationality became an advantage only when he adjusted his researched objectives away from any assumption of social affinity with these Aymara Indians.

Another type of insiderness was the American researcher who had to take up long term residence in a community in order to study their educational system who became an insider because he and his wife stayed there so long that they were indistinguishable from other residents who stayed more or less the same length of time before moving on. He became 'our' resident researcher rather than an outsider trying to find out what was going on. He and his wife thus became their own principal informants

A different type of researcher would be those who are looking into their own work environment as priests, teachers and doctors and here much would depend on whether such work is overt or covert A priest who is studying his own diocese or religious order will be doing so with the permission of his superior and informants will know this and adjust their answers accordingly. Most doctors will be researching something in which they have a long-term interest and there is no reason for anyone else to know what they are doing. The surroundings of such research would be governed by the ethical rulings of their professional organisation. Such research is covert in the sense that it is not part of such an employee's work contract but overt in the sense that they do not conceal their special interests.

The fact that researchers may be insiders in terms of their citizenship is likely to be no more than a sliding scale of nearness and distance. They may be insiders as regards the professional group to which they belong under social association with that urban-industrial culture in which they have spent most of their adult lives. But for a Javanese researcher to assume that he has much in common with rural peasants makes no sense. In such a community he is likely to be given a higher status than their own and seen to be a member of the civil servant class with whom lowly people have to act with circumspection and kept at a distance (Koentjaraningrat, 1982). Education and politics have created in most new states new class divisions.

So we can conclude that those who are researched make no distinction between the social scientist as researchers and the society or groups which they think that they represent. National researchers in reality are probably just as likely to be classified as outsiders and indeed as potential enemies since it is always assumed that the government has given them permission to be there (Naderi, 1982). They can remain outsiders for the duration of their field work however much they might remain personally acceptable to those who see advantages in their presence.

The National's Explanatory Potential

There can be little doubt that the national researcher in situations approaching their normal social environments, home, village or neighbourhood has a potential research ability over a non-national of even the most persevering and self-effacing personality. An unmarried English woman researcher brought up and educated in the south of Britain would have some limited understanding of the background of married women in a Northern industrial community centred on factory shift working. Both would have a shared knowledge of English, seen and heard the same advertisements, wireless and television programmes, the headlines of and at least some of the contents of national newspapers and some understanding of national and local politics as well as of the workings of the social services as it concerned them relating to health, the police and, of course, road use behaviour.

It may be that they have social differences based on class, speech and dress but even if that is so they are both within a single social system despite a tendency in research to underline the differences as part of the analyses required by each research project; these are usually thought to be relevant but similarities are far less interesting. The American of Japanese origin who wanted to find out about married women in an industrial environment did not want to continue as a lodger in a Japanese family. She rented a house and than found that she had obligations as a neighbour whether she was married or not and her American citizenship was irrelevant.

Such dyads may eat, dress and use quite distinct linguistic codes but the linking similarities make for an ease of entry and preliminary understandings which would take a non-national a very long period to acquire if indeed they could ever be acquired in adult life by learning rather than by socialisation.

How far would this apply in India, Malaysia and China other than nationality. There would indeed be striking differences resulting from education and a rise in social status in comparison to their parents and most of the members of their extended families whether these individuals have not travelled overseas or become half and halfs, they are now members of an intellectual class within which they would share a similar basic understandings of what is going on socially, economically and politically in their own culture. More importantly they would be able to sense their way through the intricacies of their local bureaucracies and to know how far and in what direction they can go in their enquiries. Sensitiveness to the nuances of life in a strange community may be recognised but to put this into the researcher's own behaviour is much more difficult.

But how far do these somewhat intellectual overviews make an Indian national born and at least raised in a particular locality which they have undoubtedly left many years previously understand the workings of sub-societies in Bengal, Banaras, Bangalore and Bombay. The answer must surely be with difficulty as they may not even know how much or how little they know.

An ordinary Zigua boy in Tanzania whom a non-national researcher met by accident when they were both sheltering from a rainstorm demonstrated nearly twenty different games which he played with other village children. If that is the 'specialised' knowledge of a ten years old, then any adult who has not been alienated by prolonged education outside his or her natal social environment, will have an unparalleled accumulation of local knowledge. The educated adult researchers may thus be over-confident that they have such useful accumulations of local knowledge from which they themselves may have been alienated by social mobility through prolonged education in distant institutions.

The Citizen and Suspicion of their Motives

A non-national doing fieldwork is open to any suspicion of their motives which can be thought up as the pursuit of knowledge for anything other than self-interest is not understood by most people in most cultures. On the other hand, a national doing fieldwork in any community and for any purpose unless they have socially accepted connections there already are going to be the objects of suspicion on two counts.

Firstly they are unlikely to have any concept of disinterested search for knowledge and they suspect quite rightly that they are working for their own advancement and for some outside organisation whose motives are both suspect and unknown. The ethnographer usually confronts the suspicion of having ulterior motives in the immediate encounter with and learns its existence from the people studied without such motives. Most people find it hard to understand why only the researcher is paid or wants to spend money to have this experience (Pels, 1999; 107).

Secondly, their experience of outsiders whatever their ostensibly self-assigned benign purpose or their legal right to be there, are largely seen as intruders whose arrival is followed by trouble or anticipated trouble for the community which has been entered. Any type of intrusion from government officials entails forms of control and hostile reactions to what they are trying to do even if its beneficial effects are ultimately recognised. In this respect the 'not in my back garden' reaction against planned or required changes is an almost universal reaction even for one who belongs and is seen to belong to their own Church.

In fact for many, if not most, people the experience of government is that of inspections connected with policing, taxation, agricultural controls, licensing, education enrolments, public health, road maintenance and building controls. It is within this framework that the arrival of the social science researcher must be viewed. This situation is further complicated by the fact that the academic reasons for the researcher's choice of precisely this location for study are to many of the people studied incomprehensible (Pels, 1999; 107).

Even if the choice is more by accident than planned or made as the result of a civil servants recommendations that this area has a vacant house or indeed someone there who has had some experience of dealing with strangers or internal expatriates, this is unlikely to be accepted locally as the truth.

The whole situation is based not only on the perhaps well justified suspicion of the potential objects of research that no good is likely to come to them from these encounters except for the few who may gain temporary status or employment from such projects. It is also the fact that researchers however well intentioned are not naturally endowed with the ability to negotiate with people from other cultures over their research requirements.

Any community has both power holders and those that aspire to power and both might well attempt to make researchers become part of their communal politics. There is almost always the initial dislike of those in power to have a free uncommitted outsider whether national or non-national lose in their socio-political environment.

The national researchers' political ideas may make for problems either in their view points as members of a professional elite or in the fact that their membership or affiliation to a political party may be known in the community or institution being researched. Although there is a clear distinction between being a member of the Communist

Party and being a practising Baptist, it may be more significant in guiding thinking that being a member of some national cultural organisation. Perhaps it is easy enough for a non-national whose religious affiliations may not have any deep familial and social background. However, for a Hindu of any caste or a Muslim, their religious background is automatically tied into national and local politics and almost impossible to slough off socially or intellectually.

The Political Mistrust of the National Researcher

The power holders in any society know very clearly the difference between national and non-national researchers and the fields in which they are working. The latter are quite clearly on sufferance and require the agreement of both the community, institution and the central and local governments for their presence there. The former do not have to go through any such anonymous one-sided process; they are free to negotiate their own fields of enquiry and the personal relationships involved.

So far so good but there is a more complicated sub-strata. The non-national can always be expelled or prevented from working by circuitous means if they created difficulties which outbalance the advantages of having a foreigner as a pawn which can be manipulated for the advantage of informants, leading local figures and the community.

The national researchers apart from their natal understandings will each have their own network of connections and the extent of their social and political power will not be known; informants might well be a little nervous as to how they should relate to the appearance of national researchers; on whose side are they and to whom are they reporting and to whom are they related by kinship and reciprocal social obligations.

Since they do not go away in the sense of living in another country and may well live within reasonable travelling distance of the researched, they remain a more or less resident pawn in local politics and in the personal lives of important informants. The Egyptian researcher who worked on Nubians affected by the Nasser dam was visited by some of those he knew in that work although he lived in Alexandria (Fahim, 1979).

On top of this it is obvious that if a national researcher has long-term relationships with the community which he has researched, there is no longer potentially the same range of possible detachment from the research at which most field workers aim. On the one hand they may become sympathetic to the difficulties of the lives of these people with whom he has become intimately connected; he wants to represent their misfortunes to higher political authorities while at the same time recognising that almost every community within the nation at that level of living has the same problems. The researched community feels that the researcher should represent them as a return for their cooperation in his work.

On the other hand the national researcher with his wider perspective of national issues particularly of the shortage of money, may lose sympathy with such people as the Nubians displaced by the flooding of the Nasser dam; their continuous complaints against the government and their unwillingness to cultivate part of the land allocated to them despite the money and efforts spent to meet their needs (Fahim, 1979). The state is always primarily concerned with economics, the money with which they can implement policy and it will be interested in religions as to whether they support or impede this process. They are nervous of any popular movement that is not part of their self-interested interpretation of democratic processes.

The national researcher may also have problems from the fact that with his superior access to what is going on in any community, he is likely to uncover corruption. Although researchers are studying discrete communities attempting to understand them in terms of their distinctiveness, there is always the state in the background of all that they do. The modern state has many more ways of being involved in local affairs than in previous generations. To omit the state from their work on local communities and their undertakings is almost always an error or they may be ignorant about what research is being or has been done.

The Tanzanian national villagization campaign came under criticism very early from the national university. No government can afford to ignore reasoned criticism of their policies but in this case the policy had gone too far for it to be stopped without the governing party losing prestige. Organised religions may have an important role in warning administrators of public opinion.

The state is always there and the national researchers finding out about widespread corruption and having the Israeli government's censorship and control of research in the social sciences is a concrete moral strain on national researchers which is very much in their minds while it is an abstract issue for non-national workers (Cohen, 1982).

In terms of the sensitivities of higher level politics and national dignity there may have been some preference for non-national researchers; their work can be used or ignored according to the local political situation. As foreigners the reasons for the rejection of their information are always ready to hand; they did not know enough to be able to distinguish the realities of their data and their conclusions can be ignored.

The national researcher from an insider position is likely to learn more about what is going on than a non-national. To the extent that they are involved in the immediacies of development, they may well be seen as political adversaries particularly as many social scientists are committed to change (Cernea, 1982). Logically enough social scientists are often seen to be spies and their methodological tendency to be participant observers in almost every activity builds up this picture of suspiciously purposeless inquisitiveness which does not make sense to the communities in which they are working particularly if they are non-nationals (Diamond, 1964). This is made worse by the non-national's professional obsession with the extraordinary rather than the commonplace (Naderi, 1983); it is perhaps ironic that much more is known about witchcraft than is known about the disposal of human wastes.

Conflicts may break out between the approaches of the social scientist who has no commitment to any local interests unless of course they are researching their own community and as such can be assumed to have a built-in bias; the local power groups who are committed to the *status quo* and would dislike any approach which questions this.

'In a subject where theories and methods are weak, intellectual shifts are likely to arise out of conflicts between approaches rather than conflicts between explanations will be weak and often non-comparable because they are approach specific' (Bernstein, 1974; 154). So the politically unacceptable will be attacked by the inadequacies of the methods used by the researchers rather than in terms of what they may have disclosed, and which power-holders may take as personal criticism.

Citizen social scientists may come up against trouble not only when their research closes in on subjects which are against official public practices but which have the support of a politically dominant group, but because of the ideological framework, the mental framework that sees social sciences research as a reflection of the global north-south ideological divide, with which they approach their work.

In this there are two opposing frameworks. The Western world bases its understandings on the rationality of administration in which morality together with religion is essentially a private matter. This could be described as the morality of rationality and that certain behaviour does not contribute to the public good; the religiously endorsed beating of wives, subordination of women to men, their circumcision, and public corruption are wrong on these rational grounds.

Thus social scientists may collect facts and reach conclusions which may or may not elide into the policies of those in authority. Researchers may be guided by their own personal moralities which are not channelled by religious predefinitions. Whether they get into trouble is often a matter of circumstances since their approach to what they do in the field has considerable flexibility.

At the other extreme there are Islamic societies in which the framework of thinking is that of tradition based on interpretation unalterable sacred texts. In this situation social science research and its conclusions have to be within the boundaries of what Muslim theologians lay down as being what the sacred texts seem to say about these issues.

This of course is a very restrictive framework within which to work in which the religious rationality clashes with that of Western social and indeed political science. But national social scientists are not dealing with any overall and effective restrictions on research which will vary between countries. In Saudi Arabia there is a close connection between the hegemony of the Saudi royal family and a divided but still politically influential religious elite and in Iran with its Shia religious dignitaries holding key political positions. On the other hand there are other ostensibly Islamic states with much looser interpretations of what should be done such as in Indonesia where there is a much more tentative connection between the government of a predominantly Muslim state and substantial non-Muslim minorities.

So restrictions on social science research are more likely in an Islamic state with its adherence to a single holy text and its derivative interpretations and in any single party or military controlled states such as China or Myanmar, than in Hindu, Buddhist or Christian states in which there are no such structures of authoritarian orthodoxies since their sacred texts are inexact, ambiguous and numerous.

In addition to these restrictions there is human ingenuity in the use of alternative interpretations. In such states as Saudi Arabia there is always the avenue of advice *nasima* rather than criticism *naqd* but even that has to be proffered in the form of transgressions against God's eternal commands (Asad, 1993; 200-36).

So in such circumstances much would depend on how the data is presented and to what extent it attracted the attention of political and theological authorities. It is perhaps not that Islamic theologians and political authorities with which they are institutionally interrelated, do not change but that change seeps in without attention being drawn to what is happening by social scientists. Overall it seems that social science research in authoritarian states is limited and dangerous since their association with alternatives defined by those in power as subversion would block such people from further work within their own societies.

The National Researcher and the Underside of Society

Whether it is designed or not social science researchers are either by birth members of the professional classes or become so as a result of their prolonged training and current employment; thus they are not necessarily either professionally or personally interested in the under class; those who are deprived of reasonable living conditions.

All societies and not just in the non-Western world have very large numbers of people who are seen as being outsiders and misrepresented as having no attributes making research on them a priority. Afro-Americans are an example of a community which has been consistently denigrated by researchers and politicians as having no culture of their own and of being largely parasitic on the dominant Euro-American community who provide the research supporting such views (Gwaltney, 1981).

It may well be that the Untouchable community in India is in much the same situation as not having as socially valuable a culture as that of caste Hindus. Both these communities have ways of retaining their own identities and of dealing with intrusions from the outside dominant world including researchers.

In such contexts there are particular advantages in being ethnically similar and a national but this does not provide automatic entry but only a predisposition among the researched community to give them some wider options initially. Such researchers still have to make them realize that they are not just agents of the dominant social groups surrounding them.

The National Researcher as an Employee

Unless the social science researchers have independent means and can thus choose what they work and how they do it, the researcher always has some characteristics of an employee. Of course a researcher who is employed as a teacher or nurse can do research on some matters in which they are personally interested but it has to be done covertly if they do not want to lose their jobs or overtly with the permission of their employers.

Thus it is possible for teachers to work on some private research programme while still doing their official job just as a doctor can privately work on a private interest in a particular aspect of epidemiology. Both these approaches are difficult to carry out so that others do not know so they still have to keep in mind that they are employees.

Generally speaking social science field workers are employees of a university, a government department involved in agricultural development or social welfare, a non-governmental organisation working with refugees or education or an organisation funding research from private sources such as the Ford Foundation or one dependent on government funding which they distribute to approved projects.

As receivers of money from organisations which they cannot control they are to all intents and purposes employees as the source of their funding by their agreement to support a particular project controls them. There is of course the illusion of academic freedom which is in practice always circumscribed by the factors which we have described. The researchers balance this hope against the practicalities of what they are hoping to do and where they do it under what contemporary conditions.

Of course there may be public and private codes of conduct but once the researchers have accepted this support they are no longer in any position to question the backing for their own work or the topic other than through covert manipulation as they are functionally employees.

They also start their work knowing the objectives of their employers. A researcher will very soon sense what their employers want or at least what they would find acceptable. They are not likely to be funded for the open ended type of research for which university grants may be provided. They will always recognise the economic poverty of most states in the developing world and that they would not be justified in researching subjects such as cognitive abilities. The work and the results of such long-term research would not be justified when their abilities would more sensibly be used for immediate short-term problems. Each social scientist has to weigh up the balances between the comparative needs of 'us', the researchers and their employers and 'them' who are to be researched with a view to some change which is happening or is considered necessary. There must be some duplicity in their relationships to both their employers and their informants.

An Egyptian anthropologist (Fahim, 1977) in studying Nubian resettlement schemes related to the Nasser high dam found it hard to reconcile their continued complaints and unwillingness to cultivate part of the land allocated to them with the amounts of money and effort; put into their needs as new communities when the country as a whole had financial problems. At the same time he was sympathetic towards their reluctance to take any initiatives to solve their own problems. The solution to this ambiguity probably lay ultimately with how necessary it was for that researcher to retain a paying contract from the government.

In major moral issues they can resign from employment and of course suffer the social and economic penalties of breaking their contracts or at least seeming to do so by not completing their research work in any report. In developing societies most employment for social scientists is likely to be in applied rather than theoretical work in which they are employed to look into some problems which are causing anxiety or are likely to cause problems to those in power; they would be sensible to keep this in mind when voicing objections.

Research related to the movement of populations which would become necessary because use of the building of a dam, means that the social scientists have a commitment to helping the government complete its wider objectives. All that the researchers can do is to highlight the suffering that any population movement must cause. The Chinese high dam raising the water level several hundred metres over previous flood levels must have caused massive suffering. One saw farmers cultivating vegetables on the edge of the rising water obviously not accepting the futility of their work when the dam was already a reality.

If social scientists are employed to produce reports on some areas of difficulty then what they report is the property of their employers and copyright rests with them as to what should be published or indeed they may prevent the publication of any part of what the field works have written; reemployment must depend on some measure of conformity to what these power holders want.

Von Haimendorf held the view that the information he collected from informants was his property and indeed others have held themselves to hold the copyright on what they have collected (Fisher, 1946;351). Some social scientists have seen their use of the information they have collected as needing the protection of law. Horwitz (Horwitz, 1993) had her major informants sign release agreements for her to used their information for whatever purposes she needed. Haimendorf claimed that the information he had collected from a Nepalese assistant who had subsequently become a professor in their nationals university was his under copyright. This unseemly and politically inept quarrel would have prevented him from doing any further work in Nepal. Both these approaches seem singularly out of place in the stances of contemporary research when cross-cultural cooperation in research must be the main way forward apart from the fact that they have both shown an absence of any generosity of spirit. With any change in political authority and the climate of research, people who in the past would be classed as informants may now have to be classified and treated as assistants, a challenge to the personal as well as ascribed status of the social science researchers.

The national researchers may not have as easy an access to insiders in the areas which they want to research as might be imagined. Any social scientist works hard to acquire and maintain a circle of similar professionals to help them in their work (Madan, 1982) who are at the same time rivals; this is a time-consuming process in which their work and their social lives may overlap. There is the relevant possibility of professional jealousy which may account for some hostility to the work of nationals and the relationships between researchers and key informants has to be carefully considered. Social scientists are working in fields of enquiry in which there can be no facts which have the solid factual basis of inorganic hard science.

The National as an Employee of a University

National researchers come from a university and their association with the academic world may be of immediate importance as well as much longer than any with a particular place of research. They may be directly employed so that their research will have to fit into university term times and even if they do research from their homes it will have to be subordinated to what their employers expect and indeed have a right to demand unless their contract states that it is not so, their primary duty is to teach. As the visiting Professor Bohannan remarked 'Oxford is a wonderful place in which to work if only the students stayed away'.

As the university may have provided the grant to enable the research or approved the topic covered by the researcher in his or her own time, its own status is affected by what they do and, therefore, affects their further employment and what their university considers to be the best use of their specialised talents. Political independence leaves contracts in a disputed area and the withdrawal of expatriates means that for a short period promotion will have been rapid leading to achieved status which would lead to sensitivities in interrelationships.

Whether they progress in the academic world depends not only on the value of their teaching and the quality of their research but on the reputation that they achieve among other academics which, at its extremes, may promote or block progress. In most cases this reputation is based on the tenuous professes of academic interrelationships and gossip. Since the social sciences have no hard data so much of their work is inferential rather than based on the quality of their supportive data.

As university employees, they have the distinction of not being employed by the government although the government may, in the first place, provide the university with its funding in general or for research in certain areas. There is, of course, the ideology of academic freedom which in the long run probably depends to the extent of which the university will support the public rather than private research activities of their employees.

Many Western universities have accumulated independent funding so that they are able to take a clearer line on the independence of their employee to express opinions and have practices which the wider public would not approve. In this there are limits as the publicly expressed opinions of senior academic staff that are non-white may have a slight genetic disadvantage in their cognitive capacities and that similarly women may have the same which might account for their relative absence in high level mathematics. Another was sacked for using marihuana in experiments with students. During the McCarthy period in the United States universities were not particularly prominent in support of their teachers suspected of Communist sympathies. Just as in some universities in the developing world they make no public comment about military governments and oppressive regimes. In the former cases, except for that concerning the use of soft drugs, they can be seen as moral failings on the part of the university authorities but in the latter it is simply not safe to intellectually oppose the government. No national would investigate black market activities quite so openly as a non-national may do (Green, 1981) and then leave the country in safety.

In addition many universities now operate departmental and university research committees which would have to agree to the research intentions of their staff and thus avoid their involvement in matters which would involve public opposition and questions about their judgement.

In the Western world the boundaries of acceptance for academic work do not coincide with its assumed legality combined with the fact that the university may not wish to know publicly what they know privately as it might make them liable in law as accessories after the fact.

National researchers in Western societies have certainly participated in projects that have involved law breaking over gang activities, drug taking and corruption. It would probably not worth the uproar for law enforcement officials to take action about such researchers, they would gain nothing and they would lose the opportunities of gaining some additional knowledge. Researchers will probably work out their own limits of tolerance to law breaking in terms of dangers to themselves as well as what their universities might think.

National researchers may operate in countries which have no long established tolerance of academic freedom and, more importantly, have every reason not to tolerant criticism. In any country which has a single party government and no well established political opposition, criticism of any type is seen as opposition.

For informants the fact that researchers are affiliated to a local university does give them a possible separate status to that of those directly sponsored by the government. This distinction may be an important one in which government suspicion of what they are doing aligns them with the opposition (Abu-Lughod, 1988).

Nevertheless the relationship with a local university is important as it is a not so much covert restraint on how far national researchers can go when viewing their own career prospects and ideologies as to whether endangering these is worth any oppositional disclosures. They must always be more circumspect in what they do openly unless their future is assured possibly outside their country and even more so if they are married or born into local families who might suffer from their research activities.

The National Researcher as an Employee of the Government or Religious Organisation

In many situations in developing countries the opportunities for social science research are as the paid employees of the government, in which they have little latitude to take an approach which is different to that of the government, their employers. Any idea of independence must be tied to the possibility of alternative employment, lost seniority in such a move, there are also pension and status issues.

In the situations in which they are not salaried employees of a government department or project, researchers may be hired for a specific purpose and specific period which means that they have no opportunity to go outside the terms of what they are asked to report on. They will want to establish a reputation for usefulness and with this the opportunity for further work. Their popularity with students would be a factor in which concern for their welfare might be more important than teaching skills.

Since they have been hired for a specific purpose their conditions of employment may be much the same as that of a mechanic who has been hired for repairing a piece of machinery; a short-term preoccupation. The analogy here is quite deliberate because the contract for the researchers is likely to be quite specific. The contractor is uninterested in paying for or accumulating any disinterested surrounding knowledge (Feldman, 1981).

So to be employed by a government department or an agency which gets its funds and authority from the government requires a change of mind and heart in those who become applied rather than theoretical social scientists. In this context it is salutary to remember that the possibilities of university appointments for social scientists with higher degrees in the first post-independence years and the expansion of higher education has long gone.

If these highly trained social scientists wish to use their potential expertise then they have little choice but to work for employers who are either government departments or agencies selling their research results to their governments. They are in no position to be too consciously critical if they wish to earn a living after their long years of training and idealism.

But there is a snag to this in that they do not have the specialisations that can easily be transferred from one social environment to another. A soil scientist can be just as useful in Kwangtung and Rajasthan as in Hopei and Assam with no difficulty other than the short period required for personal adjustment. Social scientists may have gained their expertise within particular cultures and this knowledge cannot be easily applied to different circumstances in which there are many unknown factors.

The contracting firm may have already made up its mind to what they intend to do which in Feldman's case was the oil fields in Alaska had to be opened up for the greater good of American society and of course for the financial benefit of the companies involved. So local public opinion was irrelevant.

Even where there is no state or private capitalist motive behind a project on which the researchers are contracted to work, they will be tied to the theme of development. In accordance with this theme there is often the imposition of schemes on communities which will not themselves benefit and indeed will involve substantial disruptions in their ways of living.

It is the imposition of rapid change and this in real terms is the common situation in which contracted researchers are likely to be involved. And they will be asked to find ways in which this can be mitigated. They are tied into a foregone conclusion and they and those with whom they now have to work with just have to make the best of the situation.

The contractors employing researchers whether private or public are specialists in their own fields and any interest in human relations will be for the running of their own organisations or departments. They would see community needs whether tribal, ethnic or occupational as standing in the way of progress. A valid viewpoint but not one which most social scientists would agree.

The time factor means that they will not have been asked to undertake community wide background research. In this sense they are narrowly defined as an employee with a job specification and they will have been employed because they already know something about the matters over which the government or contractors are concerned.

The most important relationship for such researchers is with their employers and the dimensions of the political, social and economic world in which they are operating and indeed with the few power holders who might have influence on these matters and who might read the research results. The community or issue to be researched is of secondary importance unless they have their own channels of political influence.

Thus in entering this employment or rather the requirements of their employers there will always be factors within which they have to operate such as financial limitations, time within which a project has to be completed, and the ever present limitations of the popular majority who may have no interest at all in minority issues. The researchers will also have to consider that they have been employed as political pawns just to dress up the issue to show some concern for minority issues and the humanity angle.

Then there are always unexpected factors which the researchers can use in support of their assessments such as the Chipko tree hug movement of Garhwali women to protect trees in the foothills of the Himalayas (Berreman, 1989) and the Buddhist ordination of trees in Thailand (Tannenbaum, 2000) which all caught the popular imagination and, in the latter case, got royal support.

There are also likely to be the unexpected such as the 2004 Sumatra tsunami which will have stopped major development projects in that area for a decade and the termination of aid by overseas donors because they are fed up with the extent of corruption. Much may depend on the orderliness of the national structure which enables research to be of value and its freedom from political emergencies but all in all the national researchers are less easy to push aside as they live there and have easier access to issues and supporting views.

What are the advantages of employing a social scientist? Their training and framework of research expertise provides employers, whether government departments or agencies working for government, with people who are able to assess the interrelated functions of a society or institution whether based on occupation, class, ethnicity, region or the importance of dominant figures or power groups. They are also able to criticise the work of other professionals from their own uncommitted positions. Indeed they are useful adjustable examiners of the varying situations confronting all decision makers all the time.

Preliminary Adjustments in Becoming Employees

A social scientist wishing for an academic appointment is moving from one establishment to another similar one and this whole field of employment is a mixture of academic knowledge and internal politics in which it is not too difficult to fit in because of the similarities in the social environments.

To get employment within a government department or an agency has very few similarities with the academic process. The prospective employees are working within a much broader environment in which the actual matters to be researched involve national and local politics, departmental rivalries and very limited budgets which have to be negotiated amid the claims of other departments for whatever funds are available.

Social scientists by training and the nature of their own research are individualists rather than experienced in team work; it would be rare indeed for anyone to be awarded a post graduate degree for a joint project. So they would have to learn to fit into a hierarchical decision making structure in which however right they may be, their contribution is only one element and likely to be a peripheral one as well.

A principal difficulty is that their research and whole approach is tied into completed events, they are in effect historians. As employees they are part of an on-going process and may have to learn for the first time the constraints of continuous employment and consultation (Almy, 1977). Not just to comment on the work of those whom they may consider to be misguided but to live alongside them in harmony; they are socially near and more important than the distant who are being researched. On a day-to-day basis they will have to work alongside specialists in other more exact disciplines who have well known and accepted fields of work.

They will also have to adjust to and change the feeling that a scientific fact has to be adapted to but to change human behaviour on the basis of social science evaluations, comes within the range of their general dislike of public relations and politics as manipulative without much regard for the public good, which is often politically decided upon without much public consultation

In the uncertain world of politics and development, employers may have a preference for the producers of what they take to be numerically expressed facts. They will need convincing that the social scientists producing analyses of yet more inexact variables has a value for their necessary and immediate decision making.

The successes of hard science in such matters as the increased crop yields of the Green Revolution and the control of some mass diseases are well known it is much harder to pinpoint the successes of social science which has been to contribute to broad cultural understandings; the planning engineer wants statements about what is likely to happen, not just a list of possibilities.

Scientists can put their finger on some exact element which can be related to human behaviour; crops or some humans die and they work outwards from a small number of provable facts into social environments in which there are no parallel exactnesses. Social scientists have to explain that in human behaviour there are few such facts that can be pinpointed. They are not in a strong position by saying that they have the ability to assess contributory variables which may, in some circumstances, have some effects. This is not an approach which is likely to appeal to secular or religious executives.

> Social scientists to many employers are an unknown quantity and moreover as an occupation which does not fit easily into departmental and occupational systems which have soil scientists, engineers, epidemiologists and economists who are well known by what they do and are easily slotted in as such. They have to sell themselves to market oriented employers who are sceptical of their expertise. They may be experts in the understanding of the cultural environment of Bangalore which is not, and cannot be, numerically presented. And for their alertness of mind to be of value in Banaras is not likely to be properly utilised in the conditions of short-term employment. Their useful expertise in a particular social environment is cumulative and requires a long term involvement, as well as being conversant with a wide range of related literature. Hans Cory, the Tanganyika government anthropologist, lived in the

> Lake Province for many years so was available for advice on potential changes involving the largest tribe.

They also have to acquire the tact or, more often, the diplomatic skills which are necessary in making recommendations which in effect are critical of their employer's practices and policies in which they have become entangled by the fact of their employment or because of the accidents of political change.

The 'other' with which social scientists are used to working with is no longer a clearly defined segment of society out there as the 'us' of the researcher's is now of primary importance if they want to have influence and further the results of their work.

The close association with institutional attitudes, practices and values which deal with the immediacies of cause and effect can be a shock to those who are used to the more relaxed long-term scheming of a university environment. While university tenure is a cherished goal in which success and value are vague concepts which are not usually directly subject to the crudities of value for money, there may be little in this world of applied social science. Whereas academic life has its own secretive processes for obtaining advancement and security, the ways of getting and retaining employment in the outside world require different techniques and circles of influence.

They will also have to come to terms with the fact that as employees their personal freedoms will be much more restricted since they will have to be seen to work in much the same ways as other employees. They will have to work directly on what their employers require rather than on some more personal and abstract issues which they feel should have priority.

The National Researcher and Non-Governmental Organisations

Social science has developed mainly in academic surroundings and institutions who want to use their expertise have only this source from which to recruit people with the necessary professional advice and sympathetic understandings to provide information and advice. There can be little doubt that any academically trained social scientist carries with them into the field ideas which they have absorbed in their long years within the academic environment.

There is usually an attitude of sceptical tolerance for those who run the countries of which they are nationals; the feeling that those in power do not have the moral understandings and abilities to do the job well which they themselves feel well qualified to provide detached criticism without ever having had the responsibilities which go with public service. Certainly a form of conceit particularly as few have had any experience of waged earning and situations outside their universities. They expect non-governmental organisations to provide much of the necessary criticisms

In most developing countries these non-governmental organisations, whether religious or involved in secular charities, are both linked to outside organisations and, as well, consider themselves as involved in ethical issues overriding local political considerations. Their employees or those who do research on their behalf do assume local political roles. Oxfam in Tanzania gave substantial support to the one-party state's villagization campaign which brought people compulsorily into villages from where they had lived previously in well dispersed agricultural holdings, in anticipation of social benefits which never materialised. This support continued despite the fact that observers on the ground were saying that the damage done to communities by removing them from easy access to their fields. Researchers had warned Oxfam that this would reduce agricultural output, increase the work load of women and overload the land near to these new villages leading to deforestation and erosion.

These field workers, who were employees of Oxfam, were in no better position to complain than if they had been direct employees of the government. Oxfam was operating in a one-party state and they were in no position to voice these anxieties about this unpopular programme without jeopardising their whole national operation, such as the provision of water.

The National Researcher as an Adviser to Governments

Advisers have no narrow roles and even if they are asked to look into a particular problem, there is more latitude in what they can suggest and to whom as they are often appointed because of their already established reputations and, therefore, have some political power. Verrier Elwin who had become an Indian national and an international reputation from his publications (Elwin, 1947) on Indian tribal affairs certainly had the ear of Prime Minister Nehru. As nationals they will be working from a position of already knowing the political, linguistic and social background to what they are asked to discuss.

A difficult and different development for applied social scientists is having the knowledge which they have gained in research used in litigation. In Australia aboriginal groups had taken the Federal government to court since it has been ruled that the land was not free of people with any title to the land when the first Europeans had arrived (French, 1997).

Aboriginal claimants have used national anthropologists as expert witnesses and their field notes have been subpoenaed and the evidence in them about informants memories of tribal behaviour dismissed as inadmissible evidence as it was second hand. The tribunal accepted only participant observation as evidence even though memory data is accepted as valid under tribal custom and an accepted part of social science methodology (Morton and Shaw, 2003).

The Advantages of being Employed for Social Science Research

As employees of power holders and decision makers in their societies national researchers have the opportunities to contribute to the long range good of entire communities with which they have become involved and they are often surprised that their recommendations are put into effect. It is difficult to adjust to this fact of having to take personal responsibility for what they recommend rather than seeing what they write as distant suggestions for the generalised good of society.

National social scientists in developing countries who have invested much time, effort and money as well as separation from their families, need to get employment, particularly as non-national opportunities may be diminishing. In contemporary times this is more likely to be available in the world outside academia. The institutions which for better or worse will always want assessments of how they are working or should work. They are more likely now to recognise this need and to employ researchers to look at their work This is an opportunistic world in which social scientists are well qualified to participate.

As employees of on-going and powerful organisations they are in a better position to help those who should be helped than possibly as teachers or as the writers of articles in little read professional journals. They are able to edge their suggestions into action since they are now part of the decision making process.

The Distinctions between National and Non-national Researchers

All categorisations of the distinctions between national and non-national social science researchers are based on examples at the extremes of what they represent; Malinowski as a non-national working in the Trobriand Islands (Malinowski, 1935) at one extreme and Kumar as a national working in Banaras (Kumar, 1992) at the other. There is no confusion as to under which heading these two distinguished researchers should be classified.

Although the distinction may be quite clear when the differences are between a Bengali researching Banaras or Brussels and a Belgian doing the same thing for Brussels or Banaras, this is to simplify the social environments in which these categories can be applied. In all fields of work the ability of the researcher to adapt successfully is a reflection of as much their personalities as the environment in which they have placed themselves. There can be few communities now anywhere in the world in which it might be even theoretically possible; all researchers even in their own countries are likely to be to a large extent internal expatriates by reason of language, prolonged education and social understandings of what is normal behaviour.

Cities these days will have not so much tribal enclaves which have always existed such as the Jewish ghettoes in European cities prior to World War II and the current Chinese areas in Liverpool and London but in the increasing separation of Hindus and Muslims in Indian cities.

All contemporary cities whether in Africa, Asia or in the Western world now contain enormous numbers of people from divergent backgrounds so that in the context of research the categories of national and non-national in the conditions of fieldwork are virtually useless.

An investigative journalist (Hall, 2005) or should he in reality be described as a social scientist, went to live for a year in the East End of London in an area dominated by Bangladeshi immigrants. When this Englishman tried to rent as room from a Shia letting agent he was told 'you are obviously educated and this is not a place for a person like you. Everyone here is criminal'. He describes his neighbours as Sikhs, Jews, Albanians and Afghans and indeed from any other category which can be thought of which must be the same today in Mumbai, Calcutta, Accra and New York. His experiences and sensitivity duplicate Jack London's account of the same area in 1903 in his 'The People of the Abyss'. In such a situation the category of national as opposed to non-national must be irrelevant when in that environment he was as much a non-national as he would have been living in a Mumbai slum.

Most researchers whether national or non-national combine some of the characteristics of both while the 'half and halfs' are at least committed to trying to practice from both view points at the same time. Both are committed to finding out as much as they can without bias and in the main they have studied from the same text as and along the same theoretical lines, dictated by generations of European thinkers within the tradition of the European Enlightenment. They have no difficulty in communicating with each other providing that they both use the same major language which means that much Asian research of high quality is not available cognitively in the West and *vice versa*.

Both types of researchers are attempting to carry out forms of field work which are in practice impossible. The non-nationals cannot in fact ever detach themselves from what they are observing in order to make their observations scientific. It is perhaps correct that the universal wish of researchers to become accepted as insiders comes from a human need to be loved rather more than it would be a necessary part of methodology. Nationals can never become so much a part of those they are working with as to be indistinguishable. All researchers in whatever ways they categorize themselves or are categorized, are caught in the dilemma of being inevitably and permanently outsiders while at the same time wanting to be insiders; the human clashing with the proto-scientific. Then of course there is always the difficulty that the non-national researchers usually look different, dress differently and talk differently; they are not as efficient as plain clothes policemen in becoming inconspicuous.

Both forms of research, whether assessed in terms of researchers or methodology, have profits and liabilities in the persisting conditions of developing societies in which the social science research is an almost necessary part of attempts to accelerate social and religious development. Whether or not this is an economic or a social rather than a politically justified necessity is not a part of the social science remit; they are committed to making known possible elements in human behaviour which have wide spread significance; some immediate advantage to all those involved in human betterment.

The Dominance of Demographic Factors

It is obvious enough that researchers are what they look like, about which nothing can be done, and that these obvious characteristics restrict what they are able and not able to do in the context of their attempts to approach their projects in neutrality.

The first of these is the sex of the researcher which automatically splits what they are able to do into male and female segments with knowledge of the opposite sex being obtained indirectly or from public participatory observations. Equality of the sexes, if such a thing exists, anywhere may not extend much beyond academic ideology in day-to-day practices.

The second restriction comes from age since the majority of researchers would be classified in the community in which they are working as immature adults with little understanding or experience of the 'real' world unless they have achieved status by marriage and, in the case of women, motherhood. The older the researcher the greater access they may have to those who hold power in a community or institution. It is unreasonable to think that older peopled will automatically like being asked questions by immature 'outsiders'.

Then there is also the plain fact of ethnicity; that all researchers look as if they belonged to a specific ethnic group with the whole set of stereotypes which are attached to being classified as a north as opposed to a south Indian or Chinese, Bantu, Nilotic, San or Nilo-Hamite. This classification may aid inclusion in some communities but is inevitably an alienating factor in working outside ethnic boundaries.

The Researcher as a Superior Outsider

There is also the basic fact that the national as much as the non-national is always an outsider unless an individual undertakes covert research with all its ethical and personal difficulties or is working within a purely family dimension study of their own communities but still with the restrictions of age, sex and to whom they are related and by what degree of closeness.

There is always the shared bias from being seriously educated and it is probably inevitable that the over-educated in terms of years spent in training makes them see those who have not been through the same prolonged process as being somewhat lacking in the elements of cleverness and understandings which they have achieved by a combination of ascription from birth and achieved effort.

The Classification of Nationals

Whereas non-national researchers are easily classified into a single group of people who have a passport and usually a visa and permission to do work on a specific topic in a specific area in order to enter the country, classifying nationals is far from so simple and they cannot easily be lumped together by an identity of interests or nationality.

This way of classifying researchers in a mass can only apply to small nations or sub-divisions of a nation which have distinct social and political if not religious identities; a Balinese or Bengali working on their own island, city or province might be assessed in a unitary sense. But a Javanese researcher working in Sumatra or a Punjabi researching in Pallavaram south of Madras would share very little other than nationality. They would have nothing in common except possibly the national language of their bureaucracies and even shared nationality is not a serious factor in most people's lives except when there are external threats which override more local and individual interests.

So we start with the conclusion that nationals may have certain assets for research projects such as easier access to both topic and area, knowledge of how officialdom works and the ability to make adjustments within their bureaucracies. Beyond this in many other aspects they are internal expatriates sharing many difficulties with external ones being assessed by those they are researching as foreigners. They have to learn a local language and they are usually outside the range of any ethnic togetherness and of course they may be many hundreds of kilometres from their natal areas where they might have had some built-in advantages.

There is also the divisive nature of social science training not so much that it divides the researchers from the researched, but that its format is Western created and most non-Westerners are trained along these same lines. This off-shoot of the European Enlightenment which is taught as if it was the only way in which human behaviour and societies can be understood. A pattern of belief that is based on the assumption that assessments of human behaviour have to be done in dichotomous lineal and sequential terms of 'yes' or 'no' and that individuals cannot be two 'opposing' things at the same time.

Eastern thought might well think that it is not quite so clear with the absence of philosophical and theological definitions and of any isolation of primary reasons as sufficiently adequate for behaviour when it may well have been initiated in far more distant factors. A general feeling that multiple simultaneous influences are better able to be understood as creating and influencing human behaviour which Western thought is beginning to investigate with Parallel Distributed Processing. It seems likely that nationals from cultures with many centuries of independent thought will develop social science frameworks of thinking which are not so closely confined to Western models. Further that this will develop along the lines of nationals preferring qualitative rather than mainly quantitative Western non-national methods.

5
Consequences of Research

The Consequences of Researching

'The luxurious distance that disbelief alone could afford', this evocative phrase (Davis, 1990; ix) has a number of important issues. However formally and socially close the observer of spiritual practices may be, he or she is always an outsider seeing it through the tinted spectacles of their own culture because of the arbitrariness of socialisation. They will keep their field notes in their own version of their natal language, a dominant process of translating. The partial suspension of disbelief as part of their attempted professionalism.

Disbelief is part of the contemporary even if the partial suspension of disbelief is also part of the contemporary academic climate. Neither viewpoints affect the overall sense of superiority of the involved but only visiting intellectuals. This 'luxurious social distance' within which they have been working 'on' rather than 'with' they are not working with more than sympathy uncommitted to their ways of thinking and behaving. A Sukuma drawing abstract issues was seen by a psychologist as typically schizophrenic, an answer which is little help for anyone working on such issues.

How can we get over the realism of their realities while retaining our own professionalism. Perhaps we ask too many questions which those people do not ask themselves. We look for complicated answers when the answer is usually that is what we have usually done, which the researcher knows from his or her own cannot have been the case 'The past is a foreign country where they do things differently'. This is not the answer that is confined to traditional non-literate thinkers. A recent Archbishop of Canterbury bishop decorated for getting the crew out of a burning tank, replied to an adolescent questioning him for his reasons, replied it seemed to be the right thing to do at the time. Almost no one in replying to the researcher's questions replies in the complicated form that the researcher's want.

We must surely accept that almost no one thinks in the convoluted way that researchers' hope will be evoked by their questioning. We should accept that people believe in and practice for the simplest of reasons that it seemed to be the right thing to do at the time to relieve their anxieties and distress. The researchers complicate issues for professional reasons for which the answers are usually quite simple. We end up having to write in our notes that they believe because they believe in what they believe because they believe, which is the reason for their 'bizarre' activities. There is a necessary tautology in much applied social science.

The basic difference between the categories of researchers is that one remains in the country in which the research is done but not in the locality of their applied research which he or she leaves by bus or train and the other leaves by air and produces their results outside the political jurisdiction of that country and away from the national academic establishment.

In these difficulties there are differences between transparent research into such matters as the social aspects of epidemiology and work practices involving soil fertility in which facts are clear as stemming from the project as defined in the application for grant support or opaque research.

In applied research in which social scientists are likely to find material which has discreditable implications for those in authority concerning political, social and economic aspects of internal change and international reputation. It might in fact be difficult to study any community without becoming aware of corruption, maladministration, law and order illegalities and voting fraud. There are complex moral and legal issues which are more personal and difficult for the national than the foreign researcher for whom these matters have a more detached and theoretical aspect; they can always leave the country in which they have done research and publish in safety there, because their shortcomings are controlled by government law and public opinion.

Basic Issues between the Ideal and the Actual

In whatever the social situations in which we live and are attempting to analyze, we can see some ethological foundations in the behaviour of the higher apes. They may have social groupings and strained relationships with outsiders threatening their patterns of dominances and sources of food. It is scarcely surprising that researchers are treated as outsiders and that their search for information is often seen as threatening social group organisation of the community; they get information from some people not others and this is disturbing.

Whatever religious injunctions there may be to love others, we just do not like others in proportion to the social distance from them; the researcher may be a native but he or she will always be some type of relative so they have biases more inclusive than the cultural ones of the outsider. There is always the division between 'us' and 'them'. As Europeans we are horrified by the industrialised killing of the Jews in the Holocaust, but we have not reacted with the same distress over the killing of the Pol Pot regime the Ruanda and the Sudanese Darfur genocides. It is estimated that only 21 per cent of the Cambodian Buddhist population survived execution, starvation and death from overwork (Thlon, S.163-190).

It may be Difficult to Distinguish the Ideal from the Actual

The split between the ideal and the actual may be accentuated. The model for research is Western and in a published form; a particular aspect of supposed excellence. Failure in researching or failure to complete research is never brought into evaluations of relative success. Non-citizen researchers in the late 60s in Uganda had over 30 per cent not writing up anything; a failure rate making them into academic tourists while being associates of the East African Institute of Social Research.

The model is of the individualistic and intellectually aggressive researcher working through an applied topic to the satisfaction of his or her sponsors and not one of an ongoing relationship between researcher and the researched. This is obvious enough in a capitalist Westerner researching in a Communist state but it also occurs in the fact that the social scientists are professional agnostics and that they are dealing with committed believers who may be deeply offended by their agnostic approach. The Mead-Manus islanders long-term interrelationship may well have been considered professionally suspect as her involvement ultimately it destroyed detachment, but they accepted her as bringing them medical benefits and they were publicly upset at the news of her death. The national researcher may have a pattern of social relationships which are more laid back, group sensitivity for a variety of reasons as well as being more self-effacing, less socially pushy since they may have a longer time perspective forced on them as informants may be able to keep in touch by taking a bus to his or her home.

Does the researcher have a dominant role as that or are there different roles at different times which elide or are there self-adjusting priorities. Researchers do have personal lives and the introduction to published work often contains laudatory remarks about how helpful their informant partners were. Has this always been so, or have there been failures or handicaps in the doing of research which are not mentioned.

Evans-Pritchard seminal work on the religion on the Nuer was achieved without any deep bilingual knowledge of their language and his dependence of interpreter-informants must lead to methodological suspicions of his conclusions.

The primary role of the researcher may not be clear either to those with whom they are working or in their own minds and when does citizenship arise as an issue. What are their roles as researchers in relation to their own countries or their host country, the host community researched as regards references in introductions to friends rather than acquaintances or work associates (Tanner, 2001). What are the roles of researchers in relation to grant providers, potential users of applied research and the connection with the researcher as formal or informal teacher as well as being a long-term investment in outside contacts.

How does the state view research in the abstract and the researcher in particular. Supposedly no control at all as it is in the hands of sponsoring academic or other institutions, but nevertheless access to official information or bodies will always be restricted in covet if not overt ways as in research in to British gypsies which was seen by the British Home Office as going against official policy and the use of already gathered research materials restricted (Okely, 1987). Opportunities for research may be terminated when sponsors see a draft report (Tanner, 1969, 1970) which disclosed nothing derogatory other than the unsurprising conclusion that despite the overall 'good' conditions of prison care in Kenya which the prisoners may not have had on the outside, the prisoners did not like being imprisoned which that department objected to in a draft article shown to them as a courtesy.

The researcher has always to be careful and the non-national particularly so and thereby the conscious need for a degree of duplicity in what questions are being asked and how the information is stored. In China each Peace Corps volunteer can be assumed to have their own police file (Hessler, 2001). Research tapes of interviews with citizen and non-citizen Roman Catholic priests can be 'officially' stolen or supposedly lost.

Whereas in a Western state the amount of research available may be enormous and something has been published on virtually every conceivable topic, this is not so in Third World countries where the conclusions of research may have political uses coming from no more than the reading of the brief conclusions of complex research or indeed not read at all beyond the title carrying with it implied biases. Lectures in Swahili to Roman Catholic seminarians on the contemporary problems of the priesthood can be received with some hostility as these men said these were not problems but the very nature of priestly life. It is not only a choice of words but the sense to which audiences or readers attribute to key words; Kenyans objecting to being called 'chaps' in English and the problems entailed in translation are numerous and probably insoluble (Tanner, 1993 1996, 1998).

There is always likely to be a filtering and controlling process for non-citizen researchers as in the American researching the contents of Islamic sermons given in mosques in middle Egypt, a theological topic unrelated to any political connections which was blocked off by shuttling him with great politeness and much coffee drinking between various departments in Cairo and Assyiut. Islamic social science research should be examined within the terms of 'tawhid' wholeness and 'nasiha' advice.

So far texts on social science field work have been largely written by Westerners for the use of Western researchers and it is only in India that the long tradition of research has received recognition as an important aspect of national intellectualism in the work of such researchers such as Baviskar (Baviskar, 1979) and Ramaswamy (Ramaswamy, 1979). In other countries such as Pakistan, China, Indonesia, Russia (Dragadze, 1987) and Saudi Arabia (Asad, 1993) research work needs sympathetic understanding and much self-examination, as to its implied restrictions which go with their acceptance of that research environment. The identification of the researcher as member of another religion or as an agnostic is much easier than to see either him as one capitalist exploiter.

Those researched have always to be assessed in entirely individual terms and their groupings into categories must be largely artificial because their known numbers in any country at any time is not high. Their personalities are different by every social, psychological and physiological category and the research situations are different by definition and changing all the time as their applied social research progresses.

The Ideology of Development

In the past there have been numerous examples of societies which have been changed or changed themselves but there has been no universality in this so that much change could be classified as internal. The push to change now comes into societies through the electronically assisted ear and eye from the almost overwhelming understanding of how the Western societies have reached high standards of living and the desire to become the same. This ideology of development has come from films, television, advertisements and videos (Appadurai, 1990), and seeing the wealth of tourists and indeed youthful back packers.

It is not so much that new states or old states which are underdeveloped think within patterns of development and that this is part of all discussions on national policy based on a belief indeed a hope that there is a necessary and known pattern of progress to which all societies aspire and which is feasible. This is in contrast to developed states which relate their policies on feasibility and on multi-party variations.

This is no doubt in part because the leaders of these new and old states are often doctrinaire politicians who have seen their colonial experience and past Western dominance in somewhat simplistic terms (Wallerstein, 1977); they wish to see the processes of change in their countries follow some fixed alignments of change at which their policies are directed rather than their sustainability.

There is a framework of optimism which is often reflected in the thinking of both national and non-national researchers, who imagine that changes for the betterment of these people, however defined can be engineered relatively easily using the information which they have discovered and their intellectualised understandings as outsiders. An almost mechanistic understanding that a wish can be translated successfully into action by legislation without any supporting structure.

It might be that this materialistic optimism comes from the Western framework of thinking that man can always change their social environment for the better, a refraction of the European Enlightenment. On the other hand it may be that Eastern social science thinkers may be less optimistic within their mental paradigms as both their languages and beliefs are less determined by definitions and the supposed exactness of Western instituted change.

Nevertheless at most levels of these societies the underlying pattern of secular and religious thought is envy of the better off Western societies and the belief that they have the right to such higher standard levels of living constantly refreshed by the electronic images which are flashing into their minds and rubbed in by mass tourism of well-to-do Westerners; it is the pervasive ideology of development.

The Dominant Need for Applied Social Science

Whatever the value of theoretical rather than applied social science, research is an economically expensive business and takes up much individual time during which the researchers have to be housed and fed if they are not moon-lighting from their low-paid official jobs. This accounts in part for the fact for the predominance of religious thinkers coming from Christian establishments in which costs are not much of a factor and this accounts for the fact that there is little comparable research from within the Eastern religions with their popular commitment to inactivity.

Theoretical thinking might also be correlated to the growth of universities and the plain fact that commitments therein handicap field work possibilities. There is also the availability of what might be called spare money which could be used for matters not connected with economic survival or development. Certainly it correlates to endowments which allow monasteries and colleges to house thinkers without there being any obligations for physical work, apart from the small number of individuals who are able to research what they like as they have private resources.

Developing nations have always given priority to the establishment of their own universities but find themselves caught between the acquisition of knowledge as a 'good thing' in itself but which has to be paid for and the realities of employment for graduates once the expatriate civil servants had been replaced. Makerere University College in Uganda was graduating twenty sociologists per year in the 1960s and yet the Manpower Survey estimated that there would only be employment for two in the next twenty years. During this period there was a preoccupation with status and an intellectual brain-drain as a function of political instability in many countries (Kashoki, 1982; 39-48) as well as the fact that salaries never kept pace with inflation so that cultivating their own farms and moonlighting at other jobs became inevitable. Once this brief period of accelerated promotion has been passed, the employment of graduates declines as does the status levels of employment. Thus the social scientists who wish to use their training may have little opportunity of academic employment and seek employment as short-term advisors to accepted non-governmental organisations. In 1948, the chief clerk in a district office may have had no more than primary education, while the same position at the time of political independence would have completed a secondary education. The same thing will have happened to priests in their relative education.

So the governments of developing nations are faced both with the dogma of social and political development and see the social sciences as having an obligation to apply their skills to developmental issues. In this they would prefer to employ citizens rather than imported experts over whom they have only peripheral control although their cost may be covered by donor governments or non-governmental international agencies.

Christian organisations and administrators have a general suspicion of the social sciences because of their professional agnosticism and a general reluctance to accept that they might provide useful information about the secular aspects surrounding their activities.

The role of the social scientist in the political and social environment which demands rather than just hopes for development must be more than to describe what they see in a detached way and leave it to others to make parts of their work useful in their projects. They should attempt to diagnose what the future might be and in this the ideology should be 'value accommodating' rather than 'value accepting' or 'value neutrality" (Mukherjee, 1976).

It is quite explicit that they have to relate to matters of social consequence and in Muslim states in which there might be agreement between the religious and political aspects. 'Social science cannot be and should not be practised in isolation from what is happening in the society and from what is sought to be done in it' (Dube, 1973; 21-2). In general developing nations with their urgent social and political problems are subordinated to development. Electricity and water boring require a large supply of maintenance men and financial provision for replacements.

Other national researchers cannot afford the kind of disciplinary long-term specialisations which are common in developed ones. Social scientists should develop the lateral rather than a linear approach of medical practitioners in the evaluation of social behaviour. The suspicion of power holders to applied social scientists is largely because they think rightly that they do not have to make decisions and their approach is restricted.

The Restricted Fields of Applied Work

Whereas in hard science the knowledge of what is involved is finite in contemporary understandings as the work starts from definitions accepted by most of those in those fields of enquiry. The amount of unknown factors is excitingly small in comparison to any unit of social behaviour and thus results in the steady increase in 'hard' scientific knowledge and understandings. In terms of understanding the grounds of knowledge in hard science is a restricted field.

The involvement of the social sciences is minimal except for the personal background which may account for the choice of research preoccupations, the disclosure of falsification by scientists of their results and the importance of imagination in those who become discoverers of what is new to science. 'Hard' scientific work is tied to quantitative methodologies.

The scientific acceptability work of the social scientists usually depends on their results being presented quantitatively. In this there is a need to accept the already quoted comments of the distinguished thinker Karl Popper (Popper, 1964) which can apply as well to the social sciences in general 'the triumph of social anthropology is the triumph of a pseudo- observational, pseudo-descriptive and pseudo-inductive generalising methodology and above all marks the triumph of a pretended objectivity and hence an imitation of the methods of natural science'. Once social behaviour is accepted as having some relevance the number of unknown but yet possibly useful factors becomes almost indefinitely large. Western researchers often think that it is possible to engineer wholesale change quite quickly although the structure of developing societies is also as complex as that of developed communities.

Social scientists working on either individual or secular and religious problems will always have to accept the fact that they will never know enough of the issue to be able to state with something other than personal conviction supported by evidence which they have themselves collected related to that issue in those circumstances.

This is, in fact, the usual situation because as the number of persons involved in any assessment increases beyond a social scientist and a single person, the permutations of their interrelationships and related social factors increase indefinitely. There is also the fact that as an applied project goes on, those involved will also be changing. Human behaviour is always a moving staircase of social interrelationships and material involvements; no human social behaviour can have the imposed stability of a laboratory experiment or indeed tested by repeatable experiments.

So the potential accuracy of any applied social science work will depend on how the field of investigation can be limited by initial definitions or is limited by special interests. A study of room or church design is limited by its size and its defined purpose but how the helpers and residents and this will include the cleaners will use this space, will involve enormous numbers of individual factors about which the researchers can only guess (Kashyap, 2010). Any study of equality of the treatment of women in the public service according to constitutional requirements starts with the difficulty of defining equality and the fact that every interrelationship with others and organisations has numbers of specific factors that are related to each situation which is both social as well as involving economic and personal factors.

Inaccuracy may be a built-in function of any behaviour expressed in numerical terms in which valuable and almost accurate information can be given for a situation involving a small family, but this is less possible for a situation involving a hundred people in a village or middle size manufacturing company but virtually impossible for multiples of a thousand in which suggestions and recommendations by competent social scientists may in reality may be no more than imaginative numerical constructions from their inaccurate data.

There must also be the factor as to whether there can be any reasonable possibility of their recommendations being implemented in the foreseeable future. There have been long-standing declarations of the rights of women and against the employment of children in industry but the progress towards conformity is patchy and probably for the most part ignored. Women have not produced enough political agitation to pressurize men to relinquish their social and political public domination and the employment of their children is often the only way that families can survive.

While some social scientists may value their contributions in a long-term moral perspective, it might be more socially valuable rather than just sensible to produce recommendations that can have some possibility of immediate implementations (Bello and Oyedemi, 2008). They could also see their work as producing evidence which pressure groups can use for their specialised interests (Jarikhani, 2009). Since any nation is dependent on the profitable efficiency of its industry social scientists have helped many industries and businesses to be more efficient in ways that are private to those who hire their expertise of which there are no public records (Sharan, 1997).

So applied social science may divide into work for which there are public and private benefits and immediate implementations. This will be shown in government policies and more frequently in helping the economic efficiency of factories, hospitals, farming and markets to be more efficient. It would seem that the opportunities for the profitable employment of social scientists to help the profitability of the private sector would be overwhelming. There will always be some who will work on issues which have long-term ethical aspects such as the trafficking in women and children or the social dangers of atomic power.

Restrictions on the Use of Social Science

A tool is always latent in its potentiality and there is no reason to suppose that its intended use by design will be the ways that it is eventually used. The social sciences are a collection of tools that have potentiality to be useful but what actually happens in a situation is a combination of the intelligence of the initiators of any enquiry and the situation which is being approached.

Globally there are many situations which would benefit from the detached investigations of national social scientists who are well aware of the issues confronting their own countries. Such research is not carried on because of the dangers which these men and women might encounter. It is certain that the large number of Nigerian contributions to Indian social science journals will not be read in Nigeria. When a police landrover came to the East African Institute of Social Research in Kampala on a routine business visit, a research worker threw her diary into the wastepaper basket of the expatriate Chairman. Prior to independence some administrative officers burnt confidential correspondence which might have injured some citizens afterwards.

Whatever the reasons foreigners or national expatriates, the brain drain from the developing world can safely criticise and thus avoid much of their potential influence. This applies to relatively peaceful countries but much of the world is too disturbed for even international aid agencies to and others such as theocracies and dictatorships are closed to any critical investigations even by their own nationals.

So national social scientists have to work within the permissible public dimensions of their own societies. Whether a government is overtly or covertly a one party state even the mildest of comments may well be taken as hostile criticism of what their employers in the larger businesses want investigated. What we read in national professional journals are indeed valuable contributions to national understandings within the framework of implied and understood limited permissiveness.

Ethics and Contemporary Social Science Research

Any discussion of the ethics of research is usually around the major issues of complicity in crimes and the disclosure of information. Mehta's study of Bombay involved long interviews with professional murderers and police who have done the same thing in attempting to control crime outside a paralysed legal system (Mehta, 2004) and much the same would apply to any work with criminals (Tanner, 1970). In failing to provide the police with information about crimes which have been committed, they have committed the crime of concealment and abetment.

There is also the ethical issue of using the ideas of others for personal advancement. This may be clear enough with the ideas of colleagues, but field workers certainly benefit from the ideas which they have got from informants, research assistants and the researched community in general which have only got a return in such rare cases as Margaret Mead's relationship with the Manus islanders. The Ugandans who regarded non-national researchers as sucking their blood for their own advancement, were only expressing in vivid terms what the public in general were feeling but were too polite to express directly to those visiting people.

There are two practical aspects to the consideration of the ethical issues in social science research work which are outside the boundaries of morality. Firstly if ethical considerations are to be more than a matter of dealing with contingencies, how can they be assessed in open ended research in which little or nothing is known about what may or may not be found in situations which are as yet undefined and indeed indefinable. To consider ethics in such situations would seem to be an exercise in legal imagination.

Ethical issues might arise in the course of field work just as the researcher might get ill or break a leg but such hypothetical dimensions make for anxieties in the researcher's mind which they do not necessarily need for making the best of the opportunities confronting them. Risk taking may be part of any dialectic research as in any human relationships.

The second issue is for whom are ethical issues being considered. There can be no doubt that ethical understandings are necessary to avoid exploitation in which researchers profit commercially and professionally from their work; but it is not work which has been carried out in their brains but through the medium of obtaining information from informants who in their own social situations would see the provision of any information as requiring reciprocities. It was perhaps natural that Ugandans in their gossip about field workers regarded post-graduate non-national researchers as sucking their blood. No one except these outside people got any profit which could be seen as benefiting Ugandans.

As those who are researched become more aware of the outside world, there are complications over the ownership of information. A French documentary film maker Nicolas Philibert spent six months recording the life of a small one-room rural school with its one teacher having got release forms from all those involved. The film 'Etre et Avoir' became a national and almost by accident a commercial success and is now the subject of prolonged litigation over a share in the profits. So it would be sensible for researchers to remember that tape recordings and photographs and films are seen as different to the taking of notes.

There are ethical issues in every human relationship and in primary ones behaviour is subject to social and psychological acceptability. What is acceptable outside the social, religious and political sphere in which a researcher may be at home must always be largely unknown. If researchers do not behave in ways which would be unacceptable in their own societies, they may not go far wrong and of course in this the national has perhaps greater knowledge and sensitivity to what might or might not be acceptable. Professor Evans Pritchard's injunction that researchers should behave like gentlemen is probably transferable as an ideal in any culture, but this requires much imagination whether one is working in Banaras, Birmingham (Alabama) or Bamako. The permutations over what might not be acceptable are perhaps largely a necessary anxiety for any researcher anywhere.

Research ethics may involve issues that in a cross cultural context are intrinsically wrong such as researchers conniving at incest within primary groups or ritual murder. It seems unlikely that any anthropologist knowingly rather accidentally ate human flesh. Most ethical issues are negotiable since they occur in social contexts and it is difficult if not impossible for researchers who are participating in communities. Kumar must have showed her disapproval in witnessing the Banaras police beating up a suspect (Kumar, 1992) just as Chakravarti in researching a community in Rajasthan was appalled by the villagers amoral wholly pragmatic acceptance of the necessity for bribing officials for achieving specific objectives (Chakravarti, 1979). Any researcher should be aware of ethical issues from start to finish and it should be advantage for the project to have had these considerations treated as important (Skinner, 2002).

In the end what we have in social science field work is a continuous series of situational dilemmas that involve every researcher in ethical issues. Whether they require decisions or not about how the researcher should behave may depend on their own culture based feelings as to the appropriateness or not of what they intend to do or to be involved in.

There is another ethical factor which is of greater importance than in the earlier years under colonial governments when communities did not think that they had any power over admitting researchers to their areas. The Pueblo Indians of the United States after generations of being a tourist attraction and venue for researchers, now control all such access through their own tribal councils. In most countries applications to do research by non-nationals require national academic as well as local government support The activities of non-national researchers can become the subject of diplomatic concern over their safety.

However national researchers working in their 'home' environments publishing their results in national and international journals may well have outlines published in the local language and in local newspapers so the subjects of such research may well see the results; this is a new development. The key figure in Redfield's "Chan Kom The Village That Chose Progress", had not seen the book or his photograph in it when visited in the late 60s. On the other hand a Swedish researcher of Sukuma customary law over the use of water sent all his main informants copies of his book even though they could not read English (Drangert, 1993).

Now those who have been part of research feel that they can knowledgeably discuss and comment on such published results from their own points of view (Wolcott, 1981) and their personal understandings; they have all been through the same social processes such as going to school, taking part in local politics, being ill and having family crises. In this context there is an ethical need to consult the community more widely over what the researchers have or think they have discovered. The Sukuma of Tanzania who had been informants were well able to understand their own behaviour and to distinguish it from that of other cultural groups.

When it comes to the 'truth', the protection of key informants has to be of paramount importance to social scientists which is best done by dividing up the information so that it appears to come from several sources at which informed readers can only guess. Redfield's photograph of his principle informant and the key figure in the changes about which he wrote would have been disastrous for that person in any modern community in which connected persons could have read what had been said about their own roles and those of others.

An informant at the centre of ordinary day to day affairs has to be disguised just as much as those involved in issues which verge on possible corruption and overt criminality. Informants can have their information split up as coming from unattributable commentators, as coming from other published research or from public records or by having more than one field of study so that information cannot be attributable to any single source; in this extent it is always sensible to keep informants names under cover names.

What has caused the researcher to be revolted leads to explaining away such activities in terms of psychopathology or the pressures of cultural environments. The illusion of detachment is easy when what is being observed is so obviously different obscuring the fact that there will have been important metaphysical issucs behind such peculiar and indeed intellectually interesting religious behaviour. Kuru was caused by the eating of uncooked parts of family dead by women to keep their spirituality alive.

But working to assess Christian institutions start from different presuppositions and patterns of religious behaviour. At least for social scientists trained in Western academic suppositions, all that they read and observe about the ideas and behaviour of these Christians, is not all that detached from their own past and present social environments.

We cannot know what their personal metaphysical experiences much less what their benign or malign consequences may have been, on whatever genetic predisposition they may have had within them, they will all individually have been subject to personal stresses, the accidents to which they have been subjected as well as the personal influences from accidental association with other people and books.

In this we do not know whether these influences have come from a Christian divine, devout Catholic or traditional diviner but the influences are there. These particular predispositions may be coalesced into cultural ones in which the Japanese opposed to Zunis and Tamils are likely to think in certain paradigmatic ways. It is reasonably certain that few if anyone can make a total change in their cultural dispositions. Lafcadio Hearn became ostensibly Japanese in his behaviour and in his associations through his Japanese wife but it would seem unlikely that his thoughts and dreams would not have been in English. Others such as Cushing with the Zuni may have made prolonged efforts to translate themselves into persons of another culture and indeed may have thought that they have made an emotional and well as a social transfer but they were deluding themselves.

In any assessment of religious ideas and practices whatever the social distance between them we can only guess what may be the religious thinking of others and in this we are inevitably compromised by our own socialisations as well as by the efforts of social scientists to attach neutrality to their observations and conclusions. All that they do will be reflected through the lens of their own individual and cultural socialization.

The Filter of the Social Environment

Any research into social and religious ideas and behaviour in which the social scientists are distinguished as different to those ordinarily within the community is an intrusion. The researcher's presence in any setting in which he or she is not a 'natural' and acceptable part will have some effect on the dialectical possibilities of whatever interrelationships they develop. Their questioning presence is often an affront to personal and general social practice.

Of course there are variations in this and a Swedish language anthropologist in Papua New Guinea was given the role of the ghost of a baby of his hosts who had died just before his arrival. This role was given to him when it became apparent that he did not fit into any of the secular and religious existing roles for Westerners in their experience. Then he had the difficult job of fitting into the role of ghost of a baby in pretending that he did not know matters which would obviously not be known to a Papuan baby. (Kulick, 1997; Appendix, 268-275). This very interesting role adaptation might well have been the subject of a different book.

It has always been recognised that certain types of behaviour cannot be researched by outsiders and that there are limits to the intrusive behaviour of both nationals and foreigners. In all societies people have culturally accepted claims to privacy which they are not prepared to discuss with even close friends and relatives. So social scientists have to accept that certain types of personal behaviour including religious ones will be out of their reach except by personal methodological questionable inferences.

It is rare for anyone to object to such dialectical interviews such as the Roman Catholic priest who stated that he was not prepared to discuss his religious practices with an outsider to whom he was not religiously obligated. But there must have been many others who disliked such intrusions who would have modified their replies to suit these intrusions for which they have had no previous experience.

So why should people cooperate at all into enquiries relating to the Christian denomination to which they belonged. They might believe that such enquiries have been authorised by a religious authority and that there must be good reason for such intrusions. It provides an opportunity to publicize personal viewpoints and to score points in some religious dispute and in the dull lives of subsistence farming there would be the pleasure of talking to an outsider about matters which they would normally have to be discrete or silent.

This means that any observations and conclusions are likely to be part of some scaling of inadequacy according to these peak standards rather than in terms of partial conformity. It avoids any approach which comes from the needs of potential believers. Overall this may mean that the professionally and intellectually elite social scientists are usually assessing religious behaviour in terms of the conceptions of another elite rather than 'average' thinking and behaviour. Christian theologians dislike the almost universal belief that the performance of rituals has effects independent of the moral position of the performer.

So what is observed and recorded is always filtered through some conscious and acceptable biases or unconscious ones which come from the various continuous socialisations to which these observers have been subjected to as they pass through their personal and professional lives. They are not and can never be detached observers of social behaviour and certainly not in considering ideas and behaviour as indefinable as the supernatural. 'Much has been written on how values shape the choice of a research problem and the analysis and reporting of its values which the researcher has learned in some social class, ethnic or other biographical context. Audiences help shape the direction of social science research both in the direction of particular research endeavours and over time, in the context of the researcher's careers' (Warren, 1980: 306). This important factor that data on social and religious ideas and behaviour is presented by professionals who have their own personal agendas even if they are employed by a secular or religious organisation to produce unbiased assessments. From start to finish these assessments are in the framework of 'us' and 'them' rather than tinged with the possible inevitabilities of 'we'.

The social science approach is to look at religious ideas and practices in terms of what are mainly consumer activities as we consider what a million do at a shrine or who hold a practice to be religious are the most important and prolific factors to consider in evaluating the extent of working misunderstandings. We look at the base of the pyramid of religious ideas and behaviour as it is this vast expanse of mainly non-literate emotional involvements that supports or absents itself from the more abstract and intangible theological and philosophical pinnacles of which they are usually unaware or indifferent to. A Sukuma Roman Catholic priest on commenting on the views of visiting Western theologians' aid that their dismissal of their ritual practices made it hard to see these visitors as members of the same religious denomination; they were probably unaware of the native distrust of their theological thoughts on the decisions of Vatican II.

Legal Issues

So we see that the whole field of social science research with its initial Western dominance often remains within a framework of post-colonial overtones so that a top-down structure of thinking and behaviour may still predominate.

It is hard to think of a situation in which a person's thoughts and behaviour recorded surreptitiously or in what they thought to be more or less private interpersonal conversations, come available in print to the general public without objection being taken to such disclosures particularly when it is published in a commonly understood and readable linguistic code.

Where this has occurred in Western environments over work done by Western social scientists, there have usually been such reactions. There was an uproar in the United States over the publication of a study of a small town (Vidich and Bensman, 1958) as many there felt that the pseudonym did not effectively disguise particular individuals; privacy and trust had been betrayed and reputations put at risk. The 4th July parade had a float with an image of the researcher Vidich bending over a manure pile. Two studies of an Irish community (Messenger, 1989; Scheper-Hughes, 1982) attracted an even wider range of criticisms from the people in those communities. The school master remarked 'We have our problems and know about them well enough but why has the researcher felt the need to expose this to the entire world'.

When Oscar Lewis's series on a Mexican family (Lewis, 1951, 1959) was translated and published in Mexico despite the actual family being unnamed, there were widespread hostile objections in the Mexican national press and a suit was brought against him and his publisher for obscenity and slander. In this the core factor may have been the fact that Lewis was an American, a non-national researcher who had denigrated the Mexican national image by describing the abnormalities of supposedly normal family life.

Certainly the criticisms are likely to be stronger and more widespread when the researchers are non-nationals and one can imagine the protests if the Irish research had been done by a Kenyan or Bengali. But it is prudent to remember that a national researcher may be equally foreign in terms of social distance. In fact an Indian researcher (Pandey, 1979) has worked on American Indians from which there do not appear to have been any hostile reactions perhaps in part because of physiological similarities between the researcher and those researched.

So much of metaphysics are felt rather than explicated in the individual mind that there are bound to be increased difficulties over social and religious matters and constant misunderstandings made worse by publication in a world of increasing computer communication.

Who is likely to read research findings and who is the public for which these publications are intended. There is always the factor that self-criticism is acceptable but its exposure is not. It may be the dilemma of popularising research or at least publishing it in a widely read and readable language which causes the problem from its public nature. Crudely few social scientists would pass up the opportunity to have their works published and read widely if there was an obvious financial return. Is the situation likely to be different in developing countries where the researchers are nationals and who may have to be much more careful in considering what may be the local reactions to popular publishing of their field work. Western trained social scientists are monotheists and would misunderstand Hindu polytheism and complex symbolism.

As a general frame of thinking this is clearly outdated as those who are researched become aware of their rights to be consulted over all stages of the field work. So their consent to be researched is now an important factor in the preliminaries to fieldwork; the right to be researched or not becomes important and this involves some disclosure of its objectives. We have to consider the extent to which permission to be the subject of research by an outsider covers the publication of the results to the outsider world whether in the local or a major foreign language.

If the results make the location recognisable and the identification of specific individuals possible then their informed consent becomes increasingly necessary. It would clearly be difficult to require informants to sign consent forms to the use of the information which they supply (Fleur-Lobban, 1994) although this has been attempted. This would entail all the difficulties of translation from another language or linguistic code over consent to what; a court case or indeed an appeal to a government official about such generalised permissions would lead to embarrassing rulings about getting the researched to sign blank permission.

Even the implication that those researched have some say in what is published about them, gives them the power in effect to restrict or to enforce restraint on what is published. This knowledge and its acceptance as an ethical requirement encourages or at least makes necessary a greater openness or disclosure by the researchers. This itself suggests that researchers will have two levels of information; one which they are able to discuss with those involved and in this context published and a covert one for which they will not be able to disclose their sources or their conclusions.

A more collaborative relationship between the researched and the researchers whether they are national or more particularly non-national is certainly a contemporary necessity. This is a difficult issue since one can assume that in any field work there is some sort of a collaborative relationship without which little indirect information would ever be obtained. It is not difficult to see the conflict between the extent of the obligation and the necessary professional secrecy to reduce the extent of bias. There may be social scientists who are ruthless in their pursuit of information, but their ability to get information would be different according to whether the environment involved is a family, neighbourhood, community or nation.

National Law and the Publication of Research

The research activities of social scientists are as liable to legal action as any other social activity and many universities in developed societies vet research proposals to avoid possible civil actions against their researchers and their results. Research carried out through a university requires the agreement of special committees and probably that of a safety officer as well as clearance from another committee that covers ethical issues. But this is only for research requiring funding and the university's name for getting access to a particular field of research. National researchers using their own funds and time, may not require such permissions in furthering their own interests and careers as with doctors who are continually researching their own specialisations who have always been liable to civil action over their mistakes for which may have insurance.

Often it is assumed that there are no civil law issues in researching downwards in the social scale because few of those researched would be likely to see much less read any publications coming from research on themselves. Robert Redfield (Redfield, 1956) wrote a detailed account of the Mexican village Chan Kom including a photograph of the principal initiator of the changes he described, who had never seen this book with its pictures; this seems bad manners at the very least and ingratitude for the help which he must have given to Redfield. Some insensitivity for the feelings of those from whom they get information possibly used for the advancement of their own careers.

There are now several possibilities in which researchers might become involved in disputes about the 'truth' of what they have written and published. There are growing numbers of literates in all societies from the most tribal or urban slums upwards; they can seek out through relatives, friends and journalists and increasingly have access to computer records. So there will always be gossip about what has been written about them. The universities take in students from every section of their nation who are bound out of curiosity or professional interest to seek out what has been written about their own communities. Finally national publishers in both developed and developing nations are often looking for new markets and there is an automatic attraction in publishing research on local social behaviour in a popular local language for an expanding middle class readership as well as the fact their universities pass out more students with professional interests in such local affairs.

Whether an issue becomes a legal dispute might depend on how it relates to the national culture and more particularly its dignity internationally. In Indian culture there is a tendency to use the courts as a weapon of attrition whereas in China the legal system has not been designed to encourage litigation and in Japan there is if anything an avoidance of the courts since their use is seen as a sign of the weakness of the initiator's case. In this context non-national researchers would not be affected since they would not be in the country long enough for such action to be taken; they are certainly not likely to remain there or indeed to be allowed to stay there long enough to defend such civil cases. It would be unwise politically and economically to get entangled in any such legal processes over copyright and accuracy of published data. Much the same would apply to non-nationals researching in the United States which is as notoriously litigious as India is reputed to be since a high proportion of elected politicians have graduated in law. So non-nationals if they became involved in any legal issues over their research would almost certainly be advised by their embassies to leave the country. During the Cold War American researchers who worked in Communist countries found that their reports which inferred favourably about some aspects of their political and social system found themselves personalised.

Two legal issues might result from field work. Firstly some verbal statement made to a third party about an individual who then feels that they have been slandered. In this we must remember that very little data on which social scientists rely would meet the required standards of correctness to be acceptable as evidence in court; except where the informant is reporting his own activities, much data is second-hand. There is a distinction between whispering something beside a fire or across a counter and seeing it printed for the world to see and as the subjects of research said over an Irish project, 'why did you have to write it in a way that we could read it and understand exactly what you were saying' (Scheper-Hughes, 1982).

Secondly, that something written under the researcher's name is not the truth and then the person about whom that statement was made sues for libel. This is the most dangerous of civil suits because it does not rest on words which may or may not have been recorded, have a limited audience and, therefore, become easier to defend but on something in print which has potentially an unlimited audience and no time limit. It is thus over printed reports that future legal cases might arise, not so much from those who were the subject of the research, but from those of equivalent status, particularly when the research has involved persons of high status or work in powerful institutions.

There are a number of these issues which have arisen in Ireland where published research has been read by those about whom the researchers have written. The reactions to a published study of mental illness in a particular rural community where the reactions of their most literate and self-reflexive people was harsh, swift and unsettling (Scheper-Hughes, 1982) when the researcher had contradicted a hitherto unchallenged native interpretation of their lives and created a public shame. As the village schoolmaster put it 'It is not your science I'm questioning, but this; don't we have the right to lead unexamined lives, the right not to be analysed? Don't we have the right to hold on to an image of ourselves as different to be sure but as innocent and unblemished all the same'.

The Irish may be over-sensitive to what they see as the criticisms of outsider researchers, here is an issue of loss of face in all civil litigation but might not this apply to many situations in Africa and Asia where non-national researchers have touched on the dignity of those involved once data is put to print. The Irish reactions to the published research of an American social scientist ranged from accusing him of being ill-informed, ignorant, illiterate, malicious, anti-Catholic and pro-Anglo-Irish to warning about never trusting what an Irishman says and to more general statements about the impossibility of anyone but especially an outsider, gaining an understanding of the Irish and concluding that everything he says is true but the reason he would be lynched if he returned to where he worked was that he had a right not to say it (Messenger, 1989).

The study by a national of Irish intellectual life was more complex as it touched on the connections between their university establishment and their party political connections over appointments so that she had to break down references to her sources of information by writing in an obscure manner in order to simply protect herself from worst legal threats and at best from a principal informant's undying enmity (Sheehan, 1993).

The basic issue in any civil action is the truth of what has been put into print and researchers collect information from a variety of sources of which only a small proportion will be documents obtained from an institutional source which may themselves be of questionable accuracy. Did the researcher obtain a signed release allowing the use of the material which is rarely done because it involves so much time consuming in seeking explanations.

Researchers knit together information from a variety of sources of very varying reliability and consistency which is usually reported speech of little legal validity. Social scientists would always have great difficulty in proving the truth of what they have written and indeed would be wise to back away from any such possibilities by qualifying their conclusions with possible doubt as to their unqualified accuracy; in effect to avoid any assumption of incontestable accuracy in the scientific sense of the word.

6
Methodology

The Ideological Biases in Analysis

There is the basic factor that those who evaluate social and religious practices and commitments are either social scientists with a built-in commitment to a detached and agnostic evaluation of all secular and religious behaviour so that their approach to the assessment of walking and worship start with a commitment to the same professional methodological detachment. An agnostic approach is a form of bias while its aim is scientific; it has no parallels to the ways that Chinese and Canadian scientists examine the epidemiological factors in the occurrence of a disease.

The other group of assessors of religious behaviour are theologians and those holding positions in religious institutions that are similarly committed to a viewpoint supporting forms of religious faith to which they are professionally by years of participation rather more than emotionally committed. They would look at walking and worship as starting from totally different bases. In these senses both groups are not unbiased as they enter their evaluations with pre-convictions which they consider to be both morally and professionally valid and necessary.

So there are methodologies for the collection of information about religious behaviour and commitments which are ostensibly neutral or at least aimed at neutrality but which are in practice collected by theological or social science outsiders who know that they are socially distant from the majority of the people whose religious ideas and practices they are observing. They are role playing outsiders with professional education which from the start is alien to the thinking and practices they are evaluating.

On the other hand these people from whom they get their information are both individually and communally insiders. These insiders are to a very large extent less educated and less intellectually aware of what is involved in such professional appraisals. These insiders are similarly biased as they would consider themselves to be bound by their inarticulate as well as known religious beliefs and practices and they are also aware of the social distance which separates themselves from these outsider enquirers.

From these perspectives there are biases which affect how data is both collected and interpreted. The social scientists will not give any particular value to the intellcctually inaccessible religious convictions of many of the pilgrims who go to Banaras, Lourdes and Mecca. On the other hand those with religious commitments may leave out the social factors in which some of those same pilgrims are really tourists, conforming to family pressure or see in public religious commitment financial and political advantages. It would seem to be more likely that a Western pilgrim to Assisi would be carrying a guide to its architecture than the writings of St Francis, while the pilgrim to Mecca and Banaras would not be interested in such non-religious issues and certainly in the case of Muslims carrying a copy of the Koran.

Religion and spirituality for most people is a necessity at some level of general understanding and irregular practice. These are not matters to which they have given much thought as it is an activity which is both relatively rare and to which they have never had much need to give much thought. Most people questioned would not be able to express them coherently in response to the questioning of outsiders, just as they would not be able to describe in any detail what is good food or what is a good funeral or a good celebration of the Mass.

Most people most of the time give little thought as to why they do what they do, much less how they behave in emergencies or in religious ceremonies, or whenever their emotions are involved. An analytical frame of mind is a rarity because it is not a necessity contributing to the emotional and physical effectiveness of social and religious behaviour. Social scientists are no more likely to do this for their own beliefs and practices than street cleaners, factory workers, businessmen and women and the organisers of religious group activities. So now let us look at the methods of recording putting social and religious behaviour into print.

The Recording of Secular and Religious Information

What can we actually know with any degree of confidence about the religious behaviour and commitments of those who are in fact strangers according to the categories within which social scientists box people together for bureaucratic and research purposes. The available methodologies cannot provide information about covert understandings; they are in the physical position of praying but are they praying nor can we be certain what constitutes participation in a religious ceremony. Just being there is possible participation when the church is big enough to take in all who want to come in, but Ethiopian Coptic churches of great religious importance may not be able to accommodate as many as a hundred worshippers, while thousands attend outside without being able to see or hear anything.

We can read the documentary proof that they have fulfilled certain religious obligations but this may be in order to get access to special education for their children, medical attention or in fulfilment of the requirements to gain access to an inheritance.

Finally only a minority of individuals are able and willing to talk or write about their personal commitments and understandings, so that the voluntary provision of data may well be as deliberately or unconsciously inaccurate as accurate. The pen and the tongue are always biased implements of expression. We have very little evidence that might support what these people may overtly or covertly think or behave in both religious and secular situations. Here we have the issue of triangulated probabilities; a possible accumulation of corroboration of evidence from different sources and perspectives which will align themselves towards particular conclusions but that would nevertheless not be scientific poot. There is always the factor that the wider the attempted coverage, the weaker the data. There are always methodological difficulties in getting information about religious ideas and behaviour of which only a proportion are visible or indeed readily available to those who want to understand these activities from both secular and religious viewpoints and their necessary combinations.

Observable Data

Seeing what is going on in front of the observer is the easiest method of researching social and religious behaviour but this is a crude and inadequate way of assessing faith and reasoning. Consciously and unconsciously observers pick and choose what they see and record because they are socialised to see certain specific things which leaves other activities outside any conscious realisation. In a religious ceremony in which some peopled become possessed, observers will concrete on this rather than on the passive majority.

As outsiders they are more likely to record what is strange to their own understandings; in a seminary their attention will be caught by the sounds of the talking in tongues of one individual during the recitation of the key Christian Lord's Prayer; the researcher will not pay as much attention to the hundred others who continue in silent prayer. Thus talking in tongues, glossolalia, is common enough globally so that a committed Christian might not pay much attention to such practices as it is mentioned in the *New Testament*. However Western social scientists would see it as unusual and give its occurrence particular attention. Observing cannot even begin to be described as a scientifically acceptable process and to assume its accuracy is a form of personal conceit.

It is true that one can often know how many people attend a religious ceremony as they may be counted at the door as for a football match or by immigration controls when foreign pilgrims enter Saudi Arabia for the Hajj. We can calculate how much these participants put into the local economy by their spending, because these accounts may be audited by outsiders, how many beds are available for pilgrims at Lourdes, the amount of transport used in and around Mecca during the pilgrimage season and the number of animals slaughtered there for the fulfilment of Islamic obligations and the number of bodies institutionally cremated in secular facilities at Banaras. These are all surface assessments which tell us almost nothing about why they are participating except in the primary senses that these involvements are probably in some part undertaken for religious reasons. In essence these calculations are no different to calculating the number of animals using a water-point or the numbers of people entering a market to buy fish. Animals satisfy their thirst but to parallel this with any assessments of satisfactions from religious participation would be a methodological distortion.

The most highly trained social science observer of religious ceremonies will only learn the 'where' and the 'when' but not much about the 'how' and almost nothing about the 'why' for the thousands if not the millions of individuals involved. We may want to believe or indeed assume that those attending a religious ceremony have the fulfilling of their religious needs as their primary objective. We just do not know from seeing individuals participating whether they truly meditating or just resting and what about the Muslims and Taoists in Delhi and Shanghai who were seen to be using their mobile phones while ostensibly praying in places dedicated to religious practice. How many going on the obligatory Hajj to Mecca are just ticking off a religious obligation in a list of religious communal rather than personal necessities.

Whether it is deliberately done for a certain time at a certain place or the result of the accidents of the observers just being there, observation must always be flawed because it deals with a slice of behaviour taken out of context. The attendance at Mass at St Thomas' Mount near to Madras of a passing tourist and going on an expensive collectively organised pilgrimage can only be understood if these behaviours are seen in the context of what went before and what happened afterwards for each of the individuals present. We need to know how people behave even if they are not fully aware of how a religious event has been slotted into their lives.

Observing a religious ceremony tends to be related to the timing of its start and finish as when the priest comes to the altar and when he leaves and this is to be expected as these timing are posted on the church's notice board. This timing approach is confined to the religions of the book and a clock for the timing of prayer is conspicuous in some mosques. This temporal factor is part of religious practice in the three religions of the book and has been created by a combination of literacy and organisation. For Hinduism and other Eastern religions have astrological and lunar timings but no effective collective agreed knowledge of what these might be for individual conformity.

In other religions it is hard to know when a ceremony starts and finishes as in most quasi-traditional ceremonies which starts when 'enough' people have turned up to make an implied quorum. A Hindu ceremony in a temple in southern India which lasts seven days will have had different levels of involvement for different categories of participants; it would be impossible that anyone will be in attendance from start to finish; a shift system operates for all those involved as those involved will have to eat, sleep and perform some personal functions.

Much religious activity and certainly spirituality is slotted into daily activities and churches, mosques, synagogues and temples may be empty or full quite irregularly. In Tallinn the Orthodox Cathedral was full on a weekday morning with an elderly priest holding an icon for participants to kiss and providing blessings for them, but there was not a service going on. A mosque can contain people resting in its shade seemingly asleep and services in small Coptic churches in Ethiopia have few people inside but large numbers in the surrounding courtyards. Such approaches show the social as much as the religious pattern of behaviour. These issues raise the question of what constitutes attendance at a religious ceremony; the Orthodox Jew rocking backwards and forwards in prayer throughout a flight from London to Zurich is certainly being religious as would be the same behaviour at the Wailing Wall in Jerusalem but what of those who attend Mass in a cathedral because of the beauty of the singing and those who sing in that choir because it is an opportunity to exercise a personal talent in a well accredited choir under an exceptionally competent director of music.

A single observer is always looking in one direction at a time and indeed his or her ability to observe is related to varying degrees of concentration and how long they are able to be observing, not only observing according to a schedule but doing so with the fresh acuity of the morning or at the end of a long and very hot afternoon session. Those observing a religious ceremony are usually facing the focus of attention so they are seeing the backs of other participants or the minority who are facing the other way and the situation prevents them from turning round. What the researcher can observe is often dictated not by what they want to see in a crowd but what they can see without becoming insensitive to local ideas of appropriate religious behaviour and their own need to be as inconspicuous as possible. Possibly only a single observer watching a single person carrying out a religious ritual undercover would provide harder data but the status of this biased observer would still be modifying the observed 'realities'.

Having a number of observers does not mean that they will be seeing the same things and coordinating their writings is difficult and time consuming as few if any see the same things in the same way. Their minds are always being diverted and of course their personalities may guide what they look at and see. The official orthodox focus of a ceremony may not be the points which participants find stimulating enough to record. There is always the factor of what the observer or indeed participants can see when the ceremony is shrouded in incense and poor lighting or so noisy as in the trumpet band accompanying the Easter morning Mass in the Cuernaverca cathedral that it is impossible to hear what is being said or sung by those officiating which is possibly evidence that these rituals are not important for intellectual understandings.

While there may be an orthodox focal point for the ceremony the researcher will also be interested in those who are ostensibly on the fringes of the ceremony, seated at the back, trying to keep their children quiet, hanging around the church door and providing off the scene backup playing the organ. Much behaviour is certainly connected with religion but would not involve behaviour which both secular and religious Westerners would think appropriately reverent. Such instances show the difficulties of recording religious participation which comes down to a problem of classification of what they think they are doing in relation to local rather than more general orthodoxy. We just cannot know to what extent they are conforming to what are public or private orthodoxies.

The researchers are always handicapped in their physical ability to observe and the fact that they do not receive the training in observation which would be given to doctors and detectives in their training. They may have been up the previous night seeing another aspect of the ceremony and indeed when a Hindu ceremony goes on and off for several days, so that exhaustion may cloud what they see and indeed what they are able to record. The priests in such lengthy ceremonies may work on their own shift system but the researchers cannot afford to be away resting when they may not know if some critical activity might take place. In Pangani, Tanzania attending the recitation of the whole Koran by four simultaneous readers working from a single lamp in an overheated room over sleeping children who were to be circumcised the next morning, does not make for observational accuracy then or for the next morning's ceremony. Human observations are idiosyncratic for social, physiological and psychological reasons. The 'I was there and, therefore, I know' statement has to be treated with great caution as it entails both personal and professional conceit and a personal memory competence. Memory is a transient quality under constant ongoing modification.

Observers are faced with the difficulty of reaching conclusions about what numbers of people do for most of the time at religious ceremonies for which there is a known liturgy. The ceremonies of the Coptic Church in Ethiopia are long and what the priests are doing is hidden from view behind a curtain. Those outside the curtain can only hear mumbling and even if they could hear anything distinctly it would not necessarily lead to any greater understanding since the liturgy is in a specialised Amharic religious linguistic code. So it is not altogether surprising that numbers of those attending are asleep and in some cases lying down to do so; while these may be extreme cases it is certainly not infrequent. We have to decide what part such forms of observed attendance have in the religious understandings both individual and collectively of both participants and theologians.

Indeed we have to assess whether theological and intellectual understandings have much part in the thinking of those attending religious ceremonies when it is carried out in specialised linguistic codes even in the national language under conditions which pay little attention to even the possibility of participants hearing and understanding. At the pilgrimage shrine of Katagarama in southern Sri Lanka some hundreds of women attending a Buddhist day of spiritual devotion addressed by a prominent monk using a loudspeaker, at least a third were lying down asleep. The Hindu couple being married in Mombasa, Kenya were told what to do by the officiating Brahmin and it was unlikely that they understood or need to understand the long Sanskrit prayers which were said over them to validate in their own minds and that of onlookers that they were validly married within Hinduism.

This situation of incomprehension was even more likely to occur in Chinese Taoist and Japanese Shinto ceremonies in which not only is the language specialised but the ideograms in which it is written require specialised learning so that even highly educated men and women cannot know what is written and would need to have these texts translated for them. A functionally closed world in its theology but one that is always open to complications and simplification not so much of interpretation but of symbolic utilisation. They believe and have benefit from their attendance it would seem unlikely that it is related more to status than religious understanding.

In many ceremonies we have large numbers of people seen to be doing the same thing at shrines which are the centres of pilgrimage. There is little evidence that they are carrying out their devotions in such machine like automated ways but that is the tenure of social scientists' interpretations evaluated from the point of view of different cultural backgrounds but also separated from these 'others' by social distance. Any recorded observations are inevitably taken out of these contexts and are abbreviations from the basic complicated individualism of all religious practices and spiritual understandings which may have secular origins.

Is the use of machinery any more reliable? Cameras and recording machines only record what they are pointed at and are valuable and reliable records of only that. School children being photographed in the mithrab of the Ali Mohammad mosque in Cairo and for relatives and attendants at a wedding in the Azores being photographed round the altar after the priest has left. This tell us about the limited and transient sacredness of places in which religious ceremonies take place and how people group themselves on such occasions. These are semi-religious slices out of the surrounding social environment but the use of cine-cameras complicates such issue.

Much the same would apply to the use of security cameras which are common enough in public places such as school play grounds and public squares outside cathedrals and mosques where religious activities are occurring. However, their use for research has the additional difficulties of how such a mass of continuously recorded data can be processed. Hundreds of people are doing thousands of different things in different personal contexts during a religious procession. The result of the use of these machines which are so attractive to the researchers and are often part of their basic field equipment is that they are likely to be overwhelmed with data. They have so much tape and video data that it would require large numbers of assistants to view and listen to what is available and to look for specific types of activity. Going back to listen or view this historical data would require the allocation of time competing with more immediate research needs.

It would also require new methodological techniques to cope with mass data and mechanically varied viewpoints. Even then with such a mass of recorded observations these researchers are no further forward as to why people are there in the first place and what they are personally experience. We are still left with the crudities of assessing mass participation which would be put under the one category of both devotion and indifference.

The reality of course is that social scientists use machines to record ceremonies and interviews but these masses of data usually sit in archives waiting for analysis which rarely if ever happens. These social scientists carry out their interpretation from notes which they may have made or created from their immediate memories. These recorders of data have moved on to other professional and personal preoccupations and cannot afford the time to go back in their research. A researcher may record an eight hour interview but it is rare for anyone to go back and listen to that eight hours again.

The conclusion may be that observations are doubtfully valuable as it creates the impression of scientific accuracy through the reality of personal conceit. The greatest handicap may be that the observers are convinced that what they have recorded as their personal observations are correct. This is more so when the observers have had inadequate experience of watching what may be strange or predominantly monotonous ceremonies which go on for hours in languages which not only the observer but none of those attending understand. Neither social scientists nor theologians receive any training in observation which should be part of their professional training so that they observe noisy and silent behaviour with the same attention.

It seems unlikely that observation can rarely be more than a very limited activity which gives confidence to the researchers that having seen, they are beginning to understand They certainly have had influential experiences as part of the culture shock of their field work. It is not a scientifically valid method in the context of religious ceremonies for understanding why people need and use particular religious ceremonies. Their value may be confined to the needs of administrators of religious institutions and their ceremonies who have to plan pragmatically for their efficient running. Days of prayer organised by the Cenacle Sisters require the supply of food and the disposal of waste as well as the provision of first aid and lavatories proportionate to the numbers coming. It also showed that those coming to these meetings had little contact with the devoted and committed women who spent most of the day in activities which could have been done just as well by a catering firm.

These dedicated women had difficulty in accepting that these issues were not just as essentially religious as their interpersonal contacts. All religious institutions just as much as secular ones have budgets and to keep within their provisions if they want to avoid inefficiency and chaos. There is also the basic importance in observation to have the personal physical ability see and hear what is going on which can be related to the age of the observers and their height.

Participant Observation

All social science field work starts with some form of participant observation as they enter the community in which they are going to work. Whatever their backgrounds this is going to be a new experience which is going to have a primary influence on their thinking. Whenever they enter situations in which they are not familiar, there will be culture shock proportional to the social differences. Any researcher who has returned to where they have previously conducted research living abroad, is going to be immediately struck by the differences which have occurred since they were last there between what they anticipated and what now confronts them particularly as they will have been alerted to particular aspects of religious behaviour which they had observed previously.

It is one thing to accept the need for the fullest possible participation in the researched community or institution, but it is another thing to actually do so. Joshi when he wanted to work with Hindu farmers found the villagers amused at his lack of physical stamina (Joshi, 1979). Many religious ceremonies impose strain on both participants and observers. Much the same would occur in joining an Amish or Hutterite community as well as a monastic community dedicated to round the clock prayer and work on a previously unexperienced use of time, space and diet.

It is clear that for every degree of involvement which opens up a new channel for information gathering, the researcher takes up a specific role which on the one hand provides them with some new and previously unknown areas of understanding but at the same time imposes restrictions. The Tanzanian Sukuma have so-called dance societies which have ancestor spirit connections but by attempting to belong to the Bugisu one, the researcher is excluding himself from the Bugaru one and of course the researcher would be unlikely to take on the appropriate facial markings. To study the Kenyan Legio Maria as a Roman Catholic deviation or as a genuine new Christian institutional evolvement would make it difficult to have any comparable experiences in other Christian groups in the same area. Everyone would know soon enough the primary commitment of the researcher.

An unmarried German researcher in India lived with a Hindu family in which all the women observed *purdah*, a form of institutional segregation. This made it impossible for her to move around freely until she made friends with a child welfare government official who acted both as her language teacher and chaperon (Bellwinkel, 1979) which would have still restricted the social situations in which she could participate. However hard she may have tried to avoid disturbing her hosts Hinduism is a pervasive religion so she would have been upsetting their religious understandings of purity and impurity all the time in their sexually segregated eating and socialising. However well-intentioned she may have been, she was in fact studying not only a specific Hindu household but a deviant one as well. She did not face the basic issue of what may have been in the householder's mind in inviting such persistent pollution so there must have been a hidden agenda.

In a strange way most social science researchers want to be socially invisible for professional reasons and yet be able to collect information as a person but whatever they do and whether they are nationals or non-nationals they are always someone to whom a role has been applied. In some cases they have no choice in what they are by age, sex and ethnicity but in other matters they can choose their roles by selecting what they want to be accepted as and how they can go about doing it since the role of researcher would almost always be unknown. The role of the researcher is not really accepted or appreciated and it is usually necessary to use some subterfuge such as the study of catechetical methodology or translation issues to cover the general objective of evaluation. A researcher can be accepted into a community as a teacher, nurse or seller of patent medicines The word for research in the linguistic code may be the same as that used for police enquiries.

There are serious methodological issues in using the data from the point of view of some form of participant observation. It is always the observations of one person at one place and at one time and however long that participation may be in that community, it is participation in parts of that community observed sequentially unless such selective participation is dialectically pointed at the realities of these people in their personal situations.

So the basic methodological problem in participant observation is that it is restrictive and far from unbiased situationally. No researcher can observe what she cannot see. This leaves reliability to those who live in one part of the community as a round the clock resident and perhaps not living in a separate house or tent. Observations received secondhand from informants are even more suspect as they have already been filtered through their personal conscious or unconscious biases which from the point of view of reliability is more likely to have the characteristics of formalised role related lying (Salamone, 1977). Whatever form of participation occurs the researcher takes on a role even the minimalist one of just being one of a crowd among thousands, but probably influencing the people around him or her, and it is always a restricted role controlled viewpoint. It may lead to some intuitive rather than pragmatic conclusions as to the nature of working misunderstandings in particular contexts that can be validated.

It has to be accepted that any form of participant observation is ego-centred and it cannot be otherwise and thus carries with it all the problems of such social centralisation. As in any cultural setting one sees what one is culturally trained to see and what one is physiologically capable of seeing. A literate Swahili Muslim hospital assistant in Mombasa, Kenya on being asked to write down the genealogies of all the people known to him took months of persuasion before he started to record the matrilineal rather than only the patrilineal connections as he was committed by his Islamic understandings to see just the one system of social and biological connection. The researcher whether participating as man or woman would see behaviour from that one dominant perspective. A woman researching the role of women in any religion is collecting information from women informants and from men who in talking to a woman without any pretence of providing abstract information. A male researcher would get very little data from women informants and possibly would have contact with only post-menopausal ones who have less restrictive public roles.

It may be more methodologically sound to be a sole observer with a known role in a highly structured environment like a hospital ward or a school class-room or one in which there is no restricting structure such as a railway station, market or airport in which the control is one of the area through which there is a behavioural flow (Baker, 1998; chap 7) in which the observer is undifferentiated among the many who are present. Where they can pick up overt religious signs and behaviour.

Hassidic Jewish men dancing their happiness on returning from Jerusalem in a New York airport passenger terminal. A trainee for the priesthood was asked to record over a period of months any unchristian behaviour that he could see in the London rush hour public transport, but he recorded none as that was his charitable viewpoint; he saw the moral best in all that he saw. A social scientist assessing religious behaviour in any setting would not have such a morally restrictive viewpoint. An Asian researcher assessing German religious behaviour just as an American researching Indian Christianity would not know much of what these people would acquire from their natal socialisation and thus would have to spend much time in learning what these people would class as the obvious or which any child would know.

The range of acceptability of a researcher being in a religious community and more particularly in a family in which they seek to become a full-time round the clock member is likely to change their hosts in overall ways as well as in relationship to particular day to day issues; one may be differently accepted in different seasons by different people since the family members are not one but to have different roles. Conclusions can only be specific to that particular group at that time. This odd person who wants to live with them for reasons which they will treat with some scepticism, will go through a scale of partial acceptance from being seen as a stranger, guest, potentially trainable childlike adult, simpleton unable to do the simplest of tasks known to their children at an early age to being a straightforward nuisance, an ever-present nuisance and a handicap on their usual way of carrying on who has to be endured (Briggs, 1970) for financial and status reasons; the researcher as a paying lodger is an asset but may bring disadvantages if the surrounding community does not like being 'spied' on by a stranger. This requires considerable tolerance to accept a stranger intruding in this way and by implication trying to change their way of doing things.

If the researcher expects to become one of the communities which they are researching then immediately their self-sustained and understood status of an educated and detached intellectual disappears. All types of questions develop if this researcher is trying to assess the influence of Christianity in their lives obvious enough possibly in an Amish community or a Hindu *ashram* but much more difficult to determine in mixed communities in which Catholicism and Hinduism are not quite so clearly differentiated in everyday life. They become just what they are in their host's terms by age, sex and property. They may be given classificatory kinship roles which must inevitably be daughter or son and this of course is immediately qualified by the material benefits which they should provided for their classificatory fathers and mothers. It is not a situation in which researchers can sit on personal property and say that it is mine and mine alone; their limited stocks of tobacco, personally preferred food, medicines and petrol in their transport will soon be exhausted. Assessing the influence of Christian principles on behaviour becomes personal when there are requests to help the sick and the researchers have their own transport and a suspected supply of personal medicines.

In such situations the researchers are not renting social space in which they can expect to be left largely alone to carry on with their mysterious research activities easier in a town than a village. They cannot dictate the conditions of their residence in this way unless there is already there a well understood role of lodger who then is clearly not classificatory kin. Living in a family or religious community means sharing their work since they are sharing the cooking fire and their religious ceremonials.

In all research there is the basic factor of time. The researcher may just have to wait for something to happen and which may mean that they miss something important happening elsewhere. The higher the standard of living in the community being researched the easier it is for the researcher to maintain an appearance of detachment. They may not have either the ability or the degree of commitment or stamina to sustain a strange way of living for long periods. It is no doubt upsetting to be treated as a daughter or son and then to find that one cannot live up to the social and religious obligations that go with such roles; being kin or a novice does not allow time for writing up notes when there is work to do in which the family or community expects participation as a matter of course.

The bilateral adjustments which would have to occur are probably virtually impossible to solve except at a peripheral level; the social science researcher cannot be that and a full-time participator at the same time if either role is to be performed satisfactorily. If they become truly absorbed into these cultures as classificatory daughters or sons then they will be addressed in the peremptory tones appropriate to their roles. They will not have been addressed in this way since they were in primary school and they will have long grown out of any form of kin related subordination in their own professional careers and personal lives. Overall for a variety of personal and social reasons it is perhaps prudent not to attempt full time participant observation.

Participation and Self-absorption

Researchers who observe and participate whatever their pretensions to detachment cannot be doing so. Even when they are participating in a mass religious ceremony and even if they have attended similar ones several times before, this will be an experience reacted to in an individual way, a very personal experience. Let us look at some religious experiences in which a researcher can be exposed in which his or her reactions will be entirely personal and far from scientifically detached.

Attending a Mass in the Burmese highlands with the Latin words of the priest in his vestments lit by a single candle, competing with the wind whistling through the bamboo walls. The shrouded figures of the Kachin worshippers alerted to this infrequent celebration of the Mass by the priest blowing a bugle the previous afternoon as he climbed up from the valley below to this hilltop village. In Guyana travelling with a priest to give the Blessed Sacrament to twelve Christians crippled by age or disease, knowing that the Body of Christ was with them in the car.

Whatever the metaphysical thinking of the researcher these are situations that demonstrate the importance of such rituals and the modification of the behaviour of both the researcher and the priest from this Presence. Such a researcher must see the metaphysical in a new perspective from such prolonged experiences.

The researcher attending Easter High Mass in the austere cathedral at Cuernavaca in Mexico with the altar covered by a copper reredos with a constantly moving standing congregation accompanied by a trumpet dominated orchestra. Whatever the Mexicans there may or may not have felt, it was a moving experience and the researcher's wife whispered that they had to take Communion.

During the Holy Month of *Ramadan* in which there is no eating and drinking during daylight walking with a Muslim civil servant in Tanzania during the hottest part of the day to see how the annual planting was getting on whom regularly spat rather than swallowing his own spittle. A reaction to this ascetic devotion will have been as emotional as a social scientist's first experience of spirit possession, divination 'talking in tongues' and the use of preventative magic rituals.

Self Reported Religious Activities

No individual, however well trained, conscientious or self-conscious is able to report on their own behaviour in ways which are not biased as we have seen in the above examples and indeed we can question the use of bias in such self-absorbing situations from the simple fact that their minds do not function mechanically. They are partly creatures of habit, mood and are swayed by constantly changing personal experiences and indeed by their own philosophical and religious commitments which are as much part of the thinking of a Bengali farmer as that of a Mumbai industrialist.

Social scientists are reluctant to accept that there are few if any social reasons for people to tell the truth to strangers or indeed to record in writing their social and religious thinking and activities. Informants are worried about the subsequent uses of what has been written or recorded as this recorded data is quite out of the control of either the writers or the collators. Those filling in a form about their religious activities are either acting on trust or obeying an instruction from a superior to which they may have only half-heartedly agreed. They may be far more optimistic in accepting the truth of such information than may be other professionals.

Why indeed should individuals give away personal and private information about themselves unless it is already common knowledge or they get some social return within their understanding of normal reciprocities. Most people have been brought up to be cautious about giving any information away to anyone certainly not an outsider unless they are going to profit immediately in some way from the disclosure. It is not only charitable but optimistic to think that what people say or write about their religious thinking and behaviour is related to some pragmatic quality of sharable truth.

People are progressively inaccurate about what they have witnessed quite recently and memory is widely inaccurate unless it is involved in something which has ancillary support. To remember some behaviour which has not been isolated in thought is always going to be largely provided out of obedience or some other social inducement.

Most people in most cultures would reluctantly admit that they adjust their opinions to their current needs and that would include the people they are talking to in their social and religious lives, about which in itself is likely to be both an unusual event for most people. They might give information to a priest but to be asked to explain and often enumerate a religious practice is rare indeed. This would apply more particularly to questions asked by researchers and other outsiders from whom they can probably expect no return. The Ayatollah Khomeini, the supreme Shia leader of Iran when the Shah's rule was overthrown, is reported to have said that what he may have stated last week would not necessarily be the same as what he might say the following week. But what he did say then would have been recorded and then have become part of a religious whole to which other values would be subtended. What might be considered to be the truth is very flexible in how it relates to social circumstances. Memory is always unreliable. An informant may remember that a critical event has occurred but the details of it will usually be inaccurate.

The frequency of religious participations are usually exaggerated in order to make the writers look better in their own eyes and to show conformity to the norms of the religion to which they belong. We are not certain as to what constitutes participation in their own understandings since it may involve simply standing outside the church door which is not participation according to most theological understandings but why then are they there at all. On the other hand it has to be considered religious when some are observably possessed by what they think to be overwhelming religious emotion regardless of psychological explanations may appear to deprive an individual of the wholeness of their experience.

The answers to questions posed in person is a social inter-relationship in which the person questioned is reacting to the questioner as well as the questions asked, indeed the questioner in social terms may be more important than the questions that had been asked. In a research situation this is usually between people coming from two totally different social worlds. They are intellectually different, of different ages and almost certainly look and smell different as meat eaters do in the sensitivities of vegetarians. There can be little assumption of trust which would come from some shared aspects of identity but a shared religion is certainly an important link. However much a nominally Hindu researcher may wish to disguise his caste status, but gossip will soon make his status known and his lack of apparent conformity will soon be a subject of unfavourable comment or he may be required to act as a Brahmin.

Most people having working vocabularies which do not contain many words unless there is a professional necessity to have a large one as in the knowledge of local plants and their medicinal uses if they use them in their work. A Tanzanian Sukuma or south Indian Tamil might well know five hundred plants while having a very limited vocabulary of words connected with religion largely used by people in communities outside their own because they have no need of a large religious vocabulary. For most natal speakers of English it is said that they have a basic vocabulary of about five hundred words. This means that for most people most of the time, they do not have the linguistic equipment to express themselves in phrases that carry what may be complicated ideas and personal and emotional meanings. It is certainly not evidence that these are any less complex just because their bearers cannot express them. Literacy in this respect is invariably elitist.

This inability in most societies for all men and women to express complicated social and religious feelings and understandings and even more their inability to write about such matters leads to variable understandings and misunderstandings which are usually not sorted out prior to interviews or by the administration of questionnaires. The finding out of religiously allied meanings is a project in itself and trying to do this might delay the usefulness of other findings. We have to conclude that the ability to write about personal feelings is likely to be possible for very few literates with specialised motivations and abilities.

In fact attempts to reach agreement with informants on the key words such as religion or spirituality when their cultures may not even have words for these concepts, will almost always lead to a multitude of intellectual and social difficulties even basic misunderstandings. The five million Sukuma use the Arabic word *dini* for religion probably referring to Christianity and Islam rather than for their own traditional beliefs about ancestors and unrelated spirits for which they have no collective word. These linguistic differences may make it nearly impossible to assume that those writing and talking about their religious practices and spiritual beliefs have even remotely similar meanings to those carried by the researcher's own socialisation, professional aims and understandings. A question to a Japanese as to whether he believed in God, got the reply asking what God had the researcher in mind. This was a sensible answer when there are reputed to be over a million named transcendental powers in the Japanese cultural and religious pantheon of gods and goddesses. Much the same reply might be expected from a Chinese when a recently purchased religious poster in Shanghai depicted no less than twenty gods and goddesses. We can never be sure that a respondent is answering any question in the terms which the questioner wants.

So the self-reporting of religious experiences involving spiritual beliefs are usually suspect because of the absence of details about the circumstances and motivations in which such statements have been made and their inevitable circumstantial impermanence. This does not mean that social scientists can assume that they do not express emotions and ideas which these individuals and their compatriots feel and accept as genuine. Whether they have the linguistic equipment and intellectual or emotional capacity to make such statements as perhaps no more than one in a million have such abilities whether they are praying or painting. There is always the more basic problem as to whether both parties are in fact talking or writing about the same thing as this is totally different to talking about the concrete realities of cows, crops and children. There is always the possibility that in some metaphysical circumstances, the social scientist has made the wrong interpretation and the street cleaner the correct one.

There are also striking differences in the amount of talking which will be given in reply to a question such as 'what do you do' asked of Roman Catholic priests in Zambia and Zimbabwe. This resulted in differences between fifteen minutes from one priest who thought such a question was an intrusion on his privacy and professional status to fourteen hours from another who saw the answers which he gave would give his views a wider publicity. We can reach different conclusions from the answers given by these two priests as individuals but what their relevance might be to any wider understandings about the works of the Roman Catholic Church there would be highly speculative.

A few people will like the opportunity to discuss religious understandings with someone whom they consider to be a knowledgeable outsider of equal intellectual status to themselves. This was the case with Victor Turner and the Ndembu diviner Muchona the Hornet who was isolated from his local position in these discussions and so could talk freely to this interested and interesting outsider. Some in a religious institution will also appreciate the opportunity to talk about their hopes and difficulties with an outsider when the social scientist who is professionally unlikely to disclose the individual source of his or her ideas.

There is also the problem that occurs when the information acquired is so clearly contradictory. The Japanese according to opinion polls appear to be the most secular people in the world with 65 per cent claiming to be without religious beliefs. When asked about observance 75 per cent pray to Shinto gods at the New Year although only 21 per cent affirm that they believe in their existence (Reader, 1991:5). In such situations the answers cannot be tied to anything more than circumstantial and variable 'truth'.

There are alternative methodologies which might avoid the potential unreliability of mass questioning and overall replies from informants about whom virtually nothing is known and who have no felt need to cooperate with the enquirer. By reducing the number of informants and the specific issues into which enquiries are being made, it is possible to know more about the backgrounds of informants but this is also a dialectical situation. A study in the Netherlands used fifteen informants with different religious understandings and associations with whom there were in-depth interviews (Wijsen, 2009). This was an attempt to counter intolerance by bringing people together to pray in an environment which had no specific religious associations. This approach using words and phrases allowed the researcher to find out the backgrounds of the informants in some detail and to put their remarks into specific correlations related to their personal, social and institutional orthodoxies. The use of this expensive methodology in terms of time and money reduced the unreliability of information by relating it both to the personal backgrounds of informants and their relationship to a specific project.

Surveys

Social science surveys have a long history in secular demographics and are accepted as useful for both secular and religious administrators. They provide numerical answers to whatever questions have been asked and thus provide seemingly satisfying logic to numbers of questions.

Lining people to ask them to answer identical questions is not acceptable normal behaviour in any society. It is a bureaucratic device to assist bureaucracy. Although it provides numerical answers, their accuracy is usually questionable. Censuses are a feature of every nation's life as a necessity for planning but many have very real personal reasons for evading such counts and many people culturally and behaviourally have no fixed addresses. At best a survey for religious reasons is a simplification of complex behaviour because the bigger the institution using them the less such counts can provide for individual differences.

Firstly religious ideas and practices are personal and only a part of these can be expressed in overt behaviour whether in movements, speech and much less in writing however intellectually competent an individual may be.

Although a survey can be aimed at whole populations such as the English Religious Practice Survey of 1856, those related to the needs of religious institutions are aimed at the secular dimensions of religious practice; who, what and where questions but why ones are virtually a waste of time. Mass attendance in relation to working hours in an industrial or farming parish and the numbers of children for whom a parochial school might have to provide for.

It is only rarely that a majority of any targeted population can be surveyed as interviews with nearly all the priests in Guyana and Zimbabwe or the nuns in a British order. Almost always the population has to be sampled to make any survey manageable. Random sampling assumes that individuals are constituted in social situations with fixed characteristics rather than individually varied and there can be no such assumption that any sampling will produce an average (Stinchcombe, 1980). Sampling is putting the idea of scientific accuracy into situations which can never have any such quality.

Surveys of Roman Catholic practice after the policy changes initiated by the Vatican Two Council showed in Western Europe and North America a severe decline in the number of priests there and in missionaries as well as a decline in attendance at regular ceremonies. It was not necessary to use survey methods to demonstrate these effects.

Surveys produce from their numerical answers to restrictive questions a sense of homogeneity and stability whereas in fact every population is in constant demographic and social movement never mind induced changes in behaviour from environmental factors outside their control. In most populations ten per cent or more move every year. The Roman Catholics built a substantial church in the Matumbi hills in Tanzania and yet within a few years the population of subsistence farmers had almost all moved away. A priest in Guyana undertook a village survey but by the time he had finished at the end of the village a substantial number of those he had counted initially had moved away. One of the lessons from any type of demographic survey of religious commitment is that there are movers and stayers and each block has different types of social and religious needs and involvements.

Scientific accuracy depends on the ability to replicate results in subsequent tests. There is no possibility of any such replication of human behaviour when almost every factor has to be adjusted. They are in reality different people who have been selected for that same test or the original ones who have changed since the original test.

There is of course the satisfaction of having completed a survey and to see the written results filed in a box but there are doubts whether surveys can be used for long-term planning in relation to human individuality and their personal spirituality. The increase in the number of pilgrims can be attributed to economic factors but what the religious consumers need and obtain at such places can have no simple assessments.

Secondly, social science researchers have tried in numerous ways to make surveys more accurate by trying to control the social contexts in which they are answered, but they have not been successful in developing any watertight scientific methodology (Tanner, 1992). The order and form of the questions will significantly affect the answers as not only may the participants not be sharing a language natally learnt but there will be differences in linguistic codes within which they understand key words (Schuman and Presser, 1981). How in practice can anyone distinguish accurately frequency questions as to whether they go to Mass frequently or often.

The standardisation of questions and the exact way in which they are presented cannot eliminate the variatious environments in which respondents reply. The words may be standardised but there is no way that the body language of the questioner can be neutralised (Forsyth and Lessler, 1991).

The Free-form Interview

Whether social scientists are surveying samples of large populations or seeking to get more detailed information from smaller numbers of informants, the basic situation is a face to face interview. This can vary between a relatively short-term confrontation to what from its length is clearly a personal inter-relationship.

Interviews have always fallen short of their positive goals (Burawoy, 1998) because they are primarily social relationships in which social scientists are trying to make scientific capital for which it cannot be designed. There are well-documented instantaneous effects on these relationships of age, race, gender and personal appearance. An interview with a senior Zambian priest failed to develop at all as he had assumed that the interviewer was already aware of the existing tensions over his pastoral ideas and those of the dominating missionary priesthood. These immediate almost predetermined reactions will have influences on the nature of almost all replies but the status format of the interview will also be important as to whether they are sitting side by side or facing each other in a confrontation over a table.

Then there are the meanings of the words used since religious discourse are tied to complex metaphysical understandings. A social scientist with a Hindu background whether he or she is practising that faith or not would think about and use the word 'spirit' in entirely different ways to a nominally Protestant Belgian or a practising Roman Catholic Brazilian. How these people will view and more or less understand such a word would be dictated by their cultural upbringing (Cicourel, 1982).

Then there are the environmental effects felt by both participants in an interview as to what is said because of the surrounding social, economic, political and religious situation. How can a Jesuit working in Zimbabwe speak outside the context of the surrounding violent and oppressive regime. Chinese Christians will similarly frame their replies rather more than their thoughts in terms of the one-party agnostic political system in which they live. Questions discussed half a century ago in the aftermath of colonialism will receive different contemporary answers in autocratic situations dominated by widespread corruption.

So we can conclude that any interview which is formalised in the hope of scientific accuracy is in fact too inaccurate to provide detailed verifiable information about social and religious ideas and behaviour which assessors may want to find.

The alternative is to accept the reality of the surrounding possible inferences and to let the interviewee tell her or his own story without any more interruptions beyond requesting more details. We have already described the differences in responses by priest to the one question 'what do you do'. Such a question was asked from nearly all priests in Tanzanian, Zambian, Zimbabwean and Guyanese dioceses produced quantities of varied data which could not be numerically expressed and some of which would not have been thought of by the interviewer within the paradigm of orthodoxy.

It was easy to slot such informants into the categories of surrounding influences but that did not alter the stimulating existence of the variations disclosed. In effect these interviews were the excavation of local knowledge in the terms dictated by these informants (Geertz, 1983), networks of situated knowledge (Harraway, 1991; Chap 9).

Inferred Religious Behaviour

Social scientists have probably reached the conclusion that in working to assess religious and social ideas and behaviour, trying to organise the gathering of data there can only be the illusion of conformity to the requirements of hard science. This is not a demonstration of the irredeemable shortcomings of the social sciences to provide exact conclusions to exact questions. It is a recognition that the way forward to any understanding of religious and social ideas and practices in their enormous variations can only be by inference.

Even the most experienced social scientist in reaching conclusions from their field work are likely to go further than might be justified from what they have learnt. As researchers they are people who have absorbed the attitudes and career needs of their professional colleagues and the atmosphere of scientific secularism of universities which were founded in the beliefs and practices of the European Enlightenment. The intellectual environment in which social scientists are trained whether in the East or West or in Africa is in a methodological tradition of secular questioning. It is an almost automatic professional response to the fact of religiously motivated behaviour that there are ample social and psychological explanations and that the supernatural is not a necessary explanatory factor.

In taking up a request from a religious institution to make an assessment of their work, there cannot be the professional standard motivation of social science in denying the reality of their perspective. They have to start with an acceptance of the metaphysical reality which is their basic motivation. For their work this is a reality and as we have noted earlier that a held belief has real consequences.

While they may not intend to depress the religious practices and spiritual understandings of the people and organisations they study, this is certainly their effect on religious thinkers, administrators and theologians to whom their conclusions are presented. They know from their own reading and experience that social scientists are professionally sceptical of their devotion. They too will have reacted to the production of thinkers from Darwin to Dawkins *via* Freud who have provided hostile conclusions. They perhaps do not realise that the social science agnosticism can be seen as equally scientifically defective. Such thinkers can certainly be accepted as explaining away much religious behaviour and its possibly consequent conclusions but these are partial rather than terminally limiting, explanations, always have a uniquely environmental restrictions.

The social sciences are not seen as supportive unless one of their own carries out such enquiries starting from this basis of religious commitment which explains 'in' religious behaviour rather than 'outing' it into secular conclusions. An example of this would be the Western nun who successfully investigated the ways in which Zairean nuns might develop their culturally based vocations without breaking the vision of their European founder (Burke, J.F., 1992), changing their names from 'sister' to 'mother' and having a local dress.

The views are often combined with an unconscious feeling of superiority and possibly some lack of intellectual humility in their analyses which may come from their academic and professional detachment and from any direct responsibility for their conclusions and the ways in which they are reached. The situation has been summarised by Moberg 'The immediate practical problem related to this subject is to convince religiously unbelieving sociologists (and others) that they should leave the door open to the possibility that man (i.e., every human being) has a spiritual dimension of ultimate commitment and concern even in modern secularistic societies... the situation pertinent to science and man's spiritual nature is not a battle between 'pure science' and 'religious bias'. Rather it is in every instance a case of science plus biases *versus* religion plus different biases' (Moberg, 1967). A social scientist assessing religious behaviour cannot stand when others are kneeling and in kneeling absorbs some of the emotional idealism of those kneeling around them.

It is a big methodological leap from observing religious behaviour to making statements about the reasons for such behaviour in one social setting much less to extend such conclusions to more than the one community in which they have been working over immense cultural and social distance barriers. The decisions are made in bureaucratic terms mirroring that of the surrounding secular society.

Researchers in the social sciences find it difficult to admit that they have been working from inferences rather than hard data and from an absence of definitions about the matters on which they have been working.

For others who produce results from well recorded and more easily available data, there are always these limits to such speculations. The Vietnamese and other Asian cultures have the general concept of 'hungry ghosts', the spirits of people who have not been buried with the appropriate ceremonies is not enough to explain action and reaction within one conceptual circle. When the social scientist goes beyond this primary explanation which is sufficient for those reacting to such beliefs, is to provide explanations which those involved do not consider relevant and certainly not understood by them, raises issues related to intellectual and assumed cultural superiority. Philosophical and theological issues raised by people who are both non-literate and look primitive raise intercultural difficulties of understanding.

Intellectual perspectives not only have different cultural bases but even within this as we have seen in Western thought (Kuhn, 1962) it is not only ideology that changes but hard science as well so that 'hard' conclusions of a century ago have now only relevance in the history of science. It seems more rational to accept that there can be no categorical superiority or inferiority in thought and that for all 'practical' purposes Vietnamese hungry ghosts and Sukuma aggrieved ancestors exist. The fact that pragmatically they cannot exist is perhaps irrelevant.

These researchers take a leap from information that has been quantified for institutional reasons. Quantification is useful for designing space for those who wish to worship but has very little validity in explaining why they wish to worship there in the first place. There is also the factor that the results may have had little to do with the research objectives because that was the way in which it was sorted and recorded. It would be unwise to infer from this the nature and extent of beliefs of individuals and whole communities. They must surely be tentative at best in showing the range of known possibilities leaving aside the inevitability of a further number of unknown ones, for which there is some preliminary evidence. Much of these results are tautological in which the proof provided by the data are used as its own proof.

Who is to know among the millions going on pilgrimages who are no more than religious tourists as the primary reason but that does not cancel other secondary and tertiary motivations and those that are there for more predominantly religious reasons. We know in Japan that a rising proportion of the elderly and of Chinese in Taiwan go on pilgrimage tours which in the former cases fill up the gaps created by loneliness and the latter are combined with shopping. Then in mainland China millions go to temples on their annual feast-days which involves going to the opera being performed within the temple compound, eating new food and listening to the music with perhaps a ten minute visit to the statue of the God(s) in the temple largely taken up by standing in the line to get in. The feasting held at a Cretan chapels in honour of its titular saint perhaps unused for the rest of the year, Myanmar pagoda festivals with gambling and the annual parish fetes in England, are thought by their participants to have a religious focus even though what goes on is almost entirely secular. The secular minded would see this as no more than secular entertainment and those of a religious pattern of thought would see the same activity as religiously motivated. It is necessary to be modest even charitable in conclusions when so much is outside the ability of anyone to evaluate with any degree of accuracy. There surely are examples of the way that religious beliefs lurk in the psyche of most if not all human beings to be available for crises as much as for special occasions.

Data Based on the Requirements of Scientific Methodology

Since the social sciences from their title, deal with what can be pragmatically assessed from public behaviour, private spirituality rather more than public religion is both based on metaphysical assumptions with which they can never agree since they have no physical reality. Agreement is not a necessity in taking up assessments of religious behaviour. They are employing their professional expertise to help their employers in their needs. It is no part of the contract to go further than this.

So the social sciences are left with 'relic' data which varies from what is clearly a religious fact that a mosque is a religious building and a wooden shrine under a tree has nothing to do directly with forestry. The inanimate connection is clear and that is as far as it can go without metaphysical speculations which may or may not be related to do with individual perceptions. There are no Christian objections to using a cathedral for a concert or having a tea and souvenir shops inside the nave in the Church of England cathedral in Liverpool but no one has suggested that mosques and temples should have such usages. So we are left with an enormous range of activities which have religious components and here the social sciences enter the disputable field of correlations in which a religious connection has to be admitted but cannot be proved. Secular proof is not necessary.

There are parallels here to a clinical examination of a patient supported by laboratory data which is the end of an abbreviated story coming from its own design. We have already shown that the resulting facts no matter how internally accurate they are, may give explanations that are no more than accidental coincidences as to the cause of death or the incidence of certain behaviours. Medicine claims to prove that a disease comes from certain practices after very careful epidemiological enquiries which exclude as much as include other causal factors.

In New Guinea there was an incurable degenerative disease named *kuru* after the valley in which it occurred which affected mainly women and the researchers concluded that it must be caused by a gene carried only by women (Glasse, 1967). Subsequent social science research showed that often women ate uncooked parts of their dead relatives for the religious reasoning that it would retain their spirits within the lineage and that this was responsible for the disease. In such a serious matter involving many deaths it might have been guessed that there would be religious correlations. This disgusting and revolting custom according to Western cultural standards was not given any serious attentions as a religious issue. It is possible that even missionaries may not have been aware of this secret practice.

Pilgrimages spread disease and religious emotions just as going to pop concerts and football matches just as shaking hands in a Christian service demonstrate charity.

The Russian Skopsi men who castrated themselves were clearly performing a religious act to prevent sin and just as clearly the mass suicides at Jonestown were not. The lessons which can be learned from these extreme examples are complex of which the principle one must be that the results of research may reflect the attitude of mind with which the matter is approached. There researchers make their own windows through walls of uncertainty through which they evaluate what they see beyond.

Science prefers collective data which has pragmatic bases acceptable by other researchers from which individuality has been detached as much as possible. In the consideration of the 'kuru' case the religious satisfactions which these people got from this practice were not evaluated possibly because no one involved spoke their language well enough to understand their point of view. The fact that their perspective was both credulous and ridiculous but that obscures the fact that contemporary society accepts the patterning of science with the same dominance of credulity. Few people have seen germs but it is universally agreed that they exist. So social credulity is not confined to New Guinea, The individual in their understandings are unconsciously as much as consciously holistic, the social scientist has to take a partial approach if they have scientific ambitions to accuracy.

Such extreme examples prove little beyond the extreme and attractive situations in which they occur. It would be difficult to define extreme religious behaviour as credulous because they are often unconscious lateral personal interpretations and influences.

Since it is difficult to assess religious behaviour except in relation to orderliness and its related hard facts such as a marriage ceremony in a church but Hindu marriages can occur anywhere and a marriage of Buddhists is only peripherally religious by the feasting of and donations to monks. So we can state with some conviction that a marriage celebrated in a church or synagogue has a religious base, a Hindu marriage is religious because the participants say that it is and that a marriage between Buddhists is only very obliquely religious in that monks are fed as part of a secular ceremony. These conclusions are detached from holistic preconceptions.

There are thus an enormous range of activities which can be correlated to religion but not with any scientific exactitude. There are religious ornaments, picture and gestures which are clearly connected at some time and by some people to religion and to that extent they work. Whether there is any misunderstanding is not a matter that cannot be decided in the absence of hard data. Any ostensibly religious ceremony is proportionately secular.

The Excess of Divided Information

Once we leave the over-personally debatable evaluation of an individual's religious ideas and practices which are holistic and look for the wider correlations which connect with this in any social environment, the problem is not the absence of information but a surfeit of possibilities for investigation and if anything an excess of information.

In a Western context there is a surfeit of psychological data related to religious ideas and practices which despite the accuracy of their statistical elaborations must remain of questionable accuracy. These studies are dominated by the convenient use of university students. There is little reason to presuppose that what information an individual may provide verbally or much less in writing will be as accurate as a DNA calculation in an aseptic laboratory.

Why do we assume that the information that an informant can and will provide an accurate reflection of what they do and feel about their religious ideas and practices. Social scientists hope that they are getting accurate information and that makes them half way to believing the accuracy of the information that they get. The methodologically hard science is riddled with pragmatic gaps. This information may indicate trends in how people feel that they are behaving or ought to behave.

There are even greater difficulties in accepting written information in which informants are trying to express complex ideas and behaviour with very limited vocabularies. Few people have emotional and religious vocabularies which can match and explain the complexity of their thoughts. There are bilateral misunderstandings in any use of language in which the researchers always have a known vocabulary much greater in extent than that of the people with whom they are dealing. In any society there are few who can explain an emotional issue although they are certainly universally moved by the important religious and secular realities affecting them.

There is also the factor that social scientists are not so much highly literate as committed to getting as much as possible into writing and seeing that this is professionally essential. A simple sentence has to be explained and the relationship between the two can only be inferred. Even in the most universally literate society people do not feel any compulsion to put their everyday activities into writing. They prefer to talk and this is easily transferred to the use of mobile phones but they do not write except when there are more or less socially or economically compelled to do so. There is also the fact that social scientists may be just as unable or unwilling to express metaphysical ideas verbally much less in writing as a a literate Bengali farmer.

So writing in every sense of the word is a minority activity, time consuming and inadequate for expressing much more than commonplace needs. Social scientists possibly get satisfaction from the accumulation of data, they have this to show for their efforts without regard to the fact that it would not pass as evidence in hard science or probably in a Western-based legal system court of law.

It verges on the ridiculous for people to be asked to grade their ideas and activities which might be possible for examination grading of answers by professionals with serious doubts about its accuracy but not for religious activities and it is certainly not an everyday practice in any society. All the researchers have a table of grades but they have little more than inferences to relate this to individuals and communities. An attempt to do this in Tanzania was seen to be a success as there were few refusals until the researcher found out that the respondents thought the form was a lottery with winning combination.

There is also a quantity of information about the physical consequences of religious activities (Reynolds and Tanner, 1995) but this is also from the simplistic primary point of view. People catch diseases from going on pilgrimages and the same would apply to going on package holidays or to football matches. We do not know why they have put themselves at risk. We know that monastic life and meditation significantly lowers blood pressure and that they do not spend their time in avoiding possible stress but this also occurs seemingly by sitting quietly doing nothing.

So what we have available is a very large quantity of information collected by social scientists and other professionals that is predominantly presented not only in an elitist form but under a cloak of what is really pretended accuracy when it should have been more properly presented in inferential forms. It has perhaps elevated much of their conclusions to a higher professional status than the data justifies.

There is also the difficulty that in the evaluation of religious ideas and activities much is related to idealistic conceptions of what behaviour should be rather than what is actually happening. This should be accepted as providing patterns of acceptable values isolated from anything more than personal or at most neighbourhood attitudes. This approach which in a religious sense lacks charity, makes it virtually inevitable that everyone is falling short of the religious status to which they aspire or at least nominally committed. There is also the basic fact that almost universally whether they are Hindus, Muslims or Shintoists, believers are satisfied with their performance of personally created or orthodox rituals is sufficient to bring about the real possibility of getting what they want. Implicitly possibly rather more than explicitly individuals set their own targets for religious performance.

An ideal system in terms of the religions of the book, Christianity, Islam and Judaism are provided with definitions and so the result of this recorded and defined idealism are inevitably records of short-comings. So we have examples of what people should believe in the textbooks of canon law of these three faiths and in their denominational subdivisions. Social scientists look at these textbooks of required behaviour with delight of having something of substance to work from and by which to evaluate religious behaviour. The more institutionalised a Christian denomination is, the more likely that social scientists enter their assessments from top-down literate perspectives.

When we come to religious classics of what believers should aim at such as the works of Saint John of the Cross, whoever wrote the *Bhagavad Gita*, *Al-Ghazali*, the *Dialogues of the Buddha*, these are accepted as exceptionally valuable. But they were written in the linguistic codes or specialized languages of their writers, classical Arabic, Latin, Pali, Sanskrit and subject over time to a variety of translations into other languages by parallel elitist groups. There is always the doubtful assumption that an abstract word in one language can be correctly translated by equivalent words in another with which it has no philosophical affinity. It has been suggested that even Mahatma Gandhi, an influential political and religious figure first read the *Bhagavad Gita* in English, not in Hindi much less in Sanskrit. These theological and philosophical classics are known to and used by only a minute fraction of those who think they belong to these religions. In this sense we can conclude that there will always be layered differences both lineally and laterally between what is understood and what is behaviourally demonstrated.

At one end of this scale of comprehension and utilisation comes religious writings which are no longer comprehensible by almost all the people who are alleged to be influenced by them. Even when the language has its supposedly comprehensible and commonplace forms it may not be understood as in the religious documents distributed in Taiwanese temples. Certain basic factors are referred to as religious mysteries which have to be taken on faith and perhaps should be left as such. In this what are the definable differences between the beliefs of what Mary Douglas referred to as the 'bog' Irish, the simple faithful there or in Banaras or Berlin and the sophisticated understandings of theologically trained in religious seminaries in Delhi or Detroit.

Whether these studies are done with the intention of informing fellow religious professionals and social science elite outsiders, they are top-down evaluations in which the theoretical background has to a large extent already been predetermined by these elitist foundations.

If these assessments of religious ideas and understandings were derived from bottom-up data it would be shown that these elitist understandings have only marginal influence on the ideas and religious behaviour of believers and it might provide a better grasp of social reality. Of the seventy million who are estimated to have attended the last *Kumbh Mela* how many can we estimate will have had any knowledge of the Hindu classics and the current thinking of the Hindu theologians in Indian universities and *ashrams*. How many of the millions who go annually to Lourdes are doing so with any orthodox perspectives rather than just in the hope of personal help which would seem to be predominantly achieved. Both the *Kumbh Mela* and Lourdes are examples of religious success or at least in terms of participants who appear to have got what they wanted. They are indeed only able to account for their presence there in the simplest of dogmatic phrases.

Surely a more reasonable if not rational approach would be to take social and religious behaviour and ideas from what is commonly practised and to see the thinking of theologians and philosophers for what they are in social science terms, deviants; to admit that orthopraxis in the thinking and practice of people who define themselves as Buddhists, Christians, Hindus and Muslims is religious normality and to attribute religious behaviour to other standards is creating deviancy.

These elitist paradigms which do not provide much theological and religious dignity to common practices comes from the elitist social science and theological framework within which social and religious ideas and practices are assessed and even more so when they are not assessed in referential terms.

The Usefulness of Inexactness

Since there is both individual and social environmental variability whether or not the social sciences are able to collect accurate information is really irrelevant because there is absence of uniformity when research is directed as these sources. The accuracy of sources reporting in collective terms on issues which cannot be defined suggest that these averages have the overall characteristic of rarely if ever being applicable to any individual. When such averages are presented to the people about whom they were created, the usual response that this may be your view as an outsider but in this or that situation we will react in different ways; in other words your paradigm from your perspective as an outsider may be correct but it is not really accurate in how people as individuals utilise rather than think about it if indeed they do think about it in any way that is separated from particular situations. It may be that in societies and in individuals abstraction occurs when there is both individual and cultural intellectual and semantic evolvement. Most people most of the time do not use abstractions in anything more than concrete ways. Whether individuals are tied to formulas or informal social and religious behaviour they probably accept in some subliminal way that there is a hinge of exactness, a lurking sense of trustworthy certainty about which they know little of which their behaviour is felt to derive which is provided by the background authority of their denomination or community.

There is a necessary ambiguity in the forms of more organised religions that imply certainty without in fact providing it which at the same time allows for much variability in individual religious behaviour without losing the implications of lurking certainty. Hinduism retains its popular hold without having any definitional foundation without individual Hindus without being able to illustrate this except by religious practices which show that they are not Muslims.

It is outsiders, the researchers into social and religious behaviour who formalise these inexactnesses into conclusions about variability as if it was some form of failure rather than as aspects of normality. Individuals hold to their own personal day-by-day certainties, a moving staircase of major and minor changing social and religious realities. The only certainties in this are the individual's concept of themselves as separate individuals.

It may be that the assumption that certainties exist in all varieties of behaviour including religion antedates the European Enlightenment and comes from older Greek thinking and this has become a feature of the religions of the book, the ongoing processes of logic, the construction of definitions and the dominance of those who are in fact religious lawyers.

The Eastern religions have always avoided the dead end of exactnesses and the futilities of debating in religious terms what is a fish and what constitutes cooking. The Buddha himself is supposed to have said that it was better to divide a monastery than argue points of religious difference since such metaphysical difficulties are never reconcilable by debate. Certainty could be considered a form of property, a possession from which Buddhists should be trying to detach themselves from. In such circumstances a compromise is a loss of the religious realities in which the protagonists believed.

Exactness is something which is available for the measurement of supposedly inanimate objects. However in all animate behaviour and in particular human behaviour, any statement of exactness raises issues not so much of that particular factor but the extent to which it does not apply. It has the immediate function of exclusion. The inexactnesses of the Eastern religions do not have any such exclusivities except providing an illusory dialectic of stability which the Western religious systems have pushed into the dichotomous reality of binary alternatives making exclusion much more socially divisive.

Ambiguity seems to be a valuable religious attribute in terms of its indistinctness to social science approaches and indeterminate conclusions, functional utility and it would be both prudent and more reliable to apply the same.

In any attempt to assess and indeed to pin down what appears to be a firmness in social and religious thinking and behaviour, we are inevitably faced with the use of data obtained by methods which fall short of scientific requirements. It is perhaps almost ridiculous to approach religious issues with any hopes of accuracy anymore that it would be possible to reach stable conclusions about absolutes in literature or art.

The purpose of social and religious research is to produce representations of personal realities that are as reliable as possible (Philips and Jorgensen, 2002:182). It would seem that the methodology most likely to produce acceptable results is dialogic research in which both researcher and the researched are mutually involved in the same project and their biases are accessible to analysis. The working together of researcher and informants on a common problem within some temporally acceptable parameters.

If we accept the unreliability of verbal and written statements made in the assumption of possible detachment, it would seem that only in discussion can any researcher have access to social and religious realities. It is virtually impossible to distinguish social realities and their cognitive representations (Philips and Jorgensen, 2002:196).

It would seem that only in dialogic research which is inevitably small scale because of the costs in time and funds, that there is any realistic possibility of finding the personal extent of working misunderstandings. Any expansion in scale will progressively detach conclusions from this individual reality.

As Wijsen (Wijsen, 2009) concludes for his Netherlands study of the possibilities of religious tolerance 'we must be conscious that validity as a term comes from a different language game to that of positivist epidemiology and quantitative research, claiming that scientific statements are true if there is a correspondent between reality and representations of reality. But if we accept that there is a dialectic relation between social reality and cognitive representation of reality, our representations of reality are never mere reflections of reality'.

The Divisiveness of Language

The social scientists assessing religious ideas and practices will inevitably record their findings in the linguistic code of their profession and their own socialisation. Their suggestions will be read by religious administrators and theologians who, from their long training, will have their own denominational professional linguistic codes.

It is very unlikely that these linguistic codes will be that of the people from whom they got their information with all their linguistic diversities and individual differences.

We need to understand that the difficulties of translating into writing social and religious ideas and descriptions, underlie the difficulties which social scientists have in translating into their own understandings what they hear from their informants who will range from theologians to traditional diviners, secular intellectuals and the 'simple' peasants.

Research and the Need for Deception

The word duplicity implies a conscious awareness that actions serve two contrary ends which are morally in conflict; that it is wrong to play one role while pretending to be in another. Perhaps this is to simplify a normal social situation. Everyone performs a number of roles and in order to avoid the plain fact that they will always conflict, duplicity is an unconscious normal social necessity.

Any research process is composed of innumerable inter-relationships which may be grouped but are just as likely to be socially specific. Working for a government may involve the need for some deception and of course the use of results may involve some degree of deception; the extent to which information supplied by informants is considered by them to be private property and should not be described in ways that disclose the identity of the informant.

What does come up in discussing the ethics of research are not so much the issues of duplicity but the need for it. If researchers actually did explain the objectives of their fieldwork that they were doing research for a higher degree to enable them to earn more may be an approach that they would understand and of which they would be jealous. However, to suggest that they are trying to find out more about what is happening in a community in the hope that it might lead to their betterment and the injection of some development is to become involved in political and religious processes for which they are professional barred and in any case unqualified to participate. Also to tell them that they do not know what they are looking for is unlikely to create enthusiasm for participation. Over all this hovers the problem that it is likely to occur in the beginning of field work which, if there is no shared language, will involve interpreters with a limited understanding of what they are supposed to be translating. There is no doubt ethical issues here of balancing personal gain against the use of others who are usually of a much lower standard of living to that of the researchers. Issues that involve breaking both the law and matters which would put informants into danger from their fellows or from the government as in the use of body parts in magic medicine.

No social science researcher at work is without built-in role conflicts. There is no obligation to be straight forward as a clear statement of what is being undertaken would bias the information which might be supplied. Then there are role conflicts within the individual researcher as to whether they are using what they find out for the betterment of mankind or for their own advancement, but even that is somewhat disingenuous when almost all researchers are paid for the work they do. It may be that role conflict is so much a part of the research situation that it is not so much unnoticed as constantly adjusted to as the day-to-day work goes on. Role conflicts may be internal, the workings of conscience or external relating to particular persons or groups from the obligations which come from inter-relationships with persons or families, a constant process of negotiating priorities.

The professional social science researchers must always be to some extent two-faced; they cannot disclose what their trends of thought are without in fact causing their informants to react to this information in a biased way. Even in applied research in which those involved know to some extent what is being proposed researchers cannot disclose too much without risking premature political and social reactions in which they do not wish to become involved.

In theoretical research there is a build up of understandings which those being researched may or may not understand. It is perhaps a professional obligation to disguise thoughts in order to avoid the necessity and difficulties of explaining what is not yet clear in the thinking of the field workers themselves.

It is probably safer to disguise personal status; it is certainly safer for a woman researcher to be married or to state that she is married even then she has to suffer the criticisms of why she has left her husband to work alone in a strange environment. The unmarried woman may sometimes be the object of undesirable attention although Kumar in all the years in which she researched alone in Banaras stated that she had never experienced unpleasantness of this sort except in one crowd situation. Temporary partners should state that they are married particularly as it gives them a more acceptable status in the eyes of local authorities.

It would certainly be unwise in many cultures for researchers to make the community aware of gay or lesbian relationships. Colin Turnbull's long-term companion was seen as just another researcher who conveniently happened to be an Afro-American.

The unmarried man of a mature age who is not married has lower status than the married men of equivalent age in many cultures, it might be suspected that he is not a complete man and this might pass on to his status in the research area; a suitable fiction explaining the absence of a woman might be a reasonable deception.

Much is known about the few researchers who have consciously taken on a role which deceives those who are being researched. The most extraordinary example of this must be that of Burton who in the nineteenth century successfully pretended to be a Muslim in order to get to Mecca; he was accused by his contemporaries of betraying his character as a European gentleman and a Christian (Burton, 1893;

xxi). Almost by definition this may only be possible for nationals who are better able to enter their own communities as it were in disguise. Researchers have become involved with criminal gangs or get admitted to prisons with secret identities in which there is obvious danger as in pretending to be mentally ill. In other cases the pretence of being homeless or whatever so can take over the researchers that they have difficulty in maintaining any distinctions in their own minds as to who they actually are and this can lead to the destruction of their normal private lives. Any researchers even beginning to plan total and prolonged deception need to take professional advice over what is involved irrespective of the importance of the topic which is proposed for researching.

However in many situations researchers may become involved in levels of deception which are both recognised and unavoidable even when those being researched are told from the start that the researchers are not what they pretend to be. In researching the working conditions of agricultural workers both national and non-national researchers can state that they are working on farming methods and information of their penury or the behaviour of landlords becomes a by-product of these enquiries.

Once the field of enquiry moves out of the seemingly pragmatic into the metaphysical there cannot be any such acceptance of thinking within a single framework. Asking about anything in the spirit world draws attention to its existence not its possible reality. No doubt this is an interesting philosophical issue about the reality of abstractions, but for non-national researchers to ask about witchcraft, the malevolence of ancestors and magical protective and aggressive rituals makes these outsiders acceptors of these ideas as physical realities.

National researchers might not be placed in such dilemmas as they would clearly belong to families, groups and cultures in which such ideas are part of the ways in which they come to terms with misfortune. They would not be cognitively hostile to these forms of reality, while social science researchers who tend to be both pragmatists and agnostics have difficulty in disguising their feelings.

When it comes to researching religious communities or sects there are the problems of these clashes of belief. Those being researched may not see the researcher as just an outsider interested in what they do but as just another person who should be proselytised as a possible convert to the True Faith; in functional terms a redeemable or possibly already a redeemed person seeking the light (Englund, 1996). It might be that Hindus and Buddhists would find this situation less involved in deception as their faiths are tolerant of variations while the religions of the book have a sharply defined yes or no to issues of faith.

The Impossibility of Sharing a Language

People within a shared culture share numerous commonplace situations in which there is almost automatic agreement and when and where to start agricultural work or build a house. Much social life would be impossible without large scale agreements. In developed societies those who cannot live by these common sense agreements are defined as deviants or mad.

The problems arise when people try to agree across cultural boundaries which involve language. Change the language and you change the meanings. Many languages have classification of nouns and verb tenses that involve time; some indeed do not have any way to describe an indefinite future. In Burmese a monk can only be referred to as a sacred person and it would be grammatically wrong to use the classifications relating to an ordinary man.

So the speakers of a Bantu language in Kenya would have difficulty in communicating with those who speak a Nilotic language. This difficulty is extreme in New Guineas where natally isolated communities have different languages so communication is so difficulty that they have created pigeon English as a lingua franca, which is now used in Christian ceremonies with meanings unrelated either to Christian orthodoxy or the Papuans own natal metaphysical understandings.

The fact that two people communicating are both Africans but speaking languages from different linguistic groups is an irrelevance and when the speakers are also socially distant as with American or Dutch anthropologists working in a language which has no connection with any European the possibility of metaphysical understandings is minimal. The difficulties over the meanings of words which are heavily soaked in cultural ethical and personal understandings are perhaps insuperable (Turner, 1993); a process at best of mutual interpretation between two people of different cultures wanting to reach agreement but not in terms of one culture. Silence on a particular issues may be due to previous horrifying events (Magaran, 1996).

The deeper a researcher penetrates into another culture, the greater the possibility of misunderstandings. We are all subconsciously committed to our own personal and cultural understandings. A Western European researching the use of the word 'god' has monotheistic assumptions which are not shared by most Asians.

Many languages have not been committed to writing and others have only had this commitment for a century and have not yet had any development of abstract scholarship. There is no reason to suppose that any language is superior to another. English is no doubt complex but many of the Australian Aboriginal languages are just as complex with totally different grammatical constructions. The language of the Tanzanian Sukuma has more tense forms than English. All these differences have metaphysical ramifications.

Intuitive Anthropomorphism

In suggesting that intuition is a factor in the acceptance of religious ideas, there is the likelihood that the divine figures in Christianity are both anthropomorphic and counter intuitive in seeing Christ and the Virgin Mary as human figures; and in their magical activities in human terms. This cannot occur in Hinduism as there are no humans with multiple arms or human bodies with elephant heads or indeed hungry ghosts. In southern Europe the Virgin Mary in one village is not the same divine figure as the Virgin Mary in the next village down the road.

The Chinese have lived for centuries in a highly stratified bureaucratic system of government of their metaphysical ideas and practices which are mirrored in just such a divine system which operates in the same way as their political system. With its grades of influence and power and the need for reciprocities, the gods can be bribed in the same way as officials. Most of the world anthropomorphise the divine just as Hindus feel that this is not necessary as they are more metaphysically imaginative and disregard intuition, but they may feel that their ideas are similarly intuitively correct without any need for it to be verging on the rational.

The Limitations of Trust

For someone to provide information to another who is not a close relative or perhaps not even then, involves trust and that is a scarce social commodity. It is extremely fluid in what it implies and to whom and moreover when it is always situational. The finding out of information from someone who does not offer to provide it, is always a long and difficult process. At its worst it is confrontational and at its best when the information is provided without the informant knowing that it has been provided.

Why should a stranger be trusted and indeed even a close relative who may well be rivals for affection and property in their shared community. It is a commodity which is often used to obtain some social and psychological advantages. For someone to provide information out of the goodness of their hearts seems unlikely.

Since information is a commodity what is wanted and from whom has to be assessed in social, psychological and even economic terms as trading; what is being asked for and what is being given should be assessed as profit and loss balances for those involved. To the informant this way of looking at relationships and information is always something into which they have been unconsciously or consciously socialised. The seeker of information in social science field work is almost always an outsider even if temporarily socially acceptable for reasons which are likely not to have much connection with the aims of that research.

Asking direct questions in most social situations is bad manners and rare and usually associated with officials who usually want answers to their questions as quickly as possible so that they can get on with whatever matter initiated the questioning in the first place.

Social scientists in their fieldwork are not by training patient since time and funds may be limited; they may not know what they are looking for and are as much crime detectives searching for clues. Worse from the point of view of creating enduring social relationships they are, whether they admit it or not, in a hurry; their field work has to be paid for and their time there is costed in terms of academic leave, visas and their personal lives.

It would be best, therefore, to collect information by observation and some type of participation made possible by similarities in ethnicity, age, sex and assumed equalities of education and intelligence. But this is a waiting game particularly when the information which is wanted is interior to the individual and invisible rather than socially exterior and observable.

So a short cut is the creation of trust not in the concrete sense which can be developed between people who are tied together by marriage, blood or affection, but is a created commodity between people with different interests. It seems unlikely that this can be created across the board in a community. There will always be gradations of possible closeness just as there will be gradations in accepted reliability.

A possible way in is through those people who are attracted to the researcher as a source of social and economic enrichment or who see any association with an educated outsider as an intellectual stimulus.

Initial questions might be asking them how the researchers should proceed, making them initiators as much as respondents, making them co-producers of channels of information. But of course the way forward through some sort of reciprocal trust depends on getting self-interested informants in the first place.

There is another aspect to the gaining of 'interior' information and that is getting to be known in the community not so much as inoffensive but as socially incompetent who should be helped; this can sometimes be done by the use of inquisitive children as personal tutors.

At all events trust cannot be assumed or created for detached and impersonal reasons. Working with prisoners as informants involved them in getting information and cigarettes from the researcher which could then be marketed among other prisoners.

Most people in researched communities with some understanding of the outside world would assume that the information which they have provided directly or indirectly through the ever-present notebook, is going to be sold in someway to the advantage of the researcher. It is rare indeed for researchers such as Verrier Elwin with his Indian wife to have a reputation of commitment to those researched in representing them to the outside world.

Ethics and when is a Confidence to be Respected

The basic issues must surely be that both covert and overt social science research is almost always intrusive on personal privacies as matters are found out and publicly exposed without due consideration for those about whom such exposures are made. The parallels to such exposures of private matters must be private confessions to priests, lawyers and doctors who are all bound by professional and moral obligations, in some cases protected by law, not to disclose further what has been told to them.

Any researcher must consider whether their informants are aware that what has been told to them in private could be used in writings available to the general public and even in some cases available to those about whom this has been written. It is not difficult to assume that much of the information retailed in this way would be damaging to the informants if they were known to have passed this on to a stranger; under what understandings were they passing on these facts or possibilities.

Secondly, are there aspects of confidentiality which researchers should observe and is it adequate to just change names when every community knows well enough who has been talking to these researchers and for how long. There are also legal aspects to the confidences about which the researchers become knowledgeable about which give them obligations to inform the authorities or become legally liable to prosecution. Most researchers in the course of long stays in a community become privy to much of the darker side of social life about which they should and indeed have to remain silent.

Outsiders generally in neutral social environments such as bars, trains or waiting areas for flights often receive personal information from strangers as it is assumed that they will never meet again. Except for research which only involves seeing and listening such as behaviour at political meetings or public rituals involving no person to person contact, social scientists are professional extractors of information from people who are not known to them in any personal way. The difference is that what is reported to them is written down or recorded and becomes the property of these people over which the providers of this information have no longer any control. This is why some potential informants are suspicious of researchers' questioning them and they would no longer have any control over their property or privacy. It was too easy for European anthropologists to be accused of betraying their informants (Werthein, 1972; 321-4), and it may well be that contemporary national researchers may become subject to the same accusations unless they stay clear of government officials as much as they can.

All field workers are professional outsiders accumulating data collected from individuals while viewing their behaviour in relation to others which none of those involved would want to be openly disclosed much less discussed. This is rarely data which would be accepted as scientifically valid or legally acceptable as evidence and would probably be better classified as an accumulation of gossip, dangerous in itself in any small community. 'The anthropologist who learns a great deal about his neighbours in confidence must respect that confidence except for overwhelming reasons, though it is of course conceivable that there might be occasions when it should not. No hard and fast rule can be laid down and these are matters of conscience rather than of reason (Beattie, 1965; 55). Broadening the public knowledge for academic reasons can scarcely be such a justification for disclosure even if the non-national researchers work in another country and never returns to the areas of their original fieldwork. Long-term mistrust can be as pervasive as gossip.

So researchers accumulate confidences and they have to decide for themselves how this data should be used. Notes and tapes can be and have been stolen by thieves and possibly the political police so it is prudent to remember that these materials can very easily get out of the researchers' control. Research material can often be lost under suspicious circumstances and possibly used for political purposes. It is often a reasonable precaution for any researcher to post fieldwork data home on a regular basis.

Then there is the problem of what goes into print and thus becoming public knowledge for anyone who happens to come across the publication. Unless the published research is biographical and has the permission of those involved to publish as was the case with Baba of Kano (Smith, N.1954), it is prudent to use anonymity both for both people and places without too much circumstantial identifying data. This is particularly important when the researched activities are illegal such as drug addiction (Tanner, 1966a) or cattle theft (Tanner, 1966b). or just deviant to the standards of any society's dominant elite.

The further distinction is between publishing about people and places in the 'home' environment that are likely to read or hear about what has been written or using a medium in a distant and specialised location where it is unlikely to be read by anyone who does not have a specialised interest in those matters.

There can be no clear dividing line between national and non-national researchers, but the latter have less to worry about over the use of confidences but the national must always be aware that they and the researched in some respects share a common social environment and every community now is likely to have several people of high intelligence and education who are quite capable of following up what researchers have written about their community from computers and seeing these results as hostile to their sensibilities. An Indian researcher intending to work on his own community with a minority religion received death threats to him and his family. My own published research on European behaviour in East Africa as if they were part of yet another tribally identifiable community resulted in social distancing (Tanner, 1964, 1966c). For a Westerner to study Africans or Asians is alright but for a Westerner to study his or her own expatriate community is socially suspect.

There are other issues to consider. Social scientists are not working in a social environment which is not their own just to get on with strangers, although 'just getting on with strangers' might be a valid research topic. These researchers are working for a particular aim which should have little to do with their personal feelings except that they have chosen that particular topic or agreed to do it on the suggestion of another academic. They have to ask themselves how far would they go to get the data which they consider to be essential.

When the nearly complete fossil skeleton of the proto-hominid Lucy was found in Ethiopia, a modern knee joint was needed for comparison so one was obtained from a modern Afar burial mound although warned that the locals would be outraged if they found out about this desecration (Johanson and Edey, 1981;158-9). It seems very unlikely that had an Ethiopian professional been present that such an act would have even been considered and much less discussed. A national academic in a research team would be restrictive for the study of questionable behaviour.

It seems likely that some non-national researchers see the 'other' as outside the boundaries of any necessary social and indeed ethical considerations. Non-national medical researchers in East Africa were interested in the El-Molo living round Lake Rudolph who had a low fluid intake with a high saline content; it was suggested that some teeth should be extracted from the living in order to study the effects of such unusual and limited fluid intakes. Uganda medical students sitting in on this research committee meeting became restive that this should even be considered.

Researchers may go outside the boundaries of acceptability even in their own societies in the interests of science as in the recent British case of hospital doctors retaining the organs of dead children, but this is more likely to happen in communities and under conditions of extreme social distancing.

The Social Networks Around Researchers

The non-nationals working in their own countries will be creating around themselves networks of people who will be useful to them in their research work, largely composed of fellow professionals but also some informants in key positions. These networks do not include relatives and in the western world the number of relatives is much smaller than the extended families elsewhere which have multiple uses.

It seems likely that in the developing world professional and familial networks work much closer together and that real and classificatory relatives are valuable links into many different fields of research. National researchers are going to think in terms of these relationships as part of the process of thinking about choosing and putting into action a field of research. Aspects of kinship which would help them gaining access to people, place and paper. They would be foolish not to do so when this is a common feature in most institutions and communities. Whether informants who are relatives are more reliable then those who are unrelated is a matter for speculation because they will be working from their own points of view about how their joint family is working (Gupta, 1979); perhaps it is prudent to use them as ways into sources of information and not to keep the relationships closer than is polite and necessary.

This is a bilateral process and just as the researchers use relationships to further their ends similarly the researched will see any connections with the researcher to further their opportunities in the outside world of which they are presumed to have influence (Dua, 1979).

Ethics and the Boundaries of Acceptable Behaviour

Any culture and every community has boundaries defining what is acceptable and unacceptable behaviour. This accumulation of rules, practices and customs never has any unity except in the codifications of written legal systems and even then a whole profession has developed to argue in public that particular words and sentences coincide or do not coincide with particular laws, abstract definitions and actual events which are not often so narrowly related.

So researchers are often faced with what are in effect personal boundaries within which they themselves behave in their primary relationships. These become increasingly attenuated with social distance; it is totally wrong to steal from your parents, all right to borrow and not return from friends and not as matter of any serious moral concern to cheat over your tax returns or steal the property of government or international companies and to take souvenirs from hotels when on holiday. This of course applies when people lead relatively static existences. A national from a Hindu background researching pilgrims to Banaras is working more or less in the same environment as existed in their own communities.

However, researchers do not have any simple array of standards to which they can conform even if they are working in their home communities, there are still the standards which are laid down by the profession to which they belong. Non-national researchers outside any broad understandings of their topics really have little idea as to how an outsider should behave among men and women pilgrims to Lourdes, or among market women in Bamako. The success in getting research data depends on establishing a very special role in any community which legitimates a kind of information getting behaviour which is not previously part of local social expectations; this requires these researchers to show both personal rather than professional sincerity and diplomacy (Hotchkiss, 1967; Pelto, 1974; 218).

Most social science field work is not done within home environments except for the large amount of in-house research which is done in universities using students for tests which has led to a huge accumulation of data about their psychological attributes with much less known about those who live outside the conveniences provided by any university.

So most research is done in social environments about which the field workers may know something in theory but in practice they are faced with an endless series of social and mental inter-relationships for which they have had no imaginative preparation at all; they have injected themselves into social environments in which they are in every sense aliens.

Most researchers should be sensible that they are pushing their luck when they publicly behave in ways that almost all the locals would see as suspicious. Geography researchers working near the Lebanese border wearing khaki, carrying maps, binoculars and cameras looked like every child's conception of spies (Howell, 1972); they should perhaps consider themselves fortunate not to have been shot at.

Then there is the issue of personal standards beyond which the researcher would not go. An anthropologist working on the East African coast was given the role of male 'midwife' to a key Swahili informant for his marriage which appeared at first understanding to have parallels to that of 'best man' in an English wedding celebrated in a church. What he did not know was that the first act of sexual intercourse between husband and the bride was felt to be so much potentially under the possible malevolence of outsiders, that this is done by the husband's midwife. When faced with this situation in the marital bedroom, he walked out as this was not a personal boundary as a married man which he was prepared to cross for research purposes. Even for a Hindu researcher wanting to get acceptance into a Tantric cult involving sexual excesses might well face similar personal reluctances.

Most social scientists develop a liking for the people they study and have an understanding of the conditions under which they live and cannot avoid. This humanism clashes with the formal and detached ways in which they write their reports. It is not only that they experience a double identity, an almost biographical element and an almost conscious sense of betraying them because they are not able to present this in their professional writings (Stewart, 1994).

The National and the Ethics of Research

Professional standards for social scientists must remain a matter for individual assessment since they are not accredited to any professional body which might support them in any conflicts of interests in which they might become involved. Nevertheless 'having an ethical code is a necessity in the folk epistemology of professionalism, an epistemology widely shared by anthropologists (Pels, 1999; 102). They have no corporate status in law nor can they be considered as comparable to medicine and professional bodies which exercise considerable control over both doctors and lawyers as to what they can and cannot do.

The professional standards of these two professions in most countries are based on not just on the centuries of development of their status, their links with learning and the acceptance by the state and public opinion of the facts of their activities; since society accepts these professions for what they are, their standards are maintained as much by the society itself and not just by their members.

It is not possible within the general field of social science to find any profession wide agreement as to the meanings coming from their work nor are their researchers working with state recognised and legal licensing. Even if a code of ethics should be created it is 'inert knowledge' that lacks the concrete problems in which decisions have to be made. More importantly it could not train potential field workers in making the choices between conflicting principles (Appell, 1978; 35). It is not a science within the accepted meaning of the word that hard facts are produced which are accepted by other scientists not connected with the original research work. Indeed it could be called a field of work in which opinions are formed rather than conclusions based on personalised evidence.

It would seem, therefore, that any discussion of the potential existence of an ethical code for social scientists is no more than theoretical play-acting because it comes down to what individual researchers decide that they should or should not do in the circumstances facing them. Outside the provisions of the law which apply to all people living in a country other than diplomats, there are few if any restraints which can apply to social scientists other than their own consciences.

There is an immediacy of choice in many small scale ethical issues which perhaps only in retrospect can be interrelated to major issues of ethical importance. Most field workers are involved in issues of duplicity between what they say they are doing and what they are in fact doing, a day-to-day factor in everyday life and unless it is blatant and tactless this probably remains an individual matter of conscience.

Any broadly applicable ethical issue must always be situational and capable of wide ranges of interpretation but in all nations there will be ethical facts which are imposed on the individual researcher over which they have no choice. There is firstly the legal code of the nation, then the political system as it is practised whether by ballot, bullet or bribery and finally the unwritten ethical system of whichever community is being researched as to what they do as well as say they do.

Thus ethics will always involve the individual researcher in choices and in this the national ones are less likely to blunder into difficulties either because of ignorance or because their personal values have not been created and peripherally maintained in another cultural setting; they know the social realities of caste discriminations, mother-in law avoidances and the restrictions and possibilities of private and public inter-relationships.

Perhaps the most difficult aspect of social science field work is when the researchers as individuals feel that they are participating in something which is morally wrong but feel that they are unable to make any material gesture in opposition. An agnostic is not a non-believer but one who has a set of divergent beliefs. National researchers cannot distance themselves from these situations in the ways that the non-nationals can by leaving the field through the simplicities of air travel.

There may be two levels of ethical principles which prevent researchers involvement or ethical difficulties in the first place such as pre-emptive ethical choices in which they decide not to get involved or are forced to keep silent.

Then there are the ethical principles which may guide relationships between researchers and their informants and the community from which they come. The moralities of everyday relationships which are a mixture of those learnt when they were growing up and what they have learnt professionally, only reduced to a limited extent by bureaucratic records. Burmese highland people knew the importance of written records and although they could not read kept their documents in bamboo tubes which related to decisions taken fifty years previously. Again the national researchers have advantages here as they may not have the same extreme contrasts to cope with as must be the case with non-nationals who may well have personal fixed intolerances when it comes to what they see as the unkind treatment of women, children and animals and their own personal taboos. Intellectual and personal understandings of 'their' fit uncomfortably together. It takes a very long time for a non-national adult to be socialised into patterns of behaviour of a different culture; if their children accompany them into the field they may well be envious of the way in which they appear to fit into this supposedly alien culture.

The Family Resemblance of Religious Groupings

It seems to be a valid criticism that the understanding of factors in social and religious belief and practice has tended to become exercises in intellectual specialisation which has separated such understandings from the realities of popular understanding and practice.

Hinduism is a case in point where theologians have given up trying to create exactnesses which they have achieved to some extent in some aspects of the religions of the book in their denominations.

Whether Hinduism reflects the prehistoric development of divergent beliefs and practices created by different charismatic but now unknown charismatic figures is perhaps not relevant to the contemporary mass of different cultish practices.

An American academic (Hawley, 1991) attending a south Indian religious festival was asked by someone attending whether he was a Hindu replied that he was a Jew but that Judaism and Hinduism did many similar things. But on being asked whether or not he broke coconuts or burnt camphor, he replied 'no', then he was told that he could not claim to be a Hindu.

In this brief conversation what theologians might consider to be the essential points of Hindu beliefs were not touched on. This man and without doubt the vast majority of his fellow Hindus saw their religion in terms of its practices, not their beliefs.

A pre-Vatican II Roman Catholic might similarly replied that he was a Roman Catholic because I eat fish on Fridays nor have breakfast before going to Sunday Mass.

It would be more accurate to depict religious faith in terms of the rituals which believers believe to be essential than possibly relate their faith to theological dogmas, abstract factors of which they have little understanding; nor in practice do they have any wish to further or dissolve their lack of understanding.

There would appear to be two factors here. The use of ritual acts to which are attached grandiose theological understandings and secondly the use of collective assumptions that relate to Wittgenstein's idea of family resemblance (Wittgenstein, 1953).

There has been made a connection between ritual acts and two major religions. Whether it has been taken out of context or not, it remains that and major behavioural groupings a connection has been made between minor acts in terms of time and motion, which in many countries now have political relevance. It would be difficult to find ways in which their day-to-day lives illustrate their religions' underlying beliefs about conduct.

There is little logic in connecting such infrequent but regular rituals with major theological presuppositions; there may be but not with any exactness as it is too great a leap of understanding. At least one thinker Nassim Taleb (Taleb, 2012) has postulated that human life has gained from constant disorder, and the constant mutations in social life.

It is hard to neglect such distinct signs as irrelevant. It has been pointed out with Hinduism (Ferro-Luzi, 1991) that a more concurring approach would be Wittgenstein's idea that something which may be thought to be connected by one essential common, may in fact be connected by a series of overlapping similarities feature. This would result in the followers of both major and minor religions may have some common features of which only a few may totally conform. Not all Hindus burn camphor or Christians go regularly to Mass or fast in Lent.

Observing and Participation

For the national to research some aspects of their own culture rather than the divided intellectual who has to go through a process of re-socialisation on their return from overseas can never be the same person who originally set out from his natal family and society. Whether or not for social research, there are the difficult issues of the remains of existing socialisation.

There is the need to initially recognise that by taking on a researcher role, they are no longer by any standards 'normal' citizens; they have made themselves different. 'It is not at all obvious or even plausible that a 'native' anthropologist, born and raised in a city, perhaps educated in a foreign school in his or her own country and even more likely trained abroad in Europe or America would be doing indigenous anthropology in the strict sense of the term when studying illiterate peasants in a remote corner of his or her country (Altorki, 1982).

This quote from a Saudi-Arabian woman academic raises a number of divergent issues which involve any national researcher. Whatever the social origins of the national researcher whether a Mishmi or Baluchi from remote villages, the process of education has urbanised them Then the process of education is an imposed system of acquiring knowledge which has in all probability has no obvious or indeed even intended relationship to what they might have learned had they remained in their natal social environments and moreover it is a Westernised way of learning. The adult man or woman who has been successful in this hierarchical process of accumulating status by examinations abstracted from other aspects of living has made them socially and psychologically different to those who have not been through this process. This is a much more extreme condition than higher education in the Western world does not provoke such extreme divisions.

If such researchers leave their own current social environments, almost certainly urban and predominantly intellectual in how they see the world around them, and start research outside this charmed circle, it will almost certainly be with people who are socially and economically inferior to themselves.

This social situation is not much different to Western nationals researching in their own country; the recipients of their research will have seen the researchers as social aliens and the researchers themselves will not see those with whom they work as their social equals.

On the other hand should they start to do research in the community and at the social level of which they are already a part, there are immediate dilemmas. They may feel that their primary obligations are to completing the research which they have initiated and which their families and colleagues know they are carrying out. But they are still relatives and no research objectives will ever obliterate the fact that they are still daughters and sons, grandchildren and cousins and they will always be expected to fulfil those roles. Their relatives will trivialise their research even if they know that such work is highly thought of in the outside world in which these relatives now belong professionally.

As a household member by right of birth, such researchers are immediately on call for their primary roles as relatives and neighbours. They have no immunity which would normally be given to visitors of that nationality or even non-nationals over breaches of acceptable behaviour.

Such researchers are automatically slotted into social roles appropriate to their age and parentage which both channels and restricts the possible range of their enquiries. The non-national is always some sort of stranger but the national can never get away from the fact that they are so and so daughter or son, of a certain age with an appropriate marital or non-marital status.

Access to a society by reason of birth and location does not mean access beyond their primary social roles and to obtain data about which such researchers do not immediately have the right to obtain requires careful work. 'It took six to eight months before I could develop friendships that made close observation of their daily life possible to the degree that my presence was more or less ignored' (Altorki, 1982).

But supposing a researcher and his wife come and live in a community for years to study education and are known from the start as researching into a local activity, the dilemma remains that they are their own best informants because in that community (Hennigh, 1981) they were not much different to others married couples who lived in a community of couples who have just arrived, stayed for a while and were likely to be on the move again soon as their jobs changed. It was not a field work situation as they were acceptable residents, and not just suspicious transients. This couple moved from being detached enquirers into an active involvement in community affairs in which the community saw them as a source of information. The community had an acceptable place for active newcomers and they were treated as any other community resource.

This active participation in community affairs was a highly efficient way of gaining information, it was a requirement of local citizenship to join in and it was also a psychological defence against the abrasiveness of long-term field work and counteracted the absence of academic social stimulation. Whenever the ego role dominates research dilemmas become more difficult.

There was also the factor that by becoming a part of the overt community life as not much different to others there, it was a significant short-cut away from the struggle to gain insights into alien cultural settings even if it was part of their own American public culture and it also reduced the traumas of withdrawal when they eventually had to move house to take up other work (Engelhart, 1977; 1-15). Just as anthropologists tend to think in terms of 'my' tribe, sociologists may develop an emotional attachment to the community in which they had done their first field work.

This form of active participation is only possible for nationals in that part of their own society in which their social characteristics are broadly similar to that of the field of study. Once there are social differences and any element of covert observation then the problem is broadly similar to research in a foreign environment.

The Pattern of Selectivity

No matter whether the researchers are nationals or non-nationals of whatever social and demographic characteristics, there will always be a pattern of selectivity in what they see and assess and in what they consciously at the time and retrospectively avoid seeing and perhaps unconsciously turn towards or away from in their research. At the back of any information researchers can be sure that there are still hidden factors. No one however well trained sees all parts or persons in a community in which they are working on equal terms. Indeed in crude terms we are no more capable of assessing parts of a society in equal terms than we are of accepting equality in our own lives; inequality is part of our socio-psychological make-up however unacceptable this may be in overt political terms. Mkwaja village in Pangani Tanzania had about a hundred houses divided in two by a shallow ditch which even a small child could hop over. The people in one half were ignorant of much that was or had been going on in the other half.

Every researcher not only has hang-ups which they will circle round if not positively avoid but positive preferences which come from their own backgrounds and research experiences. It seems likely that these are often ethical if not moral choices such as preferences for but not too close an involvement with the poor and envy as much as dislike of the well-to-do. The writers of a text book on interviewing stated that they had an irreducible preference for pretty women in fur coats and there can be no doubt at all that there are similar biases in all cultures and in all researchers. Most are unconscious of the ways that language can channel patterns of thought.

More is known and has been written about witchcraft, an almost universal preoccupation of anthropologists and which at most can never be described as a daily activity. In comparison very little is known about the social system in every community by which they dispose of their human wastes; not only is there a distaste for such a subject despite the fact that it is universal and inevitably frequent but in its assumed crudity, it is not likely to be seen as career enhancing unless such research is seen as part of the wider topic of public health.

We are all brought up to accept some reticence in cross-sexual interactions in which there are distressful masculine and feminine patterns of public and private conversation The researchers and their informants work within one-to-one relationships in which the ideas and practices of their separate cultures are bound to be under social and psychological strain. It is usually male researchers talking to men but rarely women except at a professional level of assumed collegiality. Women researchers are often given a quasi-male status and who are thus able to have both male and female informants but that is not the same as treating sexuality in an equally open way.

To have an abstract interesting and an understanding of commonplace behaviour which is essentially private, is not the same thing as bringing it out of this private domain into the public world of interpersonal discussion in the presence of note-books and tape-recorders.

One has only to look at the range of human behaviour and the distribution of social science information to recognise that there is, and always have been, a pattern of selectivity. This is not only governed by personal choice within their own cultural parameters but also by the ease and difficulty of potential and actual social access to what they consider researching. Most people spend their days both in public and private according to the social acceptability of individualism, but proportionately we know very little about private activities for which we have to rely on what we are told which can never have the same assumed validity as observed activity.

Whether the national or non-national researcher is better able to intrude for that is what it is, into the affairs of others with whom by definition they will always be within some category of intruding strangers must always be outside such simple categorisation and remain with the personal abilities of individual researchers with their personal aptitudes for getting information and their diplomatic persistence but it will always be selective.

The Problem of Condensation

It is not so much that people are individualistic in much of their behaviour but that their group involvements are so situational that it is rarely possible to make assumptions about the similarities of such behaviour except in very general terms such as very cold weather makes riots unlikely; in fact many of these conclusions verge on what common sense would suggest as likely.

Thus there is the problem that while social science has to accept that human behaviour is rarely similar enough to be grouped with any realistic hope of overall accuracy, it is almost invariably presented in categories as if they were similar, unless of course it is presented in qualitative terms in which numbers are not used as illustrations of perceived realities. We have already discussed that categorisation works well enough in some primary legal senses and in their extreme ranges but that the grey areas in which these categories merge are too commonplace and extensive to be ignored.

Social scientists condense primarily in order to present their findings to others in the same profession and they do not do so in consultation with those who have been researched who only occasionally see behaviour in such abstract terms uninfluenced by personalised situational factors.

If there is any such condensation in the thinking of people at any stage of their social, political, religious and economic involvements, it is in their attitudes outside their personal knowledge who are grouped together by some assumed attributes for the conveniences of commonplace biases. This occurred so frequently in all societies as to beg almost a constant as when the Sukuma, the English or Biharis refer to the attributes of the Maasai, the Scots and Tamils in terms which have little coincidence with social realities or indeed in the ways that most people refer to those who are demographically different to themselves by reason of age, sex or ethnic appearance.

It is easy to assume that some condensations have value as in the proportion of men to women in Musoma and Ngara areas of Tanzania which was so low as to make monogamy virtually impossible in the former and in the latter making women carry out many of the role requirements of both sexes. But to what extent do such condensations provide accurate and usable data which must be related to the age of the women, the number, sex and ages of their children, the viable and supportive nature of their extended families and the pragmatic nature of their relationships in terms of property holdings which make unions worth maintaining or indeed initiating. Widows cannot be inherited if there are no brothers to inherit them nor can mother's brothers in patrilineal cultures have responsibilities for their sisters if there are none in existence.

How, in fact, is it possible when the data provides no obvious groupings. In a survey of Tanzanian attitudes to schools run by Christian missions (Tanner and Mirgan, 1976) for which a sample of 5,000 were questioned from which the answers were grouped into 300 categories, but which might just as well have been six hundred and it was assumed that these were both primary and singular opinions. Nothing was known as to why each individual opinion was held or indeed whether these people ever thought in such singular rather than multiple terms. As an exercise in social accuracy it only produced answers in the form required by those making the analysis who, in fact, wanted to produce a simplification in what they should have known was much more complex and situational; a combination perhaps of the dominance of Western social science theory and non-national researchers.

It is worth considering the possibility that this tendency to condense data is at least in part comes from the sense of superiority felt by social scientists towards those they are researching. This is shown by the compulsive way in which behaviour is condensed into patterns presumably with some idea that their future behaviour can be estimated and perhaps socially and politically manipulated for the greater good of society.

We can perhaps assume that there is some collusion between social science researchers who wish to have their data in some marketable form and their principle informants who are probably stating no more than quasi-idealistic conceptions of the ways in which their society is or should be ordering itself.

Any condensations of data must be decisively inaccurate as for instance in relating high indulgence of infants to extended, polygynous, nuclear and single mother families (Whiting, 1961). What constitutes high indulgence and birth order for a start and are not all families extended to some extent in emergencies and single mothers may be living with their own mothers so that there would be a tendency towards the 'normal' indulgences of alternate generations.

The Weaknesses of Categorisations

Whether religion is a reality or not, we provide ourselves with data. Despite the fact that religious behaviour is predominantly individual and environmentally varied we try and cope with these masses of data by dividing it into categories which are then used for analysis and comparison to other analyses which use the same categories.

Virtually all social science work to which the adjective surveys can be applied uses categories and numerical analysis. There have been numerous studies of this issue largely confined to American populations (Lanson, 1978).

The commonest categorisation is that of age. Many people in the world do not know their ages and others go to considerable lengths to disguise their true ages. Age categories are usually in five or ten year blocks. This means that high proportion of the sample are near to the dividing line between two age groups. Can we really use this system of categories and assume that there will be some assessable useful differences between an informant who is 29 years and eleven months and others who are thirty and one month. Such a division may be useful in medicine but not for social behaviour. Even attributing a sex to person is often suspect since significant number of people who are hermaphrodite or at least are behaviourally sexually neutral.

Categorisation is even more questionable when it is applied to abstract words in the context of religion. Some studies have proved as near as possible that the religious elderly live longer and in better mental health than those who do not attempt to practice any faith. Such studies involving personal evaluation of their own 'well-being in which there are innumerable contributing factors. A visit, reassurance from a priest or doctor, winning a prize in a competition. Looking forward to a religious festival as it would mean visits from friends and relatives. It may be something, an isolated event at the time of the questioning which moves the division between happiness and unhappiness.

Mood swings in relation to religious and social experiences can vary in any individual from moment to moment. If religion is a personal attachment to the Divine from an individual then he or she could attribute their well-being to their religious beliefs alone. We are left with the need to make assessments of the reliability of any such statements; a difficult and expensive process involving interrelationships. Much depends on the informant's impartiality towards telling what they consider to be the truth and what may be the material benefits which they may be receiving from these associations.

Then there is the multi-dimensional aspects of any secular or religious relationship. Any form of lineal attribution of causation is nearly impossible to sustain as has been shown in the attempts to create Parallel Distributed Processing. So whatever relationships these elderly individuals have had, we have to deal with multiple causations and correlations of which only the more obvious can have received attention.

There is no reason to suppose that the usefulness of attributing his or her well-being will be the same as that of others with similar demographic categorical backgrounds. Here can be aggregate similarities but in terms of what religious executives can rely, there is always the factor of individual in persons and environment on which religious practices are based. There can be only peripheral possibility of similarities between Hindus and Muslims in East and West Bengal, between Jews in New York and Israel. The most that we can hope to gain by numerical categorisation are no more than inferences of frequency.

Satisfaction and dissatisfaction will always have substantial differences between individuals and communities. In the use of any abstract factors there can be no assumption that the meanings of a word will be the same with all the individuals involved. In terms of well-being, a definition of health cannot be usefully related to the presence or absence of professionally diagnosed illnesses or physical malfunctions.

Education, we do not know whether examinations passed have any equivalences nationally or provincially. And to what extent are the results of examinations are variable between hard and soft subjects and the standards of the examiners including corruption will vary between the Punjab and Bengali. Lower levels of assessed education may lead to envy and higher levels may not lead to any well-being. Only Christianity connects itself with literacy while other religions have their literacy confined to specialists in languages which have no spoken use and require prolonged learning with few peripheral social benefits.

Well-being associated with income is also subject to innumerable variations. As it would depend on what income is regularly available and not what they have in assets which are not realisable. A family may be poor while owning land which it dos not want to dispose of and which it does not have the manpower to farm efficiently. A family with many children and looking after their elderly parents has more demands on its harvests.

Where we might expect to find a sex differential in well-being, there are variable demographic factors. A woman may have a satisfactory family life as well a success in business running a folk art cooperative. While the divorced may have a sense of personal failure.

Well-being may be correlated to well organised village life based on kinship which cannot be a feature of more uncertain urban living in slums unless it has an ethnic basis as the Chinese have in some British cities.

Overall there is the difficulty in surveys in which the answers being provided by informants or whose answers cannot be checked. Researchers' faith in their informants probably has little reality and it would relate more to the few which they know personally from long association.

Many researchers try and grade the answers of their informants correlating them to age or their informants stating that they are frequent or intermittent attendees at religious ceremonies which might be better correlated to what these informants think they should do. An answer alleging personal high attendance may give those persons an unjustified sense of well-being.

In conclusion, numerical accuracy cannot be claimed for the results of surveys for behaviour for which there is no clear definition. We can do no more than infer trends from these results. It is just not possible to reach such levels of accuracy for behaviour with its individual variations and environmental differences in time and place. What such surveys can do is to open the mind to the variations in behaviour rather than its fixed formulation. A marriage is a legal change of the status of the couple involved but it says nothing about how such couples interpret and change their subsequent behaviour.

So a fixed question results in fixed answers to which little accuracy can be attached. Open ended questions may well produce a very wide range of answers. A study in Tanzania funded by the Ford Foundation asking sample of 5,000 adults people what was wrong with the Christian Churches today, produced answers which appeared to be classifiable under more than three hundred categories for which there would be classification difficulties of putting which statements into which category. However such a survey did produce a mass of data from which new inferences can be drawn and developed.

Psychological Field Work

In sociology the terminology and practices can be moved from the language and practices of one culture to that of another and how this is done depends upon the personality and understandings of national and non-national fieldworkers and what they undertake. Most of those studied can understand in their own languages such concepts as mother-in-law avoidance, joking relationships, family segmentation and the unity of alternate generations and the reasons for them. In going through the index of Evans-Pritchard's study of Azande religious practices, the Tanzanian Sukuma elders consulted were quite able to state that they did this but not that. This is easy for such people as these terms are based on concrete behaviour in particular circumstances and they are not based on abstract thought.

Psychology within and without a particular culture is much more difficult to transfer from one system of understandings to another perhaps because it is more complex for a variety of theoretical, personal and practical reasons. The base lines are overwhelmingly Western. A recent summation of the possibilities of integrating contemporary psychoanalysis and cognitive science surveying contemporary models (Westen, 2001) makes no mention that there may be non-Western models applicable to much larger populations than the total Western one.

Psychology is worked out in print in one of the major languages in a professional code used among the international psychological, professional fraternity which would be extremely difficult to translate from the language in which it is printed into another one outside that particular linguistic group. Abstract ideas for which there can never be cross-culturally acceptable definitions are almost impossible, if not impossible, to translate from Chinese and Japanese into German, French or English. Regarding the possible transfer into English of Chinese philosophical concepts Richards wrote (Richards, 1953; 150) 'we have here indeed what may very probably be the most complex type of event yet produced in the evolution of the cosmos'.

Much of the data is supported by inferences for which correlations vary widely in their plausibility. It would be extremely difficult to translate schizophrenia for a group of non-literate Sukuma intellectuals as they would suggest such behaviour among them is the relatively common spirit possession of successful diviners and there is just no need for another definition by an outsider when they already have the diagnosis and the cures which work well enough in that culture.

Over much depends on the researcher-researched interrelationships and the extent which this is benign. In comparison to discussing mother-in-law avoidance across cultural boundaries is relatively easy but forms of mental normality and abnormality in looking at spirit possession usually start with some assumption about normality which do not include the possibility that such people are possessed as a reality which is so common globally as to verge on normality; perhaps it is necessary to accept that spirits do exist.

All these difficulties can be summed up by the fact that it is possible to discuss cognitive matters in particular cultures but that how they work out is always both individual and situational. Rationally we should surely have to accept that two Toureg men even if they were identical twins, are inevitably dissimilar in how they react to the social realities surrounding them; why should they be possessed by similar spirits and who can possibly state that the spirits are similar.

There are indeed more important difficulties that divide the national and non-national in psychological research more than in the other social sciences in that the current base lines are European and date at most from the Enlightenment. Eastern cultures are based on ideas recorded in writing that probably antedate the former by a millennium at least. By and large Western thinking is that these concepts such as the Chinese thinking about Yin and Yang are at best archaic and related to the practices of those in fringe cults. We may be forgetting scientific fashions (Kuhn, 1970) and the varying faiths which we have in Freud, Jung, Adler and Klein.

Thus non-national researchers approaching the social science understandings of Chinese, Indian and Japanese start from a barrier of deep-seated cultural biases. It may not be any part of their training in psychology to question in these circumstances the foundations of their training. It would be difficult to find out changes in Chinese cognition when every market and temple shop contains evidence of foreign influences.

National researchers working largely within their own cultural environment but so much speaking as thinking within these same paradigms as those whom they are researching, there is no process of translation going on in their minds and no great leap over cultural divide. They are aware already that the bases of their thinking which ultimately came to be expressed in writing, are already available somewhere in Pali, Sanskrit, classical Arabic and the incredible complexities of classical Chinese with its forty-four thousand different ideograms expressing different words.

Moreover Western social science theoreticians manoeuvre around individualism. The individual is so important in Western thought and practice that it has taken on the practical characteristics of a moral and necessary 'good' and that their group involvements can rightly be considered a varying handicap on its proper development.

We can conclude that national researchers working in their home environment can certainly carry out valuable psychological work, but that in the Western world it has short-term perspective. In the non-Western world national researchers have a head-start within the intricacies of their own complexities which start from different philosophical understandings. Moreover they have the advantages of being able to work with and to develop very ancient psychological paradigms for which there is ample written background. The non-national cannot compete with what is provided by their own relatively recent written paradigms. There is always the difficulty of Westerners learning new languages which have no affinity with their own Romance languages with their linguistic affinities. Westerners are handicapped by their inability to gain any high quality understanding of other languages. KiSukuma the language of about a quarter of the Tanzanian population has the problems of having a range of verb forms more complex than English as well as the use of tones and personal pronouns reflecting status. The Christian message does not translate easily into this language.

Surveys may give satisfaction to those who use them but there will always be methodological drawbacks to any implication of accuracy. Age may not be known or disguised. Marriage may be no more than neighbourhood acceptance of a relationship, education may be peripheral and literacy may be no more than the ability with some difficulty to the reading of a simple message but not a newspaper. Ideas move with speed across any rural urban divide because most people go to outside markets, go on pilgrimages and experience change visually.

The Uses of Bias as Commonsense Normality

We have suggested that bias in both national and non-national researchers, their adherence to common sense social norms at three levels of normality and with a fourth level related to professional ideology, means that they have their minds and behaviour split four ways by the requirements of field work.

Consciousness of this normative division would initially prevent researchers from being too tied into the social realities of any close personal ties with strangers; the type of Goffmann involvement with primary relationships. Researchers may tend to cling to the social settings into which they are first introduced; it is difficult enough to get into a strange community in the first place without shifting to another one once the elements of domestic support have been organised. Relationships with important informants can become personal rather than just as producers of needed evidence.

On the other hand entering field work with an adequate understanding of its cultural elements at the tertiary level from reading published works leaves them with an inadequate understanding and acceptance of the reality that few people are predominantly governed by the standards of their cultures. They adhere to a culture often express it in ideal terms in talking to outsiders but they habitually break its rules.

The non-national researchers with their systematic categorization of social behaviour may tend to see the inconsistencies and contradictions as part of their professional logic. The national researchers sharing some of their understandings with their fellow nationals are more likely to appreciate the come and go nature of social and psychological affiliations. Their fellow nationals see no inconsistencies with beliefs in certain things at the tertiary level which is practiced in a different way at the secondary level and which form no part of the practical aspects of life at the primary one and indeed in a reversed ascending scale of social and psychological commitment.

The social science researcher may accept this for the people they are involved with and indeed on reflection see it in their own behaviour and beliefs; the schizoid nature of religious belief and practice. What complicates the researcher's approach is their proto-scientific need to make their conclusions logical; they accept role conflict and its solution as logical. They find it difficult to accept the normality of holding contradictory beliefs for which there are no solutions and which are retained at the same time as different forms of normality.

The social science researcher, particularly non-national ones should learn that illogical thinking is part of the normality of common sense behaviour and thought. We should accept the normality of 'swerving from the right line' which is imposed by both culture and professionalism because an overall right line cannot exist in any social life and psychological understandings.

7

Conclusion

The Non-national Researcher: An Overview

The primary factor is the possibility of non-nationals doing field work in another country must be political. Newly independent nations do not like nationals from the western nations doing research which may reflect on their inability to develop as quickly as their political hopes may have framed so decisively; they want to know in advance what is going to be researched and researchers who are let in have time limited visas. Academic freedom is subject to considerable circumspections and they may be sure that they are under observation by the police.

Whole countries, areas within countries and subjects may be closed off from social science research either because non-nationals will not be let in or because their own countries advise against going there because of the possibility of kidnapping. The atmosphere of restriction and covert supervision may not encourage researchers to even attempt such work.

At best, their research is constricted within short periods of work in the field and the difficulties of continued contacts within the communities with which they have worked up personal knowledge and a circle of personally committed informants. So much non-national research are one off periods of field work within a particular framework of getting something done within the time allowed which might in a number of cases be described as academic tourism; they are in a hurry.

Even if this is partially true it has to be assessed in terms of what the researchers own career ambitions are within their own countries and do not involve any long term commitment to the countries which have provided the information on which these same careers are based. They cannot plan on any assumption that they will be coming back again and again to this one community so that their research would incorporate change in persons, families and institutions. Much research is produced in terms of a static moment in time which is socially unreal.

However, they do bring into the field and into the academic contacts that they may make in the countries in which they are short-term guests, viewpoints from another culture and another set of academic understandings which cannot be based on the reading of books so that such international and possibly ongoing interrelationships are a valuable stimulus which comes from differences.

The non-national is also expensive to keep in the field and the return on substantial grants may be a low percentage in terms of the outlay which involves fares and medical support in emergencies; they have backups against misfortune. They are often without the same amount of supervision which they might experience as support in working their own countries.

They are, on the other hand, not only well funded and independent of local power structures which may give them a biased view of the realities of local life but they will always be materially and very visibly better off than the people with whom they are working and thus make them the object of much petitioning for help and far from disinterested offers of help.

On the whole they are younger rather than older and so their research work does not benefit from previous field work trips and, of course, they take a long time to get acclimatised to the conditions under which they will have to work; excessive heat, damp, debatable hygiene and lack of privacy as well as the almost total absence of easy associations with people of their own culture. Many will not have previously experienced being so totally alone in terms of the sociability to which they have been accustomed in the university environments in which they have spent the last few years. There is of course the advantage that they are not so likely to have family commitments which handicap the time that the older researcher can be actively working away from home.

The most important handicap is that of language in which the non-national unless he or she is a half and half immigrant, is unlikely to reach bilingual competence in the time allowed by their visa even allowing for preparatory work. So that possibly more than a year of the field trip will be spent in getting as fairly common knowledge of the language but not one in which they might approach the bilingual ability necessary to be able to identify and understand cultural nuances. This means that a substantial part of the grant is spent in learning back-up which does not have much to do with a complex research topic and this means that usually the researchers have a handicapped dependence on interpreters who themselves are not really bilingual apart from the reality of their own biases. While non-nationals may not necessarily get ill they are almost always going to have problems which come from being forced to eat strange food because there is no other and cooked moreover under conditions which they may not appreciate. They will often have to live under conditions which are markedly inferior to that they would have experienced in their own countries.

Non-nationals are also not likely to have local contacts which make their connections into the community to be researched which cuts down on initial introduction times. Of course there will be local academic support but they are not likely to pass onto strangers their own contacts which are often very personal.

Of course all academics whether they admit to themselves or not, are likely to have sense of intellectual superiority to the people whom they are researching but in the case of non-nationals coming from western highly developed societies this is likely to be allied to having a sense of cultural superiority as well. Perhaps a more general failing of non-nationals is their assumption of superiority regardless of age and sex in which they approach local people expecting cooperation when in terms of the local culture they are socially inferior to the people from whom they are expecting cooperation. This in part comes from the tendency to imagine that lower material complexity in many societies than they would expect to find in their own, is correlated to an assumption than these societies are similarly simpler altogether rather than just as complex as their own but in different terms.

As non-nationals there will not have been socialised into ways of getting round the difficulties of local bureaucracies or understanding the intricacies of the local power structures and how might be manipulated. As newcomers they are more likely to be biased towards those who become their earliest informants to whom they are drawn by misunderstanding over the nature of friendship which is not based on abstract goodness of heart but on social reciprocities.

Since they have not grown up in those communities into which they are now placed for research they are more likely to have illusions about their capability to have abstract understandings. They do however have the advantage that they can accumulate information which might endanger nationals and in leaving the country at the end of their allowed field work this can be publicized in safety. There is one other disadvantage in that most non-nationals come from secular intellectual backgrounds and often assess the religious activities of these communities in terms of their intellectual frailty rather than as a valuable part of their individual and collective lives. The long-term advantage of non-national researchers to a developing nation lies in the stimulus they can provide and their help in the building up of local institutions.

The National Researcher: An Overview

The primary restraint on nationals doing social science research work in their own country must be political; they have to live with what they publish and once they get a reputation for wide range of political involvements, their names will keep on coming up in computer searches. Developing nations with unstable political regimes and the recourse to violence as solutions to their difficulties do not like their own nationals researching into areas in which their failure to fulfil political promises are made public by their own intellectuals rather than their political opponents. Politicians who have risen quickly to power are usually suspicious of their intellectual superiors from their prolonged subsidised education, who they suspect are also contemptuous of them for their lack of education.

Academic freedom is an ideal which is maintained by a considerable amount of self censorship about what is researched and printed. They will certainly be on the books of the 'political' police who have the job of reporting on subversion, if national academics work consistently in such sensitive areas as voting fraud, corruption in high places and inefficiency.

Whole countries, areas within countries and subjects may be closed off to social science research because nationals will not be let in unless they already live there, such as the high Himalaya border areas of China, Pakistan and India which are of interest because of polyandry and the effects of altitude on human behaviour. The Bhasins have made this area their consistent research interest.

However nationals are better able to do research which would be barred to non-nationals because they are better able to work their way round official barriers and to wait for opportunities to do what they want rather than being tied to the impatience of their own career time-tables. An Indian woman academic had to spend two years working to get permission to do research about a small non-violent political party because the work up to independence was only seen as a physical struggle.

Their research is not so constricted to short periods of work in the field which are hard to rearrange for further visits from abroad; they can come and go relatively easily to the research areas in which they have developed interests, as in the Bhasins interest in the Himalayan region and Kumar's in Banaras; national researchers are often no more than a car or train journey away from their field of specialisations. There wili be a build-up of personal knowledge and their own circle of informants who are personally committed to them.

So national research is not necessarily one-off periods of field work within a particular framework of visas and finance and getting something down on paper before the time there runs out; they need not be in a hurry and they can thus observe change as it goes on rather than taking a more static view of social processes.

Their commitment to research is related to careers in their own countries and can involve long-term commitments to communities on which their careers have become based; a much more personal development of relationships than could be possible for non-nationals who might correspond with some informants when either of them wanted something.

However, they do bring into the field their own long term local academic contacts as well as view points which are part of their own cultural understandings from socialisation and partly from academic training within the culture in which they will continue to work. It may be difficult for them to break free of the social categories to which they belong whether of tribe or caste but of course they have the major advantage of looking much like most of the people with whom they are likely to do research.

The national researchers are less expensive to keep in the field and much research can be done within their salaries and work commitments by using their own students and the opportunities for research which start from just outside the gates of their university. Small grants can show a higher return of completed research because they can be more closely supervised.

The national researchers will have their own familial backups against misfortune and while they may not necessarily have better health than non-nationals, they are certainly less likely to suffer from the results of eating strange food. They are less likely to live under conditions which are markedly inferior to what they are used to without the options of being better able to organise something better.

On the other hand although they are not well funded which must restrict involved costs other than that of talking and walking, they are better able to be independent of local power structures so avoiding a biased view of the realities of local life. However, they will always be materially and visibly better off than the people with whom they may be studying and subject to endless importuning by people thinking that they have influence in other places or have plentiful sources of money. Nationals are better able to work their way round the petitions of people asking for help without giving offence. The Japanese have a long series of linguistic conventions for refusing something without actually ever mentioning the word 'no'.

On the whole national researchers may be older rather than younger and so their research work does benefit from previous field work trips and of course they do not have the prolonged period of acclimatisation which is inevitable for non-national researchers. They will not suffer from the social isolation of non-nationals since they will usually be able to find acceptable associations with people of their own culture and similar status. They may well have the disadvantage of family commitments around which it may be somewhat easier to organise their research as was the case with Kumar's ongoing Banaras work in which partners or spouses can be supportive.

The most important asset of the national researcher must be language in which they are likely to be natally bilingual although of course they may have to learn local linguistic codes but these will usually be within the major national languages in which they are already fluent. So less time will be spent in getting a socially competent knowledge in which they would be able to understand, identify and comply with cultural nuances. This means that less time has to be spent in learning the cultural back-up which is part of any complex topic.

This means that national researchers are less handicapped by dependency on interpreters who themselves are never as bilingual as they make themselves out to be apart from the constant difficulty of their biases.

Developing societies probably have as much dependency on networks of influence based on villages, families, classificatory kinship, in-laws occupations as well as sub-caste or class as what may have been the case historically. So there is always the possibility of national researchers having some tenuous connections with the community in which they want to work which may be usefully developed. Non-nationals have some ethical difficulties over manipulating influence which in these developing societies may be the only way to get things moving to the advantage of their research as was the case with the Hindu Indian woman wanting to research in Pakistan.

Just as non-nationals they may be unable to disguise their sense of intellectual and cultural superiority to those who are researching and we have seen how in some cases researchers have adopted an approach that informants have an obligation to provide information and indeed expecting cooperation from people who are politically inferior to the class of the researchers; this unwise approach comes from the nationals being unable to adopt a role which is independent of their pride in their own families and education which the non-nationals would be unlikely to make. Nationals should be better able to work within expected cultural obligations.

As nationals they will have been socialised into ways of getting round the difficulties of local bureaucracies as well as understanding the intricacies of local power structures. They are less likely to be tied into those who had become their earliest informants because they have a better understanding of the nature of friendship as being based on reciprocity not abstract idealism.

Since they have grown up within the broader culture in which they are researching, they are less likely to have illusions about their capability to understand their work in terms of abstract theories detached from any understanding of the macro-structures into which they have been socialised. But they do have the handicap that they cannot accumulate socially dangerous information and then publish details from the safety of another country.

They may not have the disadvantage of coming from secular intellectual backgrounds and thus they are likely to assess religious activities as a valuable but not out-of-date intellectually restricting part of individual and communal life. A researcher who is by birth a Hindu may have difficulty in thinking agnostically.

The long-term advantages of national researchers to a developing nation lies in the stimulus they can provide and the supportive environment which they can provide for non-national research efforts.

Unitary Thinking and Eastern Social Science

The distinction between Eastern and Western thinking is clear enough in some of the earliest philosophical and theological writings and since it predates social science evaluations, it is surely necessary to accept that there are long-standing differences which are the foundations of subsequent thinking. A Chinese thinker Xu Dashou wrote (Gernet, 1985; 208) "the barbarians say I believe in eternal life. It is easy to see from this that they have understood absolutely about the meaning of the word 'life' nothing". Another Chinese thinker Huang Zhou (Gernet, 1985; 205) also wrote that 'the mode of action of Heaven and Earth can be summed up in a word; it is not double'. We may question whether this thinker meant that the upper case should be used when it does not exist in Chinese.

It would seem, therefore, that Eastern thinking feels itself superior to the more recent Western patterns of thought and moreover their materialism under cuts their claim for some equality and that (M) man and (S) spirit cannot be viewed in dichotomous terms.

Although the early Jesuits spent a great amount of time trying to make Chinese literati understand that the natural soul was of a substance radically different from that of the body and inanimate things and that the soul was the exclusive privilege of mankind. They got nowhere and the Chinese thinkers concluded that the Jesuits were materialists since they deprived the universe of indivisible form turning it into brute matter directed from outside and lacking the spontaneous intelligence that all creatures display (Gernet, 1985; 146, 203). It is not our intention to initiate a discussion of these philosophical differences but they nevertheless have substance.

Some commentators would go so far as to state categorically that the social sciences in their research have to draw back from an assumption that it can imitate the natural sciences. Its open nature, constant variations and innumerable influencing factors prevents any possible foundation for accuracy with its absence of definitions and the porous nature of its physical and psychological data. Karl Popper stated (Banton, 1964; 99) that 'the triumph of social anthropology is the triumph of pseudo-observational, pseudo-descriptive and pseudo-inductive generalising methodology and above all marking the triumph of a pretended objectivity and hence an imitation of the methods of natural science'. If this is so then Eastern thought which has none of the logical consistencies of Thomistic thinking, is in a better initial position to study human behaviour outside any hope of imitating natural science which it would not be attempting to copy in the first place.

Above these methodological issues national researchers who have from birth a general knowledge of their own large scale complex societies with long literary and philosophical traditions would mean that within the thinking of Chinese, Indian and Japanese intellectuals, there are deep elements of these almost coercive understandings. These would be impossible for non-national researchers to acquire and certainly not as far as the implementation of these ideas in the practicalities of their field work (Nakane, 1982).

Cooperative Efforts in Research

Cooperation between researchers within one academic culture has always potential personal problems since the topic has the background of individual careers which would be particularly difficult with researchers of equal age and experience. Some feel that they should share data and interpretations, both here feel that to do so would mean the reduction of the importance of their own expertise. It may well work best when an obviously senior person leads and the junior benefits from attachment to a star who does not see the other as a potential rival.

What then of cooperation between nationals and non-nationals which might well have advantages to all concerned since their career patterns are within their own academic cultures and they may not see their joint work in competitive terms.

Cooperation would seem to have significant advantages. The non-national would get access to fields of enquiry which would otherwise be closed to them or would at least take significantly longer to work themselves into. An immediate benefit would be that they would not have to spend so long in language learning.

For the national there would be the advantages of better access to research funding and, at the very least, there would be the benefits of the support and encouragement from an interested partner with viewpoints and expertise from another cultural viewpoint.

A case of fruitful cooperation was the study of urban pollution in parts of Cairo and a village for which funds were provided by a Canadian source (Mehanna and Hopkins, 2000). This researched people's attitudes to garbage and sewage in their streets as well as air and water quality and noise, involving the opinions of both men and women and participant observation. The difficulties that a non-national would have had in doing such a study do not have to be listed and the predominance of the national researcher and sensitivity to his role is shown in the order of authors' names. There can be no doubt that both authors and their institutions and the national culture within which the work was done benefited.

A valid example of research work that could be done by national and non-national cooperation would be the commercial work of women (Perry, 2002). There would be a sense of shared identity between such women researchers as well as a shared need to illustrate the ways in which women have achieved some degree of economic independence.

There are two areas of research. Topics which start with people in various circumstances and which may or may not be correlatable to laws and environmental situations. Then areas of research which start with the fact that such a law, situation or international convention exists such as the existence of a new mass disease, the installation of automation or the wearing out of a natural resource to which the behaviour of the people involved can be correlated. What can we do methodologically when the characteristics of the 'Gods' change as the Hindu Goddess of smallpox has changed to include other diseases. The Peruvian American Indian miners have changed the God of mines to include other dangerous occupations.

In the first situation there are always problems related to the role of each researcher and there can be no assumptions that a Chinese, Indian, Peruvian or American researcher would be approaching the topic in the same way; the interrelationships are too personal and occur in different social and psychological environments.

In the alternative research scenario, social scientists start with facts that exist about which there can be little disagreement and the work starts from an agreed foundation. Thus the Pakistani or Ukrainian researcher would be able to state from their viewpoints what would be the consequences of these facts. In both these situations the research process would benefit from the mixture of nationals and non-nationals as well as differences in age and sex and prevent exclusive viewpoints closing off alternatives. Whatever form cooperation takes cross-nationally and cross-professionally it can be valuable as providing lateral thinking, probably as necessary in any field work involving either religious or secular behaviour.

One to one relationships in a research project can work themselves out within the privacy of such associations but the difficulties of a group or committee approach to a topic are more complex and more public, which would probably take up scarce time not justified by the results. Personal interrelationships come into prominence which have nothing much directly to do with the research and also have nothing much to do with the fieldwork problems which come from different backgrounds. Time is taken up with discussions about approaches which may have a tenuous application to particular situations and of course costs rise with the numbers involved. Social scientists are too individualistic to make cooperation an easy approach in such situations.

We must first set aside as far as possible issues of nationalism since the flow of researchers is from the developed nations with relatively stable and surplus economics as far as the backing of research goes, with their surplus of social scientists looking for field work opportunities required for obtaining their higher degrees and for the publications supporting their university positions as well as experience outside their existing professional and personal understandings. The number of non-nationals seeking to do research in these developed states is almost always from similar states and few if any come from developing nations except as a by-product of requirements for an already subsidised higher degree.

The flow of non-national researchers then is from the developed nations into developing ones clashing with new ideas of national dignity and widespread thinking that they are being manipulated generally in the interests of Western society and its intellectuals. Thus there are covert feelings of resentment and overt bureaucratic restrictions which govern both their entry into these countries and what they are permitted to research, which is probably not a feature of cross-university association. So nationalism is a factor which non-nationals have to circumvent and cope with in and around their field work.

We have seen that both national and non-national social science researchers have both advantages and disadvantages which mirror each other but on balance the nationals ones have the most advantages but are handicapped by shortage of financial and library support even with the availability of computers which are indicative of data sources but rarely supply enough information to be useful for researchers. Nevertheless despite these inevitable differences both have the same general objectives to widen the understandings of different parts of the one society for the primary benefit of its people, while still each working for the furthering of their own careers.

In the simple sense of keeping this national distinction, there would appear to be few advantages beyond purely personal academic selfishness. The distinction is restrictive as it does not enable the best use of financial and personal resources for what must surely be considered as the objective of all research, the betterment of a particular segment of mankind.

If we take the example of a research project conducted by two Americans by birth and one Indo-American on the availability of health care in Udaipur, Rajasthan (Banerjee *et al.*, 2004), we find an immense amount of information about the widespread symptoms of disease and that 41 per cent of those claiming to be doctors had no medical qualification and so on.

Whatever help this team received from Indian academics was not shown in joint authorship of the report. So we have some thorough research work done by non-nationals who then departed taking with them their expertise, having dumped their report into the laps of the provincial government and the local health authorities to react in any way that they see as politically relevant and economically affordable beyond the denial that hostile facts disclosed refer to real situations. There was apparently no contribution to the building up of any local research institution.

Surely a rule of thumb for research in countries which have limited budgets for research, would be to have most, if not all, research initiated on the basis of some equality in senior staff numbers between national and non-nationals. This would enable a flow of research funds into developing nations while the equality of researchers would be that both types would have access to stimuli from the thinking and cultural understandings of their opposite numbers. This would be particularly valuable for non-nationals to be exposed to other forms of methodologies and thinking from their professional colleagues. They would also have easier access to fields of research by the help of their local colleagues who would know their way round the labyrinths of local bureaucracies.

At the same time non-nationals would gain from the cultural understandings of national researchers with whom they are likely to be closely associated and by this sort of interactive association they will be avoiding the rather persistent local opinion that they are getting their own personal profits from whatever research they do.

This cooperation also gets over the age divide with the younger non-national benefiting from the older nationals advice over the problems of status differences in their contacts. Indeed advice as mentioned generally of how best to fit into the communities and culture which must be strange to outsiders, thus shortening the acclimatisation period.

If there is language learning it seems likely that the national partner will be able to advise on the appropriate linguistic code for the project, short cuts to the more appropriate and difficult aspects of a language rather than what might be called the touristic vocabulary. It is perhaps more useful to be able to enquire about the intricacies of spirit possession and ritual and mother-in-law avoidances than to be able to ask how cooking is done.

The national researcher benefits from assured financial support and access to wider academic resources. Just knowing that the people in other cultures think differently is not the same as encountering this in personal relationships in which the points of difference and agreement can be talked out in encounters which may last some time and which may well continue over a series of research projects and field trips and some years of collegiality.

The main difficulty over this type of long term collaboration is that university training and more particularly post graduate work is an isolating process. Cooperation in research is a learning process and is particularly so in field work when there are few others nearby to offset the problems of close and contrary associations.

What kind of cooperation can be created and developed between researchers of different nationalities and different proto-genetic patterns of thinking, but shared professional aims and understandings. An important preliminary consideration must be some recognition and understanding of the professional dignity of the nationals involved which may not be given due consideration when much of the findings and material resources may come from non-national sources.

What are the advantages of cooperation with a non-national for national researchers. Any cooperation is likely to be stop-and-go so that there are not the complications of joint work between nationals who might not be able to avoid each other socially when there are professional differences of opinion about their joint work. Secondly, the non-nationals are likely to belong to or be connected with universities or institutions which are well-funded, stable, not subject to direct political pressures and which will usually look favourably on this form of international cooperation.

The national researchers have access to research facilities and academic backup which are provided as a matter of course for field workers whom they support. They can be helpful in providing documents by e-mail which not so long ago would require physical visits. Above all the non-nationals with whom they are cooperating come from different cultures and the covert and overt biases which they carry with them should not be seen just as regrettable aspects of Western and Japanese socialisation. The bases for a constantly active and stimulating dialectic between different and valid points of view. Above all these non-nationals, whatever their achieved social and ascribed physiological status, provide automatic differences with which the nationals have to cope rather than simply classifying them into a rag bag of unacceptable views based as much as anything on bilateral political prejudices.

What does the non-national gain from cooperation with specific nationals. There is an immediate compulsory social nearness to a national which in the field would require months if not years to acquire. The immediate access to the national's knowledge of likely behaviour and plausible explanations of the background to much of the seemingly unusual behaviour of the people with whom they are working. For the non-national the nationals provide innumerable short-cuts which would otherwise have wasted much scarce time.

If the cooperation in a joint project exceeds a simple twinning and the research is in fact run by a committee composed of equal numbers of nationals and non-nationals, then there are likely to be cultural difficulties. The Westerners there would need finite decisions to be reached by vote as quickly as possible which does not fit easily into the practices of other cultures in which people talk out difficulties into compromises rather more than clinical solutions. Any form of voting may decide issues satisfactory for short-term solutions but obscuring longer term implications as well as making the outvoted minority a permanent hostile social force.

Most social scientists aim to help the societies in which they work and since most nationals and non-nationals work in developing countries, it is the form of research most appropriate to these conditions with which we should conclude. Low cost applied rather than theoretical field work about matters which involve cross boundary issues and inter-cultural cooperation. The Western academic may feel that he should concentrate on theory, while those elsewhere, faced with national issues of immediate importance, may feel that such total concentration theory is an indulgence.

Throughout our study it has become clear that national social scientists do not have the resources to carry out expensive time consuming research without funding, while the non-nationals working in isolation are perhaps in danger of becoming a focus of animosity of those who do not have the advantages of isolation and abstraction from the realities of living in poor countries with uncertain and corrupt political systems.

The way forward must surely be to increase the amount of research with funding depending on the necessity of cooperation so that both nationals and non-nationals benefit from working together.

Bibliography

Aborisade, R. 2009. The role of motivation in enhancing job commitment in Nigerian industries. A case study of Energy Foods Company Limited, Ibadan. *Journal of Social Sciences*. 19(2), 149-154.

Abu-Ghazalah, S. 2008. Human spatial behaviour in a public housing project at Amman, Jordan. *Journal of Social Sciences*. 16(2), 103-114.

Abu-Lughod, L. 1988. Field-work of a dutiful daughter in AlTorki in AlToreki, S. and C.F. El-Solh (eds). Arab women in the field studying your own society. Syracuse. Syracuse University Press. 139-161.

Almy, S.W. 1977. Anthropologists and development agencies. *American Anthropologist*. 79(2), 280-92

Alutu, A.N.G. and V.E.I. Audu. 2009. Female participation, communication and technological development in Nigeria. Implications for early career guidance. *Journal of Social Sciences*. 19(2), 163-166.

Acharya, T. 2009. Strategies for overcoming barriers to education development of Scheduled Caste students of Cuttack city. *Journal of Social Sciences*. 21(2), 85-89.

Acharya, T and D.K. Behera. 2005. Factors influencing the educational achievements of Scheduled Caste and General Caste students of Cuttack Municipality Corporation. *Orissa. Journal of Social Sciences*. 10(3), 215-222.

Adelekabn, M.L. *et al.* 2000. Trend analyses of substance use among undergraduates of University of Benin, Nigeria. 1988-1998. *African Journal of Drug and Alcohol Studies*. 1, 39-52.

Adewale, R. 2005. Violence in the citadel. The menace of secret cults in the Nigerian universities. *Nordic Journal of African Studies*. 14(1), 79-88.

Adeyemi, M.B. 2010. Cultural influence militates against effective data collection in the field. The case of two African countries. *The Anthropologist*. 12(4), 246-249.

Aeri, P. and D. Jain. 2010. Effect of employment status of mothers on conceptual skills of pre-schoolers. *Journal of Social Sciences.* 24(3), 213-215.

Agar, M. 1996. The professional stranger. London. Academic Press.

Agar, M. and J.R. Hobbs. 1982. Interpreting discourse. Coherence and the analysis of ethnographic interviews. *Discourse Processes.* 5, 1-32.

Altorki, S. 1982. The anthropologist in the field. A case of indigenous anthropology from Saudi Arabia. In H. Fahim. (ed). Indigenous anthropology in non-Western countries. Durham.88 North Carolina. Carolina University Press. 167-175.

Anuradha, K.N. and M. Komala. Impact of non-formal education on all round development of preschool children. *Journal of Social Sciences.* 6(1), 21-23.

Apollo, M. *et al.* 2006. Eco-consciousness for poisonous and injurious plants among urban dwellers of Bhubaneswar, Orissa, *Journal of Human Ecology.* 19(4), 239-248.

Appadurai, A. 1990. Disjuncture and difference in the global cultural economy. *Public Culture.* 2(1), 1-24.

Aref, F. 2011. Capacity development of community organisations for tourism development and planning in Shiraz, Iran. *Journal of Human Ecology.* 33(3), 197-201.

Asad, T. 1993. Genealogies of religion. Baltimore. Johns Hopkins University Press 1996. The concept of cultural tradition in British social anthropology. In J. Clifford and G.E. Marcus. (eds). *Writing Culture: The Poetics and Politics of Ethnography.* Berkeley. University of California Press. 141-164.

Asadollahi, A *et al.* 2011. Does child maltreatment connote wicked in adulthood? A study among delinquents in Ahwaz penitentiaries. *Journal of Social Sciences.* 28(1), 55-63.

Asokhia, M.O. 2010. Enhancing national development and growth through combating cyber crime/internet fraud. A comparative approach. *Journal of Social Sciences.* 23(1), 13-19.

Asuzu, C.C. 2009. Shift duty and stress coping strategies among nurses in the University College Hospital, Ibadan. *The Anthropologist.* 11(3), 153-159.

Attoh, F. 2009. Trafficking in women in Nigeria. Poverty of values or inequality? *Journal of Social Sciences.* 19(3), 167-171.

Aujla, P. *et al.* 2008. An ergonomic study of muscular fatigue during ironing clothes with selected irons. *Journal of Human Ecology.* 24(1), 31-4.

Awasthi, S. and M. Bhandari. 2006. Identification and prioritisation of barriers to quality performance in medical education and patient care in medical university in India. *Journal of Social Sciences.* 13(2), 157-162.

Azim, S. 1997. *Muslim Women Emerging Identity*. New Delhi. Rawat Publications.

Babu, K.S. 1998. The educational status of child labourers and the Special Schools in gem polishing industry of Jaipur. *Journal of Social Sciences*. 2(4), 265-271.

Bakhshi, E. *et al.*, 2008. Impact of occupational stress on home environment. An analytical study of working women of Ludhiana city. *Journal of Human Environment*. 23(3), 231-5.

Balis, A. *et al.*, 2010. Marital adjustment of childless couples. *Journal of Social Sciences*. 24(1), 73-76.

Bandopadhyay, T.K. 2007. Universal education and its impact on child and adult labour markets. A note. *Journal of Social Sciences*. 14(3), 273-279.

Banton, M. 1964. Anthropological perspectives in sociology. *British Journal of Sociology*. 1.5595ii2ar.

Barash, D.P. 2012. *Homo Mysterious: Evolutionary Puzzles of Human Nature*. New York. Oxford University Press.

Batibo, H. 1985. La ke Sukuma. Langue Bantu de Tanzania. Paris. Editio Recharche sur les Civilisations.

Baviskar, B.G. 1979. Walking on the edge of factionalism. An industrial cooperative in rural Maharashtra. In M.N. Srinivas *et al.* (eds). *The Fieldworker and the Field*. Delhi. Oxford University Press, 154-200.

Behera, D.K. and S. Patel. 1997. Trapped in the development wrap. The case of the project affected Parsas of the Indravati Valley in Orissa, India. *Journal of Social Sciences*. 1(2), 113-123.

Bello, O. and D.T.A. Oledemi. 2009. The impact of abattoir activities and management in residential neighbourhood: A case study of Ogbomosa, Nigeria. *Journal of Social Sciences*. 19(2), 121-127.

Bera, S. 2004. Food and nutrition of the Tibetan women in India. *The Anthropologists*. 6(3), 175-180.

Bernardi, L.B. 1959. *The Mugwe: A failing prophet*. A study of religion and public dignity of the Meru in Kenya. London. Oxford University Press.

Bernstein, B. 1974. Sociology and the sociology of education. In J. Rex (ed), *Approaches to Sociology*. London. 153-170. Routledge and Kegan Paul.

Berreman, G.D. 1989. Chipko movement to save the Himalayan environment. In C. Borden. (ed). *Contemporary Indian Tradition*. Washington DC. Smithsonian Institute.

Bhardwaj, S.M. 1973. *Hindu Places of Pilgrimage in India: A Study of Cultural Geography*. Delhi. Thomson Press.

Bhasin, A. *et al.* 2009. Consumption patterns of ghee in Udaipur City. *Journal of Human Ecology*. 25(2), 121-125.

Bhattacharyya (Thakur), M. 2001. Street food vending in Guwahati: A survival strategy. *Journal of Social Sciences*. 5(1-2), 27-131.

Biradar, N. and K. Sridhar. 2009. Consequences of 2003 drought in Karnataka with particular reference to livestock and fodder. *Journal of Human Ecology*. 26(2), 123-130.

Bisht, B.S. and B.P. Kothari. 2010. Influence of accessibility to the infrastructure and natural resources on lifestyle and workload of rural women: Scenario of Indian Central Himalaya. *Journal of Human Ecology*. 31(1), 27-35.

Bolla, C.R. *et al.*, 2011. Utilization of Emergency Management and Research Institute (108 EMRI). An emergency response service in Khammam District, Andhra Pradesh, India. *Journal of Human Ecology*. 34(1), 49-52.

Bonny, B.P. and J. Mathew. 2010. Farm transition network. Participatory approach to reinvent university agricultural extension in India. *Journal of Social Sciences*. 23(2), 171-178.

Bowen, L. 1964. *Return to Laughter*. New York. Doubleday.

Brass, T. 2003. The sabotage of anthropology and the anthropologist as saboteur. *Journal of the Anthropological Society of Oxford*, 180-286.

Brown, R. 2012. *Through the Eye of the Needle: Wealth, The Fall of Rome and the Making of Christianity in the West 350-550 AD*. Princeton University Press.

Burton, R.F. 1893/1964. Memorial edition. *Personal Narrative of a Pilgrimage to Al-Medina and Mecca*. New York. Dover.

Cai Hua. (1977). A society without fathers or husbands. The Na of China. A. Hustuedt, A. (trans). Massachusetts. Zone Books.

Castenada, C. 1968. *The Teachings of Don Juan: A Yaqui Way of Knowledge*. Berkeley. University California Press.

Cernea, M. 1982. Indigenous anthropology and development oriented research in Fahim, H. (ed). *Indigenous Anthropology in Non-Western Countries*. Durham. North Carolina. Carolina University Press. 121-137.

Chagnon, N.A. 1983. *Yanomamo: The Fierce People*. New York. Holt Rinehart and Winston.

Chakavarti, A. 1979. Experiences of an encapsulated observer A village in Rajasthan in M.N. Srinivas *et al.* (eds). *The Fieldworker in the Field*. Delhi. Oxford University Press. 38-57.

Chanchal, N.P. and P. Seetharaman. 2008. Acceptance of functional garments for paralytics. *Journal of Social Sciences*. 16(2), 151-154.

Chandra, A. 2009. Child labour. A study from anthropological perspective with special reference to glass industry in Ferozabad. *The Anthropologist*. 11(1), 15-20.

Chandran, D. and K. Raman. 2009. Awareness and problems in implementing knowledge of managerial systems in medium sized business organisations in Malaysia. *Journal of Social Sciences*. 19(2), 155-161.

Chantia, A. 2008. Effects of inbreeding on health among Dhankut. An endogamous group of Bahraich, Uttar Pradesh. *The Anthropologist*. 10(3), 219-223.

Chattopadhyay, M. and S., Sanyal. 2007. Incidence of occupational disease among mica workers of Jharkhand. *Journal of Human Ecology*. 21(1), 59-61.

Chaudhuri, N.C. 1951. The autobiography of an unknown Indian. Berkeley. University of California Press. 1959. *A Passage to England*. London. McMillan.

Chaurasia, R. and M. Shukul. 2006. Home; Is it the safest place. *Journal of Social Sciences*. 12(3), 171-176.

Chawla, P.K. and S. Sharma. 2007. Nutritional status and mental ability of school girls (7-9 years) as influenced by nutritional counselling. *Journal of Human Ecology*. 22(1), 1-5.

Chowdhury, A. 2008. The cultural construct of troubles with boys in India. *Journal of Human Ecology*. 24(4), 297-203.

Comte, A. 1975. *Auguste Comte and Positivism. The Essential Writings*. New York, Harper Torchbooks.

Cuisenior, J. 1982. Indigenous anthropology and cultural heritage in H. Fahim. (ed). *Indigenous Anthropology in Non-Western Countries*. Durham. Carolina University Press. 61-71.

Dambisya, Y.M. 2004. The fate and career destinations of doctors who qualified at Uganda's Makerere Medical School in 1984; a retrospective cohort study. *British Medical Journal*. 329.600-1.

Datta, P. 2005. Nepali female migration and trafficking. *Journal of Social Sciences*. 11(1), 49-56.

Deb, R. 2010. Knowledge, attitude and practices related to family planning methods among the Khasi tribes of East Khasi Hills, Meghalaya. *The Anthropologist*. 12 (1), 41-45.

Deji, O.F. 2005. Membership of co-operative societies and adoption behaviour of women farmers. Implication for rural development. *Journal of Social Sciences*. 10(2), 145-7.

Desjarlais, R. 2003. Sensory biographies. Lives and deaths among Nepal's Yolmo Buddhists. Berkeley. University California Press.

Devi, H.S. and K.S. Singh. 2007. Bio-cultural aspects of the Meitei women football players of Manipur. *Journal of Human Ecology*. 21(4), 251-6.

Devi, V.S. *et al.* 2006. Reproductive outcome in the wives of traffic policemen exposed to automobile exhaust. *Journal of Human Ecology*. 20(2), 77-82.

Dew, K. 2011. Pressure to work through periods of short term sickness. *British Medical Journal*, 343.30 July. 218-9.

Dey, S. and S. Goswami. 2007. Birth rate and death rate of Meghalaya (1976-2001). A study of trend and its inter-relationship. *Journal of Human Ecology*. 21(2), 105-108.

Dhingra, R. *et al.*, 2007. A study of certain selected variables (family environment and social adjustment) related to hearing impaired children. *Journal of Human Ecology*. 22(1), 83-7.

Dhingra, N. *et al.* A comparative study of understanding of menstrual process among married women belonging to two ecological settings. *Journal of Human Ecology*. 22(3), 261-6.

Diamond, J. 2005. *Collapse: How Societies Choose to Fail or Survive*. Harmondsworth. Penguin.

Dimuna, K.O. 2011. The social effects of the built environment. A case study of selected buildings in Benin City, Nigeria. *Journal of Human Ecology*. 34(3), 189-196.

Dragadze, T. 1987. The field-work at home—The USSR. In A. Jackson. (ed). Anthropology at Home. London. Tavistock. 154-163.

Drangett, J.O. 1993. Who cares about water. Household water development in Sukumaland, Tanzania. Linkoping. *Studies in Arts and Science*. 85. Linkoping University Press.

Dua, V. 1979. A woman's encounter with the Arya Samaj and Untouchables. N.M.N. Srinivas *et al.* (eds). *The Fieldworker and the Field*. Delhi. Oxford University Press. 115-126.

Dube, S.C. 1973. *Social Science in Changing Society*. Lucknow. Lucknow University Press.

Du Boulay, J. 2009. *Cosmos, Life and Liturgy in a Greek Orthodox Village*. Limni. Denise Harvey.

Durkheim, E. 1961. The Elementary Forms of Religious Life. New York. Collins.

Dwivedi, P. and A.N. Sharma. 2007. A study on environmental sanitation, sanitary habits and personal hygiene among the Baigas of Samnapur Block of Dindori District, Madhya Pradesh. *Journal of Human Ecology*. 22(1), 7-10.

Dyaram, L. and T.J. Kamalanabhan. 2005. Unearthed. The other side of group cohesiveness. *Journal of Social Sciences*. 10(3),185-190.

Egbochuku, E *et al.*, 2009. Analysis of the use, dependence and source of knowledge of stimulants among Nigerian university undergraduates. *The Anthropologists*. 11(3), 213-218.

Egbochuku, E.O and J.O. Akerele, 2007. Stimulant use as correlate of abusive behaviour among Nigerian undergraduates. *College Student Journal*. 41.50-58.

Enayatullah and Zeba. 2003. Domestic violence. A content-analysis based study of atrocities against women in Jharkhand. *Journal of Social Sciences*. 7(1), 65-8.

Englund, H. 1996. Witchcraft modernity and the person. The morality of accumulation in Malawi. *Critique of Anthropology*. 16.257-279.

Eswarappa, K. 2009. Role of NGO in the development of Sugali M. A case study of a settlement in Andhra Pradesh. *Journal of Human Ecology*. 27(2), 115-122.

Evans-Pritchard, E.P. 1939. Nuer time reckoning. Africa. 12, 189-216, 1940. The Nuer. Oxford. Oxford University Press.

Fahim, H. 1979. Field research in a Nubian village, the experience of an Egyptian anthropologist in G.M. Foster *et al.* (eds). *Long-term Field Research in Social Anthropology*. New York. Academic Press.

Feigenblatt, O.M. von. 2010. A brief analysis of popular aesthetics in Thailand. Subjective culture *versus* objective culture. *Journal of Social Sciences*. 22(1), 61-63.

Feldman, K.D. 1981. Anthropology under contract. Two examples from Alaska in D.A. Messerschmidt. (ed). *An Anthropologist at Home in North America*. Cambridge University Press.

Ferro-Luzi, G.E. 1991. *The Polythetic- Prototype Approach to Hinduism* in D. Sontheimer and H. Kulke. Delhi. Mandhar.

Fleur-Lobban, C. 1994. Informed consent in anthropological research. We are not exempt. *Human Organisation*. 53(1), 1-10.

Fuller, C.J. 2002. *The Renewal of the Priesthood. Modernity and Traditionalism in a South Indian Temple*. New Jersey. Princeton University Press.

Gadon, E.W. 2004. Annapurna Ma, priestess and healer. Women's agency in folk culture of rural Orissa. *Journal of Social Sciences*. 8(2), 87-92.

Gajdusek, D.C. 1973. Kuru in the new Guinea Highlands in J.D. Spillane, (ed). *Tropical Neurology*. Oxford. Oxford University Press.

Gandotra, U and D. Shah. 1997. *Aged's Old Age Problems and their Attitudes Towards Life. City in Maharashtra, India.*

Gandotra, V. and M.T. Jha. 2003. Female headed households. A data base of North Bihar. *Journal of Social Sciences*. 7(4), 315-321

Gautam, S. 2005. Concept of general consideration for preschool children (2-4 years) among rural mothers of Palampur Tehsil. *Journal of Social Sciences*. 11(3), 253-4.

Geertz, C. 1973. Linguistic etiquette in J. Pride and J. Holmes. (eds). Sociolinguistics. Harmondsworth. Penguin. 169-179. George, P.R. *et al.* 2009. Socio-economic profile of rural women and the role of animal husbandry intervention in a suicide affected district of Kerala. *Journal of Human Ecology*. 27(1), 41-44.

Gholifar, E. *et al.*, 2010. Effective factors in agricultural apple waste in Islamic Republic of Iran. A comparative study. *Journal of Human Ecology*. 32(1), 47-53.

Gill, S.K. and N.D. Gopal. 2010. Understanding religious practice in Malaysia. *Journal of Social Sciences*. 25(3), 135-146.

Ginsburg, F. 1993. Aboriginal media and the Australian imagery. Public Culture. 5. 557-578.

Glock, C. and R. Stack. 1965. *Religion and Society in Tension*. New York. Rand McNalty.

Gluckman, M. 1962. *Essays on the Ritual of Social Relations*. Manchester. Manchester University Press.

Goyal, R. and P. Kaur. 2007. Mothers interaction with children. A study in three income groups. *Journal of Human Ecology*. 22(2), 89-92.

Goyle, A. *et al.* 2004. A profile of roadside squatter settlements and their families in Jaipur City. *Journal of Social Sciences*. 9(1), 13-18.

Grelotti, D.J. and T.J. Kaptchuk. 2011. Placebo by proxy. *British Medical Journal*. 343.24 September. 599-600.

Grewen, R.H. 1981. *Magendo in the Political Economy of Uganda; Pathology, Parallel System in Dominant Sub-Mode of Production*. Institute of Development Studies. University of Sussex.

Gulati, N. *et al.*, 2009. Opinion of trainees regarding drafting and paper pattern technique. *Journal of Human Ecology*. 26(3), 209-213.

Guria, M. *et al.*, 2009. Awareness level of family planning in school going adolescent girls of different socio-economic groups in rural sectors, West Bengal. *Journal of Human Ecology*. 27(2), 101-104.

Gupta, K.A. 1979. Travails of a woman fieldworker. A small town in Uttar Pradesh. In M.N. Srinivas *et al.* (Eds.). *The Field Worker and the Field*. Delhi. Oxford University Press.

Hamada, T. 1997. Japanese corporate environmentalism: A new industrial standard for excellence. *Journal of Social Sciences*. 1(3), 201-208.

Hasalkar, S. *et al.*, 2002. Influence of locality on consumer behaviour while purchasing household equipment. *Journal of Social Sciences*. 6(4), 237-240.

Hasalkar, S. *et al.*, 2005. Entrepreneurship qualities of members of self help groups in Dharwad District of Karnataka State. *Journal of Social Sciences*. 11(3), 229-231.

Hassan, S. and A.A. Malik. 2009. Standardization of Karachi domestic violence screening scale—Urdu version. *Journal of Social Sciences*. 20(2), 83-90.

Hearn, Lafcadio *alias* Koizumi Yakumo. 1894. *Glimpses of an Unfamiliar* Japan.

Hennigh, L. 1981. The anthropologist as key informant inside a rural Oregon town. In D. A. Messerschmidst, D.A. (ed). *The Anthropologist at home in North America*. Cambridge. Cambridge University Press. 121-132.

Hessler, P. 2010. *River Town: Two years on the Yangtze*. London. John Murray.

Hill, S.F. *et al.*, 2004. Mortality among 'never smokers' living with smokers.

Two cohort studies. 1981-4 and 1996-9. *British Medical Journal*. 328. 979-83.

Hotchkiss, J.C. 1967. Children vane conduct in a Ladino community of Chiapas, Mexico. *American Anthropologist*. 69. 711-718.

Howell, N. 1990. *Surviving Fieldwork. A Report of the Advisory Panel on Health and Safety in Fieldwork*. Washington, DC. American Anthropological Association Publication. 26.

Indu Menon, M. 1981. *Status of Muslim Women in India*. A case study of Kerala. New Delhi. Uppal Publishing House.

Ismail, H. *et al.*, 2003. Customer satisfaction factors and its relationship with customer loyalty in semi-conductor industry. *Journal of Social Sciences*. 7(1), 37-45.

Jenkins, W.D. *et al.*, 2011. Use of the internet and self-collected samples as a sexually transmissible intervention in rural Illinois communities. *Sexual Health*. 8.79-95.

Johanson, D. and M. Eddy. 1981. Lucy. *The Beginnings of Mankind*. New York. Warner Books.

Jororgensen, D. 1981. *Correspondence*. Man(ns).16(3), 470-2.

Jose, J. and B. Abraham. 2010. Inference model for computer literacy and usage pattern among rural population of Piravom Grama Panchayat, Ernakulam District, Kerala, India. *Journal of Social Sciences*. 24(3), 149-154.

Joseph, S. and P.M. Mathew. 2005. Effects of inbreeding in the Mudugar and Irular tribal populations in Kerala. *Journal of Human Ecology*. 17(4), 247-250.

Kadt, E. de. 1970. *Catholic Radicals in Brazil*. New York. Oxford University Press.

Kang, T. and S. Jaswal. 2006. Relationship of parental education with parenting patterns. *Journal of Human Ecology*. 20(2), 87-9.

Kartal, H. 2009. The ratio of bullying and victimization among Turkish elementary school students and its relationship to gender and grade level. *Journal of Social Sciences*. 19(1), 109-119.

Kashoki, M.E. 1992. Indigenous scholarship in African Universities. The human factor in H. Fahim. (ed). *Indigenous Anthropology in Non-Western Countries*. Durham. North Carolina. Carolina University Press. 35-51.

Kaundal, R. and A. Sharma. 2007. Problems of household waste disposal. *Journal of Human Ecology*. 21(3), 199-201.

Kaur, G. and S. Chhikara. 2008. Assessment of multiple intelligence among young adolescents (12-14 years). *Journal of Human Ecology*. 23(1), 7-11.

Kaur, R. and S. Jaswal. 2006. Strategic emotional intelligence of Punjabi adolescents. *Journal of Human Ecology*. 20(1), 49-52.

Karar, A. 2010. Impact of pilgrim tourism at Hardwar. *The Antrhropologist*. 12(2), 99-105.

Kashyap, S.N. 2010. Designing criteria for storage spaces in old age homes in India. *Journal of Human Ecology*. 32(2), 109-112.

Kassilly, F.N. and H.M. Tsingalia. 2009. Persistence and loss of cultural values of Tiriki sacred groves in Hamisi District, Kenya. Implications for management. *Journal of Human Ecology*. 27(2), 137-141.

Katoch, M. *et al.*, 2009. Awareness among adolescents towards maternal empowerment. *Journal of Human Ecology*. 25(1), 45-50.

Kautiliya. 1997. *Arthasastra*. R.P. Kangli. (trans). New Delhi. Motilal.

Khan, A.S. and M.S. Ali. 2009. Mangroves living at the edges. A social survey based on environmental issue. *Journal of Human Ecology*. 25(2), 75-7.

Khatibi, F.S. and M. Indira. 2011. Empowerment of women through self-help groups and environmental management. Experience of non-governmental organizations in Karnataka State, India. *Journal of Human Ecology*, 34(1), 29-40.

Kulick, D. 1992. *Language Shift and Cultural Penetration*. Cambridge University Press.

Kishwaria, J. *et al.*, 2004. Consumer awareness regarding legislation organisations and consumer protection laws. *Journal of Social Sciences*. 8(1), 69-72.

Kishtwaria, J. *et al.* 2007. Ergonomic evaluation of kitchen work with reference to space designing. *Journal of Human Ecology*. 21(1), 43-6

Koch, T. 2011. *Diseases Epidemics on the Ground*. Chicago. Chicago University Press.

Kochar, V.K. 1977. Sanitation and culture. Behavioural aspects of the disposal of excreta in a rural West Bengal region. *Indian Journal of Preventative and Social Medicine. 8.142-15.*

Koentjaraningrat. 1982. Anthropology in developing countries. In H. Fahim. (ed). *Anthropology in Non-Western Countries*. Durham North Carolina. Carolina Academic Press. 176-192.

Konar, A.K. 2009. A paradox of corporate perception and perpetuation of conceptions. *Journal of Social Sciences*. 18(2), 81-93.

Kotwal. N. *et al.* 2007. Causes of school dropouts among rural girls in Kathua District. *Journal of Human Ecology*. 22(1), 57-9.

Kotwal, N. *et al.* 2008. Impact of TV advertisements on buying pattern of adolescent girls. *Journal of Social Sciences*. 16(1), 51-55.

Kumar, D.V. 2010. Rajukulas and Relus of Visachapatnam. A study of their potable water. *The Anthropologist*. 12(3), 197-200.

Kumar, M. 2008. A study in social dynamism of village 'Arya Nagar' in District Hisar. *Journal of Social Sciences*. 16(2), 121-126

Kumar, S. 1988. *The Artisans of Banaras: Popular Culture and Identity*. Princeton. Princeton University Press.

Kumari, R. and I. Grover. 2007. Waste generated and adoption of waste management practices among rural households in Haryana. *Journal of Human Ecology*. 22(4), 355-360.

Kwatra, S. *et al.*, 2010. A comparative study on the manual beating of paddy and manually operated paddy thresher on farm women. *Journal of Human Ecology*. 132(3), 183-187.

Ladd, J. 1957. *The Structure of a Moral Code. A Philosophical Analysis of Ethical Discourse Applied to the Ethics of the Navaho Indians*. Cambridge, Mass. Harvard University Press.

Lakshminarayana, J. *et al.* 2011. Associated risk of morbidities of tobacco smoking among opium consumers in rural areas of Rajasthan. *Journal of Human Ecology*. 33(1).

Lanson, R. (1978). Thirty years of research on the subject of the well-being of elderly Americans. *Journal of Gerontology*. 93. 109-25.

Lansing, J.S. 1991. *Priests and Programmers. Technologies of Power in the Engineered Landscapes of Bali*. Princeton. Princeton University Press

Lewis, O.1951. Life in a Mexican village. Tepoztlan. restudied. Urbana. Illinois University Press. 959. *Five Families*. New York. Basic Books.

Macionis, J. 1989. *Sociology*. Engelwood Cliffs. Prentice

Madu, S.N. *et al.* 2003. Some perceived parental undesirable behaviours predicting child sexual, physical and emotional abuse. A study among a sample of university students in South Africa. *Journal of Social Sciences*. 7(2), 111-119.

Madan, T.N. 1975. On living intimately with strangers. In and T.N. Madan. (eds). *Encounters and Experience*. Delhi. Vikas, 131-156.

Mahakud, N.K. and B. Panda. 2005. The third dimension of education. Its relevance in the new millennium. *Journal of Social Sciences*. 11(1), 29-33.

Malhotra, K.C. *et al.*, 2001. *Cultural and Ecological Dimensions of Sacred Groves in India*. New Delhi. INSA.

Malinowski, B. 1961. *The Argonauts of the Western Pacific*. New York. Dutton.

Malik, S. *et al.*, 2005. Promoting social competence of 6-8 years old socially incompetent girls. *Journal of Social Sciences*. 10(3), 233-6.

Malik, P.R. and S. Balda. 2006. Bright underachievers. Prevalence and profile. *Journal of Social Sciences*. 12(3), 159-161.

Maliki, A.E. 2006. The Implications of Rational Emotive Behaviour Therapy on Genitally Mutilated Females. *Journal of Human Ecology*. 20(2), 117-120.

Mangalore, R. and M. Knapp. 2007. The cost of schizophrenia in England. *Journal of Mental Health Policy Economics*. 10. 23-41.

Marwick, M.G. 1964. Witchcraft as a social strain gauge. *Australian Journal of Science*. 26.

Mascarenhas-Keyes. S. 1988. The native anthropologist; constraints and strategies in research in A. Jackson. (ed), *Anthropology at Home*. London. Tavistock. 180-195

Mathew, D. and P.V. Habeeburrahman. 2008. A methodology for the quantitative assessment of the primary social impact of agricultural technologies. *Journal of Social Sciences*. 17(3), 193-199.

McKusick, V.A. 1973. Genetic studies in American populations with particular reference to the Old Order Amish. Israeli *Journal of Medical Science*, 9. 1276-84.

Mead, M. 1935. Sex and temperament in three primitive societies. New York. New American Library. 1956. *New Lives for Old: Cultural Transformation-Manus*. 1928-1953. New York.

Morrow, 1964, The Paliau movement in the Admiralties 192 New Haven Yale University Press. 1972. Fieldwork in high cultures. in S.T. Kimball and J.B. Watson. (eds). *Crossing Cultural Boundaries: The Anthropological Experience*. San Francisco. Chandler. 120-132.

Mehrotra, N. and S. Batish. 2009. Assessment of problems among elderly females of Ludhiana City. *Journal of Human Ecology*. 28(3), 213-216.

Mehta, S. 2004. Maximum city. Bombay lost and found. London. Headline.

Messinger, J. 1989. Inis Beag revisited. The anthropologist as observant participant. Salem. Wisconsin. Sheffield Publishing.

Meti, R. and G. Saraswathi. 2007. Impact of nutrition intervention programme on performance of high school Kabaddi players. *Journal of Human Ecology*. 22(4), 337-344.

Miller, D.B. 1976. *A Genius like Feeling for the Social Stuff South Asia*. 6.112-120.

Milne, L. 1924. *The Home of an Eastern Clan*. Oxford. Clarendon Press.

Milne, L. and W.W. Cochrane. 1910. *The Shans at Home*. London. John Murray.

Minocha, A.A. 1979. Varied roles in the field. A hospital in Delhi. In M.N. Srinivas *et al.* (eds). *The Fieldworker and the Field*. Delhi. Oxford University Press. 1201-215.27-140.

Mishra, S. 2007. Household livelihood and coping mechanism during drought among Oraon Tribe of Sundargarh District of Orissa, India. *Journal of Social Sciences*. 15(2), 181-186.

Mondal, N.I. *et al.,* 2009a. Family structure, economic security and educational status of rural Chakma in Chittagong Hill Tracts of Bangladesh. *Journal of Social Sciences*. 19(3), 229-234.

_______2009b. Factors influencing infant and child mortality. A case study of Rajshahi District. Bangladesh. *Journal of Human Ecology*. 26(1), 31-39.

Mukherjee, R. 1976. The value base of social anthropology. The context in India in particular, *Current Anthropology*. 17. 71-95.

Murai, Y. and Y. Tsurumi. (eds). 1992. *See Asia Beyond Shrimps and Lobsters*. Tokyo. Osakuyo-Sha.

Murphy, M.S.R. *et al.*, 2007. Place of birth. Why urban women still prefer home deliveries? *Journal of Human Ecology*. 21(2), 149-154.

Mwilawa, A.J. *et al.*, 1998. Traditional range resources utilization. Experience gained among the pastoralists of Tanzania. *Journal of Social Sciences*. 2(1), 53-57.

Myrdal, G. 1944. An American dilemma. *The Negro Problem and American Democracy*. New York. Harper and Brothers.

Nagar, S. *et al.*, 2005. Situation of girl child in Kangra District of Himachal Pradesh. *Journal of Social Sciences*. 11(1), 71-76.

Naidu, M. 2011. Indigenous cultural bodies in tourism. An analysis of local 'audience' perception of global tourist consumers. *Journal of Social Sciences*. 26(1), 29-39.

Nandi, S. and S. Sawkar. 2007. Intensity of artificial lighting in living room and study area of urban residential homes in Dharwad City. *Journal of Human Ecology*. 21(1), 63-4.

Nanjunda, D.C. and M. Annapurna.2006. Small hands in Silicon City. Some facts and experience at grass roots level. *Journal of Social Sciences*. 13(2), 151-156.

Narahari, S. *et al.* 2009. A study on paediatric practices. *The Anthropologist*. 11(20), 147-149.

Nawng, K.M. 1942. The Kachins of the Hukawng Valley. Translation and notes J.L. Leyden. Bombay. Privately printed.

Nayyar, P. *et al.*, 2007. Causes and constraints faced by women entrepreneurs in entrepreneurial process. *Journal of Social Sciences*. 14(2), 99-102.

Nasser, R. *et al.*, 2008. Gender differences on self-estimates of multiple intelligences: A comparison between Indian and Lebanese youth. *Journal of Social Sciences*. 16(3), 235-243.

Nema, A. and K.K.N. Sharma. 2009. Perspectives of family planning among youth of Jabalpur City, Madhya Pradesh, India. *The Anthropologist*. 11(3), 173-179.

Nenty, H.J. 2010, Analysis of some factors that influence causal attribution of mathematics performance among secondary school students in Lesotho. *Journal of Social Sciences*. 22(2), 93-99.

Nikkhah, H.A. *et al.*, 2011. The effect of non-governmental organizations approach on women's empowerment in Shiraz, Iran. *Journal of Human Ecology*. 34(3), 179-187.

Oboh, V.U. and R.M. Sani. 2009. The role of radio in the campaign against the spread of HIV/AIDS among farmers in Makurdi Local Government area of Benue State, Nigeria. *Journal of Social Sciences*. 19(3), 179-184.

Ogunbiyi, J.O. and J.O. Ajiboye. 2009. Pre-service teachers' knowledge of and attitude to some environmental education concepts using value education stratagems. *The Anthropologist*. 11(4), 293-301.

O'Grady, S. 2012. *And Man Created God*. London. Atlantic.

Ojogwu, C.N. and A.N.G. Alutu. 2009. Analysis of the learning environment of university students in Nigeria. A case study of the University of Benin, *Journal of Social Sciences*. 19(1), 69-73.

Okely, J. 1987. Anthropology and autobiography. Participatory experience and embodied knowledge. In J. Okely and H. Callaway. (eds). *Anthropology and Autobiography*. London. Routledge.

Okwoche, V.A. and C.P.O. Obinne. 2010. Comparative analysis of socio-economic characteristic of rural women co-operators in Nigeria. Evidence from Benue State. *Journal of Human Ecology*. 32(2), 119-125.

Okwu, O.J. 2006. A critique of students vices and the effect on quality of graduates of Nigerian tertiary institutions. *Journal of Social Sciences*. 12(3), 193-198.

Onemolease, E.A. and S.O. Alakpa. 2009. Determinants of adoption decisions of rural youths in the Niger Delta Region of Nigeria. *Journal of Social Sciences*. 20(1), 61-66.

Ong, A. 1985. The production of possession spirits and the multi-national corporation in Malaysia. *American Ethnologist*. 15, 28-42.

Orwell, G. 1946. *Animal Farm*. New York. Harcourt Brace.

Padhy, S. 2008. Ethnobiological analysis from myth to science. IX. Pancha Yajnya (Five Sacrifices). The composite principle for applied human ecological environment. *Journal of Human Ecology*. 23(2), 151-158.

Pandey, T.N. 1979. The anthropologist-informant relationships. The Navajo and Zuni in America and the Tharu in India. In M.N. Srinivas. (ed). *The Field Worker and the Field*. Delhi. Oxford University Press.

Pardeshi, G. 2009. Women in total sanitation campaign. A case study from Yavatmal District, Maharashtra, India. *Journal of Human Ecology*. 25(2), 79-85.

Parkin, D.J. 1971. Language choice in two Kampala housing estates in W.H. Whitely (ed). *Language Use and Social Change*. Oxford. Oxford University Press.

Passikoff, R.1997. *The Limits of Consumer Satisfaction*. Brandweek. 38(9), 17.

Pasternack, B. 1989. A conversation with Fei Xiaotong. *Current Anthro*pology. 29(4), 637-662.

Paswan, S. *et al.*, 2005. Empowerment of senior citizens for retired life. *Journal of Social Sciences*. 11(3), 255-256.

Popper, K. 1964. Quoted in M. Banton. Anthropological perspectives in sociology. *British Journal of Sociology*. 15, 95-112.

Poyil, M. 2009. Farewell ritual and transmigratory souls. Secondary funerals of the Attappadi Kurumbas. *The Anthropologist*. 11(1), 31-38.

Prakash, B. 2000. *21st Century Development Challenges*. Chandigarh. Commonwealth Secretariat.

Prakash, N. 2001. Relevance of social science concepts to health systems management. *Journal of Social Sciences*. 3(1 and 2), 133-137.

Pruthi, N. *et al.*, 2004. Problems encountered while dressing and undressing by persons with upper amputated limb. *Journal of Social Sciences*. 9(2), 91-93.

Punia, S.S. *et al.*, 2007. Psycho-social status of senior citizen and related factors. *Journal of Human Ecology*. 22(3), 255-259.

Rahman, M.M. and A. Begum. 2010. The strategy of empowering poor for wetland resources conservation in Bangladesh. *Journal of Human Ecology*. 31(2), 87-92.

Ramachandran, B. 2004. Transmutation of economy and transference of status. A case study from tribal Wayanad. *Journal of Social Sciences*. 9(1), 1-4.

Ramaswamy, E.A. 1979. Being where the action was. Trade unions in Coimbatore. In M.N. Srinivas *et al.* (eds). *The Field Worker in the Field*. Delhi. Oxford University Press. 173-183.

Ramya B. and Rudramma. 2007. A study on the relationship between age at maturation and adjustment pattern of adolescent girls in Mysore City. *Journal of Human Ecology*, 21(1), 21-25.

Rani, R. *et al.*, 2006. Gwender differentials in reading behaviour among children. *Journal of Social Sciences*. 12(2), 125-127.

Rantanen, I. and R. Tuominen. 2011. Relative magnitude of presenteeism and absenteeism and work related factors affecting them among health professionals. *Archives Occupational Environmental Health*. 84, 225-230.

Rao, V.L.N. *et al.*, 2006. Illness and treatment among Khonds of Visakhapatnam District. Andhra Pradesh. *Journal of Human Ecology*. 20(2), 83-6.

Ray, S. 1998. Health seeking in two squatter groups behaviour: A case study approach. *Journal of Social Sciences*. 2(4), 273-79.

Redfield, R. 1950. Chan Kom. The village that chose progress. Chicago. Chicago University Press.

Reddy, S. 2007. Mega tourism in Andaman and Nicobar Islands. Some concerns. *Journal of Human Ecology*. 21(3), 231-9.

Regassa, N. and A. Yusufe. 2009. Gender differentials in migration impacts in Southern Ethiopia. *The Anthropologist*. 11(2), 129-137.

Richards, A.I. 1953. Towards a theory of translation in A.F. Wright (ed). *Studies in Chinese Thought*. Chicago. Chicago University Press.

Richardson, F. 1980. *The Statistical Study of War*. Berkeley. California University Press.

Rilwani, M.L. and F.E. Agbanure. 2010. An assessment of the environmental impact of asphalt production in Nigeria. *The Anthropologist*. 12(4), 277-287.

Ritu Singh, S.K. *et al.*, 2007. Impact of women's education level and employment status on parent-child relationship. A case study from Ludhiana City. *Journal of Human Ecology*. 21(2), 125-134.

Robbins, J. (2001). God is nothing but talk. Language and prayer in a Papuan New Guinea Society. *American Anthropologist* (ns), 107, 901-912.

Rogerson, C.M. and G. Visser, 2006. International tourist flows and urban tourism. *South Africa Urban Forum*. 7(2), 199-213.

Rojas-Rueda, D. *et al.*, 2011. The health risks and benefits of cycling in urban environments compared with car use. Health impact assessment study. *British Medical Journal*. 343, 13 August. 356.

Rokeach, M. 1964. *The Three Christs of Ypsilanti*. New York. Knopf.

Sachdeva, R. *et al.*, 2006. Efficacy of nutrition counselling on the nutritional and haematological profile of elderly males of urban and rural areas. *Journal of Human Ecology*. 20(1), 37-41.

Saenpradit, K. *et al.*, 2009. Potential development of Lam Rehung Taw Glawn performance or Isan musical folk drama in northeast Thailand. Pakistan *Journal of Social Sciences*. 6(3), 164-7.

Saini, S. and S. Jaswal. 2009. A comparative appraisal of quality of life of aged living with sons and living with daughters. *The Anthropologist*. 11(2), 139-146.

Sandhu, S. and P. Sandhu.2008. Adequacy of amount of light for performance of selected tasks in selected households tasks in Ludhiana. *Journal of Human Ecology*. 24(2), 111-116.

Sandler, A. 2005. Placebo effects in developmental disabilities. Implications for research and practice. *Mental Retard Disability Research Review*. 11, 164-170.

Sargent, R.P. *et al.*, 2004. Reduced insistence of admission for myocardial infarction associated with public smoking ban. *British Medical Journal*. 328, 979-83.

Sarikhani, N. 2008. Muslim women's work participation in India. *Journal of Social Sciences*. 17(3). 219-222.2009. Level of awareness of Muslim working women toward their rights in Islam. A case study in government offices in Mysore. *Journal of Social Sciences*. 18(3), 163-171.

Sayaranan, R. 1979. Problems of entry. Sri Lanka, Zambia and Australia. In M.N. Srinivas *et al.* (eds). *The Field Workers in the Field*. Delhi. Oxford University Press. 246-265.

______, 2010. Status of homeless women and children in Karnataka State based on Census of 2001. *The Anthropologist*. 12(2), 119-125.

Saran, A.K. 1958. India in Rousek. J.S. (ed). *Contemporary Sociology*. New York. Philosophical Library. 1013-1034.

Sarkar, S. 2005. Women as paid domestic workers. *Journal of Social Sciences*. 11(1), 35-41.

Scheper-Hughes, N. 1982. Saints, scholars and schizophrenics. *Mental Illness in Rural Ireland*. Berkeley. University California Press.

Shutz, A. 1962. On multiple realities in Collected Papers, Volume One.

Scott, J.C. 1969. The analysis of corruption in developing nations. *Comparative Studies of Society and History*. 11. 315-341.

Sen, J. 2007. Awareness of AIDS control and sexual behaviour of youth in a town of Assam State. *Journal of Human Ecology*. 22(3). 187-200.

Sharma, A. 2002. *Women in Indian Religions*. New Delhi. Oxford University Press.

Sharma, B.D. 1978. *Tribal Development: The Concept and the Frame*. New Delhi. Prachi Prakashan.

Sharma, M. 1997. Indigenous views of altruism. *Journal of Social Sciences*. 1(2), 99-101.

Sharma, N. and P. Kanwar. 2007. Perception of rural and urban homemakers regarding ban on polythene use in the State of Himachal Pradesh. *Journal of Human Ecology*. 22(4), 309-312.

Sharma, R. *et al.* 2007. Extent of female school dropouts in Kangra District of Himachal Pradesh. *Journal of Social Sciences*. 15(3), 201-204.

Sharma, S. and S. Jaswal. 2006. Migration and magnitude of psychological distress. *Journal of Social Sciences*. 12(3), 225-229.

Sharan, A. 1997. Commitment among the industrial women workers: An assessment. *Journal of Social Sciences*. 1(4), 292-299.

Sheykhi, M.T. 2001. Urban problems and contrasting values with special reference to Tehran: A sociological appraisal. *Journal of Social Sciences*, 5(1-2), 119-125.

Shukul, M. 2007. Investment in human capital by families. *Journal of Social Sciences*. 14(2), 109-113.

Sidhu, K. 2011. Agro-climatic zone wise analysis of women in farming in Punjab. *Journal of Human Ecology*. 33(1), 47-52.

Sidhu, K. and S. Kaur. 2006. Development of entrepreneurship among rural women. *Journal of Social Sciences*. 13(2), 147-149.

Sidhu, K. *et al.*, 2007. Prevention and cure of digestive disorders through the use of medicinal plants. *Journal of Human Ecology*. 21(2), 113-116.

Sheehan, E.A. 1993. The student of culture and the ethnography of Irish intellectuals. In C.B. Britten. (ed). *When They Read What We Write*. Westport. Conn. Bergin and Garvey, 75-89.

Singh, C.K. and S. Chikra. 2005. Socio-emotional development of pre-schoolers and effects of facilities available. *Journal of Social Sciences*. 10(2), 141-143.

Singh, C.K. *et al.*, 2007. Teaching strategies used by early childhood teachers of Haryana and Chandigarh (U.T.). *Journal of Human Ecology*. 22(1), 11-14.

Singh, K. and P. Agrawal. 2007. Perceived sex role and fear of success. A study on urban working women. *Journal of Social Sciences*. 15(1), 65-69.

_______. 2007. Masculinity and femininity among working women in Indian urban culture. *Journal of Human Ecology*. 21(2), 135-8.

Singh, S. 2007. Being a criminology ethnographer in a South African prison. A search for dynamics and prevalence of HIV/AIDS in the Westville Prison, Durban, South Africa. *Journal of Social Sciences*. 15(1), 71-82.

Singh, S.K. 2004. Road accident analyses. A case study of Patna City. *Journal of Urban Transport*. 3(2), 60-75.

Siwach, M. 2008. Impact of home environment on the scholastic achievement of children. *Journal of Human Ecology*. 23(1), 75-77.

Skinner, J. 1997. Doing anthropology as action or inaction. *Anthropology in Action*. 4(2), 13-16.

_______. 2002. Considering ethics. From classroom teaching to research committee vetting. *Anthropology in Action*. 9(3), 25-27.

Smith, C.S. 2001. *Ecology, Civil Society and the Informal Economy in North-West Tanzania*. Aldershot. Ashgate.

Smith, N. 1954. *Baba of Kano: A Woman of the Moslem Hausa*. London. Faber.

Somarsa, H. *et al.*, 2009. Supernatural power of the spirit of Boa Phankan with natural resource management in Thung Kula Ronghai, Thailand. Pakistan. *Journal of Social Sciences*. 8(3), 121-4.

Sobha, I. 2007. Green Revolution: Impact on Gender. *Journal of Human Ecology*. 22(2), 107-113.

Southwold, M. (1978). Buddhism and the definition of religion. *Man*, 25(2), 208-229.

Srinivas, M.N. 1976. *The Remembered Village*. Berkeley. University California.

Srivastva, S.K. and S. Agarwal. 2004. Do the visual media contribute to violence against women. *Journal of Social Sciences*. 9(1), 63-5.

Sweeney, 2006. Personal knowledge. *British Medical Journal*. 332. 129.

Pels, P. 1999. Professions of Duplicity: A prehistory of ethical codes in anthropology. *Current Anthropology*. 40(2), 101-136.

Stewart, S. 1994. *Crimes of Writing. Problems in the Containment of Representation*. Durham. North Carolina. Duke University Press.

Taleb, N.T. 2012. Antifragile. *Things that Gain from Disorder*. Harmondsworth. Penguin.

Tannenbaum, N. 2000. Protest, tree ordination and the changing context of political ritual. *Ethnology*. 29(2), 109-127.

Tanner, R.E.S. 1963. with D.F. Roberts. The effects of parity in birth weight etc. in a Bantu sample. *British Journal Preventative and Social Medicine*. 17(4), 209-218.

Tanner, R.E.S. 1958. Introduction to the northern Sukuma's idea of the Supreme Being. *Anthropological Quarterly*. 29(2), 45-58.

_______1958. *Sukuma Ancestor Worship and its Relation to Social Structure*. Tanganyika Notes and Records. 50, June.

_______1964a. *Cousin Marriage in the Afro-Arab Community in Mombasa, Kenya*. Africa. 34(2), 127-138.

_______1964b. Conflict within small European communities in Tanganyika. *Human Organisation*. 23(4), 319-327.

_______1966a. Drug addiction in East Africa. *International Journal of the Addictions* 1(1), 9-29.

_______1966b. Cattle theft in Musoma 1958-60. *Tanganyika Notes and Queries*. 65.31-42.

_______1964c. European leadership in small communities in Tanganyika prior to Independence. *Race*. 7(3), 289-302

_______1969. The East African experience of imprisonment. In A. Milner. (ed). *African Penal; Systems*. London. Routledge and Kegan Paul.

_______1970a. Homicide in Uganda 1964. *Uppsala*. Scandinavian Institute of Africa.

_______1970b. Three studies in East African criminology. The selective use of legal systems. *Uppsala*. Scandinavian Institute of African Studies.

_______1970c. An East African prison. *Uppsala*. The Scandinavian Institute of African Studies. 1978. Rumour and the Buganda emergency. *Journal of Modern African Studies*. 16, 329-338.

_______1993. East African ideas and translation: A bilateral process. *Anthropos*. 88, 29-37.

_______1996. Some reflections on a foreigner's of Swahili. *Nordic Journal of African Studies*. 5(1), 107-117.

_______ 1998. The reception of the New Testament in Swahili. Some criticisms and comments on its use among the Sukuma of Tanzania. *Missionalia*. 26(2), 245-259

_______ 2001. Informants and researchers; cooperation, self-interest and reciprocity: An examination of changing relationships. *Journal of Social Sciences*. 34, 279-290.

_______ 2009. Tribal psychotherapy. *Tribal Tribune*. 6(1),

_______ 2011. Chance and Probability. *The Limitations of the Social Sciences*. New Delhi. Concept.

Tiwari, P. and A. Sankhala. 2007. Prevalence of obesity, weight perception and dietary behaviour of urban college going girls. *Journal of Human Ecology*. 21(3), 181-3.

Turnbull, C. 1973. *The Mountain People*. New York. Simon and Schuster.

Turner, V. and E. Turner.1978. Image and pilgrimage in Christian Culture. *Anthropological Perspectives*. Oxford. Blackwell.

Upadhyay, S. *et al*:, 2011. Nutritional status and knowledge of hill women on anaemia. Effect of various socio-demographic factors. *Journal of Human Ecology*. 33(1), 29-34.

Vaid, S. and N. Sharma. 2005. Political rights for women. Special reference of Jammu and Kashmir State. *Journal of Social Sciences*. 11(3), 233-237.

Vaid, S. *et al*., 2007. *Type and Selection Process for Pre-School Children*.

Vyas, N. and S. Batish. 2009. Involvement of women in direct selling enterprises. *Journal of Social Sciences*. 21(3), 191-196.

Varadachar, B.D. 1983. The bottom view up. Some cognitive categories in M.N. Srinivas *et al*., (eds). *The Fieldworker and the Field*, Delhi. Oxford University Press. 127-149.

Vidich, A.J. and J. Benshan. 1968. Small town in mass society. Class. *Power and Religion in a Rural Community*. Princeton. New Jersey. Princeton University Press.

Voas, D. 2008. The continuing secular transition. 25-48. I D. Pollack and D.V.A. Olson (eds). *The Role of Religion in Modern Societies*. London. Routledge.

Vig, D. and I.J.S. Jaswal. 2009. Perception of parents about their relationship with teenage sons and daughters. *The Anthropologist*. 11(3), 189-193.

Vijalaxmi, K.G. and A. Uroof. 2009. Influence of maternal factors on mode of delivery and birth weight in urban pregnant women. *Journal of Human Ecology*. 245(2), 133-136.

Volker, C.A. 2008. *Papua New Tok Pisin English Dictionary*. Melbourne. Oxford University Press.

Wahab, A. and M. Ahmad. 2005. Consanguineous marriages in the Sikh community of Swat. Pakistan. *Journal of Social Sciences*. 10(3), 153-157.

Werthein, W.F. 1972. Counter *Journal of Human Ecology*. 21(2), 117-118.

Yadav, S.K. 2006. Human health implications due to water toxicity by pulp and paper mill. *Journal of Human Ecology*. 20(2), 91-6.

Yadav, S.P. *et al*., 2011. Awareness and practices about silicosis among the sandstone quarry workers in desert ecology of Jodhpur, Rajasthan, India. *Journal of Human Ecology*. 33(3), 191-196.

Zhang, M. *et al*., 2011. Self correction of refractive error among young people in rural China. Results of cross sectional investigation. *British Medical Journal*. 343.

Subject Index

Name Index